Nature-Friendly Land Use Practices at Multiple Scales

REBECCA L. KIHSLINGER

JAMES M. MCELFISH JR.

ELI Press
ENVIRONMENTAL LAW INSTITUTE
Washington, D.C.

Mixed Sources
Product group from well-managed
forests, and recycled wood or fibre
www.fsc.org Cert no. SW-COC-002483
© 1996 Forest Stewardship Council

FSC

Printed in the United States of America
ISBN 978-1-58576-140-1

Chapter Two, "Views of a Conservation Biologist" by Dan Perlman, previously appeared
in *Lasting Landscapes: Reflections on the Role of Conservation Science in Land Use
Planning*, copyright Environmental Law Institute 2007, used by permission.

Chapter Three, "Bridging the Gap: Incorporating Science-Based Information Into Land
Use Planning" by Bruce Stein, previously appeared in *Lasting Landscapes: Reflections
on the Role of Conservation Science in Land Use Planning*, copyright Environmental
Law Institute 2007, used by permission.

Contents

Acknowledgments

The authors thank the Wildlife Habitat Policy Research Program (WHPRP)—managed by the National Council for Science and the Environment and funded by the Doris Duke Charitable Foundation—for financial support of this work. We are grateful for the substantial contributions of ELI Research Associate Jesse Oppenheimer for research and writing of the Santa Lucia and Summit County case studies. We also thank from ELI, Scott Schang, Vice President (Publications and Associates); Carolyn Fischer, Books Editor; Linda Johnson, Managing Editor; and William Straub, Desktop Publisher for their excellent work on putting this book together.

For their work on Chapter 2 and Chapter 3, respectively, we thank Dan Perlman and Bruce Stein.

Special thanks to the WHPRP program committee and staff—Chris Bernabo, Jim Boyd, Kim Elliman, Dennis Figg, Tom Franklin, Mike Harris, John Kostyack, Luther Propst, Alan Randall, Mark Shaffer, Peter Stein, Bob Szaro, Sara Vickerman, and Christina Zarrella—for their guidance and support.

In addition, we gratefully acknowledge the assistance of the following people who provide us with valuable information and guidance: Joyce Ambrosius, Tom Anderson, Andy Backman, Steve Barker, Kristine Bentz, Bridget Burnell, Jim Curnutte, Kristin Dean, Debbi Edelstein, John Ervin, Abigail Fateman, Erica Fleishman, Tom Gray, Lisa Guthrie, Suzanne Klimek, John Kopchik, Tom Kroening, Michael LaBossiere, Jacob Martin, Paul Morrow, Kate Noonan, Brad Olson, Donald C. Outen, Terry Palmisano, Jim Patchett, John Pitra, Charles Rich, John Roberts, Shannon Schwab, John Shepard, Jim Sulentich, Lisa Taylor, Roxanne Thomas, Holly Vaughn, and David J. Yocca.

About the Authors

 REBECCA L. KIHSLINGER is a Science and Policy Analyst at the Environmental Law Institute (ELI). She is the lead editor of ELI's 2007 publication, *Lasting Landscapes: Reflections on the Role of Conservation Science in Land Use Planning* and the lead author of a chapter on "biodiversity corridors" in *Sustainable Urbanism: Urban Design With Nature* (John Wiley & Sons, Inc. 2008). Kihslinger has also been a contributing author of ELI research reports related to wetland buffers and habitat banking and has developed a wetlands mitigation training course for land trusts. In 2006, she earned a Ph.D. in animal behavior from the University of California at Davis, where she studied the effects of hatchery rearing practices on salmon development.

 JAMES M. MCELFISH JR., directs the Sustainable Use of Land Program at ELI. He is the author of ELI's 2004 book, *Nature-Friendly Ordinances*, several books about mining regulation, book chapters on state and local environmental laws, and approximately 60 ELI research reports and scholarly articles, mostly relating to water, wetlands, land use, and habitat. McElfish served on the American Planning Association's Directorate for its *Growing Smarter Legislative Guidebook*. He is a graduate of Yale Law School (1979) and Dickinson College (1976).

Contributors DAN PERLMAN and BRUCE STEIN are Ph.D. scientists and leaders in biodiversity conservation and education. Dr. Perlman is Associate Professor of Biology and Chair of Environmental Studies at Brandeis University. He is coauthor of three textbooks on conservation biology and ecology. Dr. Stein, formerly Vice President and Chief Scientist for NatureServe, is the National Wildlife Foundation's Associate Director of Wildlife Conservation and Global Warming. He was lead editor of *Previous Heritage: The Status of Biodiversity in the United States* (Oxford University Press, 2000).

Preface

Ecologists know they have a problem. Every landowner or regulator of land makes decisions concerning areas whose boundaries bear little, if any, relationship to ecologically defined functions.

This has become known as the problem of scale.

Solutions such as ecoregional planning or conservation planning are frequently proposed. But what can a landowner do when such plans are not yet in existence? Or where the information available in a plan does not match the spatial and time scale of the decisionmaker, who is almost always concerned with a different set of issues with their own elements of scale? Can landowner decisions accommodate uncertainty and changing answers about the science?

The research for this book began as a National Council for Science and the Environment-administered study seeking to determine how state and local land regulation and management programs focused on other primary objectives could generate ancillary benefits for wildlife.

We soon realized that in addressing this question, we were seeing practical answers to the problem of scale. And we were seeing similar answers for land use decisions at different scales.

These answers are rooted in institutional choices. Rather than restating biological conservation principles in a nested hierarchy of plans, the answers involve the construction of systems that can allow entry of, and use of, new information. Such systems can make excellent use of large-scale conservation plans, where these exist, but do not depend upon the prior existence of such plans. Land use decisions are not one-time decisions, but involve multiple institutions whose participation in land management continues over time and area.

The case studies that follow, preceded by essays by Dan Perlman and Bruce Stein, show how systems solutions offer practical approaches to a problem that bedevils ecologists while too often escaping the notice of land use decisionmakers.

CHAPTER ONE

The Scale Problem for Land Use Decisions

Habitat loss, fragmentation, and degradation are the major causes of imperilment for most threatened and endangered species, as well as the most significant threats to ecological systems and the natural services they provide.[1] As the U.S. population grows, developments associated with urbanization and exurbanization will continue to be significant threats to these systems.

Indeed, two million new housing units may be built annually to meet the demand of the next 100 million U.S. residents that are expected over the next 35 years.[2] This new development is likely to hit imperiled species and habitats especially hard, as areas, such as California and Florida, with high numbers of endangered species are likely to experience disproportionate population growth.[3] California's population is expected, by some estimates, to increase by as much as 46% by 2025.[4] Development associated with that population increase could add 185 species to that state's list of imperiled species—an increase of nearly 10%.[5]

Communities, public agencies, and developers that make habitat conservation an important secondary objective of their plans, policies, and projects will be increasingly important conservation agents. Through their planning and regulatory activities, local governments have the ability to influence the pattern and extent of development on private lands and the amount and pattern of land conserved for wildlife. Local decisionmakers set the overall vision for types of development and future land uses in a community through master planning, green infrastructure planning, and comprehensive planning. Local resource regulations and zoning ordinances can limit development in sensitive ecosystems such as wetlands, riparian corridors, and critical habitat. Further, locally implemented state and federal programs not principally focused on habitat conservation, such as source water protection and wetland mitigation programs, can have ancillary benefits for the conservation of ecosystems.

Nature-friendly developers can also make substantial contributions to land conservation in the context of development. Green development plans can preserve open space and protect critical habitat, while improving overall

1

environmental quality by reducing motor vehicle use, promoting redevelopment of older industrial and commercial sites, and reducing impervious surfaces.[6] Private development can also provide habitat corridors, adequate riparian buffers, and protected areas of core habitat. Incorporating green design or smart growth principles into the development process creates communities that both respect the environment and foster economic development, providing unique and effective opportunities for conservation. The U.S. Green Building Council has recently developed standards for environmentally superior development practices for its Leadership in Energy and Environmental Design for Neighborhood Development (LEED–ND) pilot program.[7] LEED–ND-certified developments can be encouraged by strong local environmental protection ordinances.

Because local communities, agencies, and developers can have a major effect on development across the landscape, they should play a vital role in effective conservation. However, local governments generally have jurisdiction over relatively small areas and their decisions are defined by political jurisdictional boundaries. Developers and other landowners generally focus on lands that they own. Habitat conservation, on the other hand, requires thinking and planning at much larger regional scales. Thus, the scales at which local governments plan, or that developers plan and develop, or within which state agencies operate programs such as those dealing with water supply or recreation, often do not correspond to the scales at which biologists and ecologists advise that we plan and manage for long-term ecosystem viability and resilience.

The Issue of Scale

Although state and federal governments and some regional authorities play a role in regulating and managing land, local governments have most of the responsibility for making land use decisions. State enabling laws, growth management laws, and home-rule powers provide local governments with the legal authority for planning, zoning, site review, and subdivision decisions.[8] Although local governments can consider factors related to biodiversity conservation in land use decisions, local government concerns are generally related to advancing the "public health, safety, and welfare"—the classic definition of local land use regulatory authority. Where local plans do consider environment and biodiversity conservation, ecological issues outside of the planning boundary are usually not addressed.

Effective planning for ecosystem conservation, in contrast, requires thinking and planning at both site-specific and regional scales. Ecological processes from species' life history events, e.g., nesting, foraging, and reproduction, to climate variability, to wildfire regimes, to speciation, occur over both narrow and broad spatial scales—and everything in between. What's more, many of these ecological processes depend on the natural variability, or patchiness, of the landscape, which occurs at both large and small scales. Landscape and open space planning efforts, carried out by state governments or national and international conservation organizations, provide opportunities for planning effective habitat conservation at the regional level. However, local governments or landowners are not often required or motivated to plan within a larger regional planning framework. In fact, local government planning efforts are typically disconnected from one another.[9]

This mismatch in the scales at which land use planning, regulation, and development are carried out and the scales at which we plan and manage for long-term ecosystem viability is a major challenge for effective conservation. The large number of local planning bodies, often operating with limited capacity, makes it difficult to address this challenge. But disconnected local decisions can result in cumulative, negative effects on the landscape, and ultimately lead to missed opportunities for regional conservation.

Both the natural features and processes on specific sites and the regional ecological context of the parcel should be considered when making decisions about land use.[10] Take, for example, a single hypothetical parcel in a landscape (Figure 1). The site may represent any parcel of land over which a land use decision could be made, e.g., a single privately owned parcel, a proposed subdivision, or an entire zoning district. In our hypothetical scenario, the natural features within the borders of our undeveloped site include a segment of a small creek with associated wetlands, patches of native prairie vegetation, and a modest patch of oak/hickory forest (Figure 1a). In addition to the natural features on-site, a plan for development within the site would typically consider the political/built landscape within and outside of the site's borders, including the existing infrastructure and the location of commercial centers and schools, and account for zoning districts and the effects of the proposed development on property values (Figure 1b). The effects of surrounding land and water management may also be considered as neighboring uses may affect the viability of the development.

From an ecological perspective, however, the role a parcel plays in the larger ecological landscape will depend on the natural resources found on the site and in the surrounding landscape. It may be difficult to understand the regional importance of each of these resources when they are viewed collectively as a complex natural landscape. However, resolved individually as a component or layer of the larger ecosystem, the significance of the site to the ecosystem of

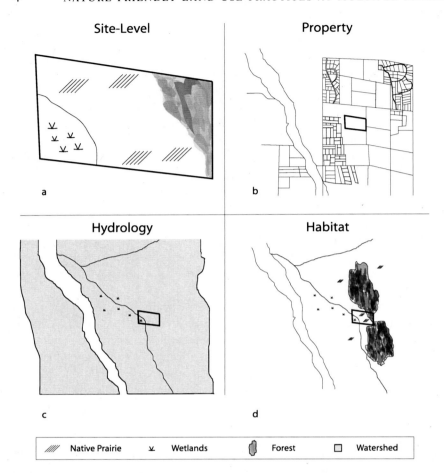

Figure 1. A depiction of a hypothetical parcel—containing a segment of a small creek with associated wetlands, patches of native prairie vegetation, and a modest patch of oak/hickory forest—over which a land use decision could be made (1a). In addition to considering the political/built landscape within and outside of the site's borders (1b), the regional ecological context of the parcel, including its hydrological (1c) and habitat (1d) characteristics, must also be considered in order to make informed assessments of the potential impacts of development on the site.

the region can be better understood. A site's hydrology or vegetation or its role in larger scale ecological processes can then be addressed individually for its contribution to the larger landscape. For example, in our hypothetical scenario, a small creek flows through the western portion of our site. Within the boundaries of the site, the creek supports aquatic and riparian wildlife and habitats as well as surrounding wetland habitat and wildlife (Figure 1c). Regionally the portion of the creek found in our parcel is a critical part of a larger stream ecosystem and ultimately contributes to the health of the larger watershed. Development (on-site), resulting in increases in the amount of impervious surface or changes to the flow or quality of the creek, can result not only in changes to surface and groundwater quality (on-site), but can also affect the hydrology of the regional stream system or even the entire watershed.

Viewed from another layer, our site contains patches of native prairie vegetation, while the northeast corner is dominated by oak/hickory forest (Figure 1d). In our scenario, these habitats have ecological significance, both within and outside of the boundaries of the site. The patches of prairie are among the last remaining examples of the habitat in the region and serve as important refuges for the native species that depend on these ecosystems. The modest forest patch within the site serves as an important ecological corridor between two larger patches of forest outside of the site; the connected forest patches serving as critical habitat for wide-ranging species. Although development on this site may result in only a small loss of habitat, destruction of these regional connections may result in a landscape-scale effect. Similarly, the role of our parcel in larger scale ecological processes, such as wildfire regimes, climate variation, and species life history characteristics, e.g. reproduction, dispersal, and migration, is also important to consider. For example, our site's wetland habitat is a major stop-over site for migratory waterfowl. Determining the significance of the stop-over to the sustainability of the species may require detailed information about the biology and life history characteristics of the migratory species, but can help inform nature-friendly land use decisions.

Visualizing the role that any given parcel or its individual resources play in the sustainable function of the regional ecosystem can help a local planner or decisionmaker determine the "ecological address" of the site. Armed with this "address" landowners or land use regulators can make more informed assessments of the impacts of their development decisions. Thinking about land uses at multiple scales requires the planner or local government to collect and analyze information on the parcel and its place within the larger ecosystem—information that may be available through local natural heritage programs or existing conservation planning efforts. Knowledge of the parcel's contribution to the function of the different components of the landscape or in turn the complex ecosystem as a whole increases the chance that ecosystems and the services they provide will be conserved.

Outcomes of the Mismatch in Scale

The local nature of land use planning means that over time many small decisions are made by a variety of individuals, e.g. planners, county boards, elected officials, representing a number of institutions and agencies. Each of these individual decisions may not result in detectable changes in ecosystem function, but incrementally the land use and development decisions made at the parcel, site, district, city, and county level can have significant effects on the ecology of the landscape at much larger and smaller scales.[11]

It is not easy to establish, however, the effect that many small, individual land use decisions can have on the conservation of species populations. Thus, development projects are often approved without addressing the collective impacts of approved projects over time. There are data demonstrating the cumulative impacts of land uses on species and habitats. For example, in the Tensas watershed in Louisiana, the number of forest species and population densities of forest interior species were shown to decline with the cumulative losses associated with many small development projects.[12] In Sonoma County, California, urban and vineyard land uses were shown to have cumulative and non-linear negative effects on the quality of salmon spawning habitats.[13] These types of data, however, are relatively rare. Thus, convincing a decisionmaker, or the public, that incremental decisions can affect the conservation of a habitat that occurs over a much larger landscape can be difficult. An individual jurisdiction containing only a small portion of a habitat may not be motivated to protect the habitat within its boundaries if its actions are not sufficient to significantly affect the conservation of the targeted habitat or species.[14] From the decisionmaker's point of view, it can be politically challenging to make future land use decisions based on cumulative impacts of past land uses.

On the other hand, local governments and other entities do invest considerable resources in protecting habitat and open space. Indeed, over the last decade, voters across the country have passed increasingly large numbers of state and local bond issues that support conservation financing to preserve habitat and open space and protect farmland.[15] These acquisition areas can be important habitat for local species—in addition to providing recreation and scenic benefits for the community. However, these conservation lands are often disconnected from a regional framework leaving only small, isolated habitat patches within any local community.[16] Such patches can become further isolated and degraded as development proceeds[17] and often have uncertain long-term sustainability as smaller patches are more susceptible to the effects of surrounding land uses.[18]

The disconnected nature of local planning can result in lost opportunities to connect these small patches preserved by numerous local entities to regional reserves and corridors, and ultimately lead to lost opportunities for regional conservation.[19] For example, local open space programs rarely collaborate regionally to meet regional habitat management goals.[20] Further, where regional conservation plans exist, local governments often do not include provisions in their local plans or regulations that acknowledge these regional efforts. Such fragmented local land use and management structures have resulted in some large-scale ecosystems, such as the Everglades, continuing to decline, despite regional plans for their conservation.[21]

At the same time, plans at a larger scale are not always translated into parcel-level or site-level activities that could provide meaningful value. Tree canopy retention practices, invasive vegetation prohibitions, stormwater management policies preserving base flow and preventing blowouts of stream banks, and limits on fences in wildlife corridors are site-level practices that can contribute meaningfully to achievement of a larger ecological vision if a connection is ever articulated.

Obstacles to Addressing the Issue of Scale in Planning

Access to applicable and reliable scientific information such as maps of regionally significant ecosystems, priority species distributions, or ecologically unique or sensitive areas, as well as data on the potential effects of development on regional ecological processes, is key to addressing the scale problem. However, these data may not always be readily available in a format that is useful to planners. For example, the science should be tailored, if possible, to target species and ecosystems for conservation. Each target species may utilize the landscape differently depending on its life history characteristics, e.g., habitat that appears to be connected for one species may not be sufficiently connected for another species. However, the scale at which data are collected and mapped can determine the types of decisions that can be informed by science.[22] Ecological communities that occur at fine spatial scales, such as riparian habitats, may not be discernable in more coarse-scale maps.[23] As minimum mapping unit increases (coarser scale) the number of habitat types that can be counted as well as the number of vertebrate species that can be detected decreases. Relative "hotspots" of species' richness may also shift across the landscape with changes in mapping scale.[24] More refined scale data targeted to focal species and habitats may be needed to plan and determine the effects of land use decisions at a site, city, or county level.[25]

Although routine access to the scientific information necessary to integrate regional ecological principles into land use decisionmaking over time is important, there is still a general lack of local application of science information in the fact base of local plans and implementation practices.[26] Cross-sectional studies of local plans and plan implementation policies have found that the fact base of plans was particularly weak for dimensions related to wildlife habitat and watershed science.[27] A study of 32 high-quality comprehensive plans revealed that the plans pay much less attention to hydrological, nutrient, and wildlife flows and more attention to "livability" values such as social cohesion, attractive buildings, safety, accessibility, and visually pleasing landscapes.[28] Further, high biodiversity within a community does not always translate to high-quality plans. Instead, human disturbance or threats to biodiversity are often the most significant factors related to plan quality.[29]

The ability to gather and interpret the scientific information necessary to think at broader scales is made more difficult because many local planning departments (outside of the larger metropolitan areas) operate with a small paid staff and stretched budgets.[30] Few departments have the resources to train staff in ecology or conservation biology, and there are still few true "hybrids"—experts in both biological science and planning.[31] However, the fact that local land use planners and regulators make many of the decisions about the use of land across the landscape means that they are increasingly going to play a central role in regional ecosystem conservation efforts. A new generation of "conservation planners" is needed that can more effectively link ecology and land use.

Collaboration among multiple local jurisdictions can help individual communities as well as developers address the problem of scale. However, most jurisdictions are often not equipped or motivated to collaborate with neighboring jurisdictions[32] and there are few regional bodies with broad power over land use.[33] A Florida study evaluating the "collective capabilities of local jurisdictions to manage large transboundary ecological systems" found significant gaps in the management of southwestern coast, southeastern coast, and central Everglades ecosystems, indicating that multiple local entities are not effectively managing these larger ecosystems.[34]

In most states, state policy usually does little to encourage collaboration among local land use agencies.[35] Many states provide authority for local governments to incorporate biodiversity in making land use decisions, however only a few states identify statewide or regional goals for land use planning.[36] There is also a general lack of coordination among state agencies that make land use decisions. Many state programs make decisions within a narrow program-specific focus, such as water resources or farmland preservation.

Opportunities to Address the Problem of Scale

Conservation biologists have made considerable progress over the past 20 years in determining how the size, shape, and connectedness of habitat affect the sustainability and persistence of species and natural processes across the landscape. The availability of such data and a structure through which to incorporate the information are critical to overcoming the problem of scale.

Planners do not have to rely on expensive environmental consultants to develop this information. There are several existing and readily available sources of data related to species and habitats, their condition or conservation status, and how they will be affected by proposed activities. State natural heritage programs, for example, have for 20 years been cataloging data on the plants, animals, and ecological communities in each state that can be used in land use planning and resource management.[37]

However, planners are often looking for ecological "rules of thumb" on how much land to protect, the adequate size and location of habitat corridors, riparian buffer widths, and the maximum distance between isolated patches. The Environmental Law Institute's (ELI's) *Conservation Thresholds for Land Use Planners*—a review and synthesis of information from the biodiversity conservation literature—provides land use planners with targets to achieve when making decisions about how much land to protect, the adequate size and location of habitat corridors, riparian buffer widths, and the maximum distance between isolated patches.[38] Such rules of thumb may be useful when detailed, case-specific information is deficient and access to scientific expertise is limited. However, planners should consider these as a baseline from which to launch more tailored and in-depth assessments based on local species and habitats. Local biologists, natural resource managers, or environmental consultants may be able to give guidelines or specific information for defined cases.

A number of tools have been developed to enable landowners and regulators to visualize the effects of their land use decisions on the broader landscape and incorporate regional conservation into planning, e.g., NatureServe Vista, CommunityViz, and LandScope America. For example, NatureServe Vista allows a user to map the biological features of a site and generate a conservation value for the features in order to evaluate how plans and development proposals will affect the natural features of the site.[39] LandScope America, being developed by NatureServe in collaboration with the National Geographic Society, will show users how the landscape of the United States is changing or might change over time and will also help users visualize individual sites of interest in a regional and national conservation context.[40]

In some urban areas, Councils of Governments offer a regional framework informing land use decisions.[41] Where they exist, large-scale conservation plans can also be an excellent source of information and can provide a framework for local planning.[42] State conservation plans, green infrastructure plans, habitat conservation plans (HCPs), and ecoregional plans developed by conservation organizations identify opportunities for landowners and land use regulators to protect regional resources and meet regional conservation goals. Further, each state has developed a State Wildlife Action Plan which sets priorities for conservation of critical wildlife habitat within the state.

Regional HCPs

The purpose of a regional HCP is to provide a coordinated approach to regulatory requirements concerning the conservation of species listed as threatened or endangered under the federal Endangered Species Act (ESA), while providing a framework for regional habitat conservation. The HCP planning process was intended "to integrate non-Federal development and land use activities with conservation goals, resolve conflicts between endangered species protection and economic activities on non-Federal lands, and create a climate of partnership and cooperation."[43] Over the past 10 years, HCP planning efforts have largely evolved from small-scale, single development-focused plans to large-scale, multi-species plans that allow for a coordinated, proactive, and regional approach to conservation and regulation. Regional HCPs allow local agencies to control endangered species permitting as well as local development decisions. The newer HCPs not only prioritize where to conserve habitat, but also prioritize where to develop and what kinds of development should take place where. In addition, plans may encourage municipalities and counties to adopt habitat conservation as a factor in local land use plans, ensure that species and their habitats are preserved in a regional context, facilitate preservation of habitat connectivity and wildlife corridors, and encourage private landowners to engage in habitat conservation.[44] HCP planning efforts also enable local agencies to receive state and federal conservation funds that are reserved for HCPs.

Green Infrastructure Plans

Green infrastructure plans identify:

> [an] interconnected network of waterways, wetlands, woodlands, wildlife habitats, and other natural areas; greenways, parks, and other conservation lands; working farms, ranches and forests; and wilderness and other open

spaces that support native species, maintain natural ecological processes, sustain air and water resources and contribute to health and quality of life.[45]

Green infrastructure planning offers a structure through which to conduct more coordinated regional conservation in the context of current and future developed lands—ensuring that priority habitats are preserved and new development is constructed in appropriate areas.[46] For example, Maryland's Green Infrastructure Assessment identified a network of two million acres (or 33% of Maryland's total area) of land that provide important ecosystem services.[47]

State Conservation Plans

Several states have conducted statewide conservation assessments which recognize the integration of conservation science and land use planning and how the two fields can be integrated more effectively to conserve biodiversity.[48] These large-scale planning efforts, such as Florida's Closing the Gap, New Jersey's Landscape Project, Maine's Beginning With Habitat, Maryland's Green Infrastructure Assessment, Massachusetts's BioMap, and Oregon's Biodiversity Project, map priority resources and habitats for protection statewide and outline strategies for the conservation of biodiversity.[49] For example, the BioMap was a Massachusetts-initiated inventory of biodiversity throughout Massachusetts using natural heritage data in order to identify "core habitats" and "supporting landscapes," and to compare those lands with lands that were currently protected and other lands that could benefit from future protection and management.

More recently, each state has completed a State Wildlife Action Plan, which sets priorities for conservation of critical wildlife habitat within the state. The State Wildlife Action Plans, prepared by all 50 states and 6 territories and submitted to the U.S. Fish and Wildlife Service in 2005,[50] identify species of conservation concern, provide information on the extent and conditions of habitats essential to conservation of species, identify problems and priorities for conservation research, describe proposed conservation actions and priorities, propose monitoring plans, and offer plans for coordination with public and private entities.[51] These nonregulatory strategic documents provide opportunities to enable local governments as well as numerous public and private actors to participate in wildlife conservation. All of the state plans identify local land use planning as a strategy for wildlife or habitat conservation.[52]

National or Ecoregional Plans

A number of conservation organizations have undertaken efforts to identify conservation priorities at larger scales—ecoregional to global.[53] The Nature

Conservancy's (TNC) ecoregional planning framework assesses biodiversity and threats over broad areas of land and water in order to select and design "networks of conservation sites that will conserve the diversity of species, communities, and ecological systems in each ecoregion."[54] Ecoregional planning is part of TNC's overall conservation framework that follows identifying conservation priorities in an ecoregion with site planning, taking conservation action, and measuring success.[55]

Several international conservation organizations have developed approaches to identify and conserve priority sites (World Wildlife Fund's Global 200 Ecoregions, Conservation International's "hotspots," and Wildlife Conservation Society's Living Landscapes). The National Gap Analysis Program identifies state by state the "gaps" in the coverage of vegetation and vertebrate species in reserves throughout the United States.[56] The Yellowstone to Yukon (Y2Y) Conservation Initiative is working to coordinate agencies, organizations, and individuals working in the region between Yellowstone National Park in the United States and the Yukon Territory in Canada.[57] The Y2Y initiative has identified priority areas for conservation for grizzly bears, birds, and fish and developed comprehensive, large, landscape-scale conservation strategies for these species.

Collaboration among local government agencies (professional planners, transportation and stormwater engineers, and parks and recreation designers) and among local and state agencies can offer opportunities to address the problem of scale and more effectively manage regional resources. What's more, high-quality plans in one jurisdiction may actually improve the quality of plans in neighboring jurisdictions if there is communication and collaboration among jurisdictions.[58] Further, state and local open space conservation programs could use existing conservation plans, such as the State Wildlife Action Plans, to help prioritize land acquisition decisionmaking[59] or could coordinate with green infrastructure programs to address issues of species and habitat loss.[60]

Law and the Scale Problem

Through their land use planning and regulatory powers, local governments can encourage landscape conservation at multiple scales—from parcel-level site review decisions to countywide master planning. A variety of measures, such as transfer of development rights (TDRs) programs, conservation easements, tax incentives, rezoning, and overlay zones, can help direct development away from sensitive habitat areas.[61]

Laws can contribute to the creation of scale problems. Local governments developing plans and zoning ordinances are, by definition, providing for development and land use within the geographically limited boundaries prescribed by law. State laws that govern river corridor protections are often narrowly written, where they exist at all. Laws may favor on-site mitigation of habitat or wetland impacts, absent a recognized watershed plan that provides for a wider scope of response.

At the same time, properly constructed laws can play a critical role in requiring consideration of scale issues by local governments and by applicants for development approvals. They can set up a basis for the development of watershed organizations and new institutions, as well as establish monitoring and adaptive management programs. When read carefully and creatively, they can often provide a source of authority for forward-looking plans, regulations, and public investments.

Each case study in this book has some elements of law entwined with the resolution of the issue of scale or multiple scales. In some instances, a planning and regulatory approval regime requires evaluation of wildlife corridors and habitat. In others, a regulatory issue like wetlands, water pollution, or drinking water supply is used to address related issues of habitat and ecological function. In some, legal creativity enabled nonprofit groups to do what oft-changing governments and private developers cannot. In still others, the response to a mandate to avoid "taking" threatened and endangered species provided a basis for new implementation mechanisms and new decisionmaking bodies.

At the federal level, the ESA is the most important regulatory law driving the preservation of particular wildlife habitat on privately owned and state-owned lands.[62] Although the ESA can be an effective tool for species conservation, it is generally reactive to the status of particular species rather than approaching ecosystems and their associated species holistically. The ESA can be implemented locally through planning leading to a federally approved HCP with a permit authorizing "incidental take" of threatened or endangered species. The Coastal Zone Management Act provides funding and authority for state governments to develop coastal plans and to ensure consistency of federal activities within these special areas.[63] Other federal laws administered by the U.S. Department of the Interior, the U.S. Department of Agriculture, the U.S. Environmental Protection Agency, and the U.S. Army Corps of Engineers, among others, support wildlife conservation,[64] conservation activities on farms and forests,[65] and protection of water quality, drinking water supplies, and wetlands and waters.[66] These laws set standards that in most cases affect multiple landscapes and activities situated within a hierarchy of ecological scales, even if the law applies to an individual permit or parcel of land. For example, decisions made about the siting of wetland mitigation projects must be made within the context of a watershed approach to ensure the sustainability of mitigation sites as well as to provide for regional conservation of resources.

State laws directly govern private activities, and they provide local governments the authority to regulate land use and development. State land use planning enabling laws determine what local governments may consider when writing land use plans and adopting zoning and other regulations. A 2003 study found that all 50 states have provided at least some authority for local governments to address biodiversity, habitat, or related concepts when carrying out land use planning and zoning.[67] State endangered species laws also help to conserve wildlife and their habitat.[68] State critical areas laws, such as those in Florida and Maryland, provide planning and regulatory protection to vulnerable areas of the landscape and watersheds that need particular scrutiny to prevent development activities from impairing ecological functions.[69] States can encourage local governments to make nature-friendly decisions by providing financial incentives and accessible scientific information to local communities, by mandating strong environmental provisions in local plans, and by establishing collaborative partnerships with local governments.[70] And of course, state laws establish the rules for conservation easements, for land trusts, for water supply and infrastructure, and for logging, mining, land clearing, and management of species (including invasive species). States provide the most substantial legal venue in which regional conservation planning or data can be incorporated into decisions that are binding on local governments and private property users, thus linking site-level decisions to wider landscape or ecologically informed goals.

Local communities make a range of land use decisions and affect land use at several scales within their jurisdictional boundaries. They have a range of tools for incorporating conservation biology at multiple scales. For example, local communities are including natural resource and biodiversity protection elements in local plans and regulations, establishing the framework within which other conservation decisions can be made, guiding zoning decisions, targeting acquisition areas, siting roads and other infrastructure, managing stormwater, and prescribing limitations on development practices.[71] Coordination of activities and ordinances with adjacent local units of government and with state or regional plans can produce profoundly important benefits.

Local governments can guarantee that a site-level nature-friendly land use also ties into maximizing ecological benefits and maintaining ecological function as part of the larger matrix of watershed and habitat lands. At the site level, local governments can require development applications to include specific information on habitat areas, species, and biodiversity concerns; discourage development in sensitive areas through prohibitions, regulatory reviews, or impact fees; and can encourage appropriate development through zoning and subdivision ordinances. For their part, private developers and public agencies can also contribute to wildlife conservation by reducing the footprint of developments and infrastructure, and connecting conservation areas with similar areas on adjacent parcels. Nature-friendly ordinances can also encourage conservation developments by requiring or encouraging practices that set aside open space identified as important for habitat, preserve wetland and stream buffers,[72] and avoid building in areas that contribute to the resilience and ecological function of other areas.

What Land Use Practices Achieve Conservation at Multiple Scales?

Land use practices, if they are to be nature-friendly, must help to preserve functional ecosystem processes. A few years ago, we published a brief set of guidelines for taking these into account when making land use decisions. (See box, p. 16.)

This book presents different ways in which land use decisionmakers have effectively engaged the issue of scale in practice and on the ground. These individuals and institutions have worked across jurisdictional and ecological boundaries.

Connecting conservation science with decisionmaking is the subject of the next two chapters by Dan Perlman and Bruce Stein, prepared for an ELI conference bringing together the nation's leading conservation scientists and planners. Reprinted from *Lasting Landscapes: Reflections on the Role of Conservation Science in Land Use Planning*,[73] these chapters frame the issue of scale in the broader context of the integration of conservation principles in land use planning. Many of the obstacles to overcoming the problem of scale are those that also plague the implementation of proactive conservation planning, such as lack of information, capacity, and coordination.

In Chapter 2, Perlman, of Brandeis University, presents the view of a conservation biologist on the opportunities and barriers to integrating conservation biology principles into land use planning. Perlman discusses several ways in which land use planners and regulators can make use of conservation biology, describes "several key areas of conservation biology research that would be

Conservation Guidelines for Land Use Decisions

Overarching Guidelines

1. Examine impacts of local decisions in a regional context.
2. Examine impacts of local decisions over time, considering foreseeable future changes in the landscape.

Practice Guidelines

1. Maintain large areas of contiguous habitat and avoid fragmenting these areas.
2. Maintain meaningful connections between habitat areas.
3. Protect rare landscape elements, sensitive areas, and associated species.
4. Allow natural patterns of disturbance to continue in order to maintain diversity and resilience of habitat types.
5. Minimize the introduction and spread of non-native species and favor native plants and animals.
6. Minimize human introduction of nutrients, chemicals, and pollutants.
7. Avoid land uses that deplete natural resources over a broad area.
8. Compensate for adverse effects of development on natural processes.

Source: James M. McElfish Jr., *Nature-Friendly Ordinances* (ELI 2004), adapted from Committee on Land Use, Ecological Society of America, *Ecological Principles and Guidelines for Managing the Use of Land* (2000).

especially useful for improving the effectiveness of conservation efforts on the ground," and considers "ways that conservation biologists and land use professionals can work more closely together." Perlman also discusses the importance of understanding the landscape context when making land use decisions. In Chapter 3, Stein, of NatureServe, presents a policy perspective on integrating science-based information into land use planning. Stein discusses the reasons for the continued disconnect between the conservation science and land use planning communities as well as the opportunities available to broaden the interaction and integration of the two disciplines.

Next we present eight case studies at different scales (Chapters 4–11) of local and state entities that have made habitat conservation an important secondary objective of their plans, policies, and projects: from small private developments to statewide initiatives. The case studies highlight opportunities for conservation (1) realized through private investments in land development, (2) led by local governments, and (3) achieved as benefits to state programs not principally focused on habitat, and show the conditions for their success. In each case, ecologically meaningful conservation became part of the objective, and in each case the entities are working across boundaries to address regional conservation issues.

The first three case studies focus on private land developments that incorporate habitat conservation at the site level in ways that also support regional habitat needs. Coffee Creek Center is a mixed use, new urbanism conservation development located on 640 acres in Chesterton, Indiana (Chapter 4). The developers set aside a 151-acre preserve on the property and formed the Coffee Creek Watershed Conservancy to restore the preserve. The conservancy has expanded its mission beyond the borders of the site to include the protection, restoration, and enhancement of the entire Coffee Creek Watershed. The General Motors Lansing Delta Township Plant site, located on 1,100 acres in Michigan, is an example of the over 400 corporate habitats certified under the corporate Wildlife Habitat Council Certification Program (Chapter 5). The plant's wildlife habitat team worked with wetland management and ecological restoration experts to create a plan for habitat preservation at the facility and worked with community groups and local agencies to consider regional conservation concerns. The Santa Lucia Preserve is a luxury conservation development/preserve located on 20,000 acres in Monterey County, California (Chapter 6). The developers set aside nearly 18,000 acres of the site as open space connected to regional parks and conservation areas and helped establish the Santa Lucia Conservancy to manage the restoration of the ecological values of the land complex.

The second set of case studies focuses on local government land use planning and growth management actions. The East Contra Costa County Habitat Conservation Plan/Natural Community Conservation Plan identifies a preserve system of between 23,800 and 30,300 acres of land to be connected to existing regional conservation lands within a 174,000-acre planning area in a rapidly growing region of California (Chapter 7). Baltimore County's integrated use of planning and environmental regulation and links to Maryland's broader conservation initiatives make the county a strong example of both site-level conservation and landscape-scale conservation not driven by ESA concerns (Chapter 8). Baltimore County's landscape approach has achieved results that are relevant beyond its own 388,000 acres and is discussing the need for a regional framework for planning. Summit County, Colorado (396,000 acres), has adopted a wildlife habitat overlay district that establishes a wildlife-focused development review procedure that uses regional and state-based information to protect the wildlife habitat and species of the county and region (Chapter 9).

The final set of case studies offers examples of ways to implement environmental and infrastructure programs aimed at other goals that can generate wildlife habitat conservation and restoration benefits if managed to do so. Fall River, Massachusetts, participated in a collaborative deal with state and conservation organizations to effectively meld source water protection under the Safe Drinking Water Act to conserve thousands of acres (14,000-acre focus area) of its reservoir protection lands and integrate them with other private and public conservation lands as part of the Southeastern Massachusetts Bioreserve (Chapter 10). North Carolina developed the Ecosystem Enhancement Program in 2003 to identify lands and waters important for wetland and stream conservation throughout the state using a watershed-based approach (600,000-acre watershed areas), and to target wetland mitigation funding associated with transportation permits under §404 of the federal Clean Water Act on such lands and waters (Chapter 11).

We conclude with six "lessons learned," demonstrating the key elements that allow land use entities to overcome the scale barrier. The key elements provide planners, developers, and government agencies with some "best practices" for the design and implementation of local land use programs and projects that promote regional conservation.

Key Lessons

Confronting the problem of scale does not require a land use decisionmaker to hire an expensive consultant or develop a regional conservation plan or even to make conservation the primary focus of the program. Instead, the entities in our case studies addressed the scale issue through *institutional* choices—by constructing or making use of existing systems or plans that can allow entry of, and use of, new information; by collaborating with multiple institutions across regions; and by educating the community about the value of ecological systems.

As the studies illustrate, and as explained further in Chapter 12, the six key elements to address the problem of scale successfully are: (1) creating and sustaining an independent entity focused *primarily* on habitat to ensure that the focus on conservation will be maintained over time and to stimulate regional conservation projects outside the initial project areas; (2) maintaining access to authoritative conservation science over time to ensure that management of the project is dynamic and addresses ecological and physical change; (3) articulating a commitment to habitat goals to "brand" the project, program, or place as nature-friendly and help to expand and adapt conservation over time; (4) identifying regional habitat conservation opportunities and sources of funding to accomplish regional habitat conservation goals; (5) educating the surrounding community to improve citizen involvement in the project or place and public interest in wildlife conservation; and (6) achieving outside, external certification and recognition to ensure continuity and durability of the habitat goals over time.

Notes

1. David S. Wilcove et al., *Leading Threats to Biodiversity: What's Imperiling U.S. Species*, in Precious Heritage: The Status of Biodiversity in the United States (B.A. Stein et al. eds., Oxford Univ. Press 2000).

2. Arthur C. Nelson & Robert Lang, *The Next 100 Million*, in Planning (American Planning Ass'n 2007).

3. Wilcove et al., *supra* note 1.

4. Paul R. Campbell, *Population Projections: States, 1995–2025* Current Population Reps., Population Projections, May 1997, at 1-6 (P25-1131).

5. Roger M. Brown & David N. Laband, *Species Imperilment and Spatial Patterns of Development in the United States*, 20 Conservation Biology 239-44 (2006).

6. John R. Nolon, Open Ground: Effective Local Strategies for Protecting Natural Resources (ELI 2003).

7. U.S. Green Building Council, *LEED for Neighborhood Development*, http://www.usgbc.org/DisplayPage.aspx?CMSPageID=148 (last visited July 23, 2008).

8. ELI & Defenders of Wildlife, Planning for Biodiversity: Authorities in State Land Use Laws (ELI 2003).

9. Samuel D. Brody et al., *Evaluating Ecosystem Management Capabilities at the Local Level in Florida: Identifying Policy Gaps Using Geographic Information Systems*, 32 Envtl. Mgmt. 661-81 (2003).

10. Reed F. Noss, *Conservation Thresholds: Overview and Commentary*, in Lasting Landscapes: Reflections on the Role of Conservation Science in Land Use Planning (Rebecca L. Kihslinger & Jessica Wilkinson eds., ELI 2007) [hereinafter Lasting Landscapes].

11. David M. Theobald, *Challenges in Bridging Conservation Science and Land Use Planning*, in Lasting Landscapes, *supra* note 10.

12. David M. Burdick et al., *Faunal Changes and Bottomland Hardwood Forest Loss in the Tensas Watershed, Louisiana*, 3 Conservation Biology 282-92 (1989).

13. Kathleen A. Lohse et al., *Forecasting Relative Impacts of Land Use on Anadromous Fish Habitat to Guide Conservation Planning*, 18 Ecological Applications 467-82 (2008).

14. Theobald, *Challenges in Bridging Conservation Science and Land Use Planning*, in Lasting Landscapes, *supra* note 10.

15. Trust for Public Land, *Land Vote*, http://www.tpl.org/tier2_kad.cfm?folder_id=2386 (last visited July 23, 2008).

16. Philip R. Berke, *Ecology and New Directions for Land Use Planning: Barriers and Opportunities to Change*, in Lasting Landscapes, *supra* note 10.

17. Timothy Beatley, *Preserving Biodiversity: Challenges for Planners*, 66 APA J. 5-20 (2000).

18. Gary K. Meffe & C. Ronald Carroll, Principles of Conservation Biology (Sinauer Associates, Inc. 2d ed. 1997).

19. Reed F. Noss, *Context Matters: Considerations for Large-Scale Conservation*, 3 Conservation Mag. 10-19 (2002).

20. Reid Ewing et al., Endangered by Sprawl: How Runaway Development Threatens America's Wildlife (Nat'l Wildlife Fed'n (NWF) 2005).

21. Brody et al., *supra* note 9; Stephen S. Light et al., *The Everglades: Evolution of Management in a Turbulent Ecosystem*, in Barriers and Bridges to the Renewal of Ecosystems and Institutions (Stephen S. Light et al. eds., Columbia Univ. Press 1995).

22. Craig R. Groves, Drafting a Conservation Blueprint: A Practitioner's Guide to Planning for Biodiversity (Island Press 2003); D.M. Theobald, *Challenges in Bridging Conservation Science and Land Use Planning, in* Lasting Landscapes, *supra* note 10; D.L. Perlman, *Views of a Conservation Biologist, in id.*

23. David M. Stoms, *Effects of Habitat Map Generalization in Biodiversity Assessment*, 58 Photogrammetric Eng'g & Remote Sensing 1587-91 (1992).

24. Timothy H. Keitt et al., *Detecting Critical Scales in Fragmented Landscapes*, 1 Conservation Ecology 4 (1997), *available at* http://www.consecol.org/vol1/iss1/art4/.

25. Stoms, *supra* note 23; Brown & Laband, *supra* note 5.

26. Berke, *Ecology and New Directions for Land Use Planning: Barriers and Opportunities to Change, in* Lasting Landscapes, *supra* note 10.

27. *Id.*

28. Philip R. Berke & M. Manta-Conroy, *Are We Planning for Sustainable Development? An Evaluation of 30 Comprehensive Plans*, 66 J. Am. Planning Ass'n 21-33 (2000).

29. Brody, *supra* note 9.

30. Arlan M. Colton & Sherry A. Ruther, *Beyond This Point, There Be Dragons: Charting the Waters of Natural Resource-Based Land Use Planning in Pima County, Arizona, in* Lasting Landscapes, *supra* note 10.

31. *Id.*

32. Ewing et al., *supra* note 20; Brody et al., *supra* note 9.

33. Ewing et al., *supra* note 20.

34. Brody et al., *supra* note 9.

35. Planning for Biodiversity, *supra* note 8.

36. *Id.*

37. NatureServe, *Visit Local Programs*, http://www.natureserve.org/visitLocal/index.jsp (last visited July 23, 2008).

38. ELI, Conservation Thresholds for Land Use Planners (2003).

39. NatureServe, *NatureServe Vista Overview*, http://www.natureserve.org/prodServices/vista/overview.jsp (last visited July 23, 2008).

40. NatureServe & National Geographic, *LandScope America*, http://www.landscope.org/preview/Home.html (last visited July 23, 2008).

41. Berke, *Ecology and New Directions for Land Use Planning: Barriers and Opportunities to Change, in* Lasting Landscapes, *supra* note 10.

42. Groves, *supra* note 22.

43. U.S. Fish & Wildlife Serv., *Habitat Conservation Planning Handbook*, http://www.fws.gov/endangered/hcp/hcpbook.html.

44. *Id.*

45. Leigh A. McDonald et al., *Green Infrastructure Plan Evaluation Frameworks*, 1 J. Conservation Planning 6-25 (2005).

46. Mark A. Benedict & Edward T. McMahon, Green Infrastructure: Smart Conservation for the 21st Century (Sprawl Watch Clearinghouse 2001).

47. Maryland's Green Infrastructure Assessment & GreenPrint Program, *Homepage*, http://www.greeninfrastructure.net/sites/greeninfrastructure.net/files/1-mdgreeninfrastructurecasestudy.pdf (last visited July 23, 2008).

48. Defenders of Wildlife, Integrating Land Use Planning and Biodiversity (2003).

49. *Id.*

50. Plans were required under Pub. L. No. 106-553 (2000), codified at 16 U.S.C. §669c.

51. Association of Fish & Wildlife Agencies, *State Wildlife Action Plans: Eight Required Elements*, http://www.wildlifeactionplan.org/pdfs/eight_elements_handout.pdf (last visited July 23, 2008).

52. Defenders of Wildlife, Linking Conservation and Land Use Planning: Using the State Wildlife Action Plans to Protect Wildlife From Urbanization (2007).

53. Kent H. Redford et al., *Mapping the Conservation Landscape*, 17 Conservation Biology 116-31 (2003).

54. 1 Craig R. Groves et al., Designing a Geography of Hope: A Practitioner's Handbook for Ecoregional Conservation Planning (TNC 2000).

55. TNC, *Conservation Action Planning*, http://conserveonline.org/workspaces/cbdgateway/cap/index_html (last visited July 23, 2008).

56. J. Michael Scott et al., *Gap Analysis: A Geographic Approach to Protection of Biological Diversity*, 123 Wildlife Monographs 1-41 (1993).

57. Y2Y, *Our Role*, http://www.y2y.net/Default.aspx?cid=97&lang=1 (last visited July 23, 2008).

58. Brody et al., *supra* note 9.

59. ELI, The Nature of Open Space Programs: Linking Land Protection and Biodiversity Conservation (2007).

60. Ewing et al., *supra* note 20.

61. James M. McElfish Jr., Nature-Friendly Ordinances (ELI 2004).

62. 16 U.S.C. §§1531-1544, ELR Stat. ESA §§2-18.

63. *Id.* §§1451-1465, ELR Stat. CZMA §§302-319.

64. *Id.* §§777-777k, 669c, 669e.

65. *Id.* §§3831-3836.

66. 33 U.S.C. §§1342, 1344 and 42 U.S.C. §§300f to 300j-26, ELR Stat. SDWA §§1401-1465.

67. Planning for Biodiversity, *supra* note 8.

68. Defenders of Wildlife & Center for Wildlife Law, Saving Biodiversity: A Status Report on State Laws, Policies, and Programs (Defenders of Wildlife 1996).

69. *E.g.*, Md. Code Ann. Nat. Res. §§8-1801 (West 2003).

70. Robert McKinstry, Biodiversity Conservation Handbook: State, Local, and Private Protection of Biological Diversity (Island Press 2006); Berke, *Ecology and New Directions for Land Use Planning: Barriers and Opportunities to Change, in* Lasting Landscapes, *supra* note 10.

71. McElfish, *supra* note 61.

72. *See, e.g.*, ELI, Planner's Guide to Wetland Buffers for Local Governments (2008).

73. Lasting Landscapes: Reflections on the Role of Conservation Science in Land Use Planning (Rebecca L. Kihslinger & Jessica Wilkinson eds., ELI 2007).

CHAPTER TWO

Views of a Conservation Biologist

Dan L. Perlman

Many aspects of modern human society draw heavily on the basic sciences. Good engineering depends on a solid understanding of physics, just as materials science and public health depend on chemistry and basic biomedical sciences respectively. Land use planning calls on conservation biology for guidance, and conservation biology is based in turn on the science of ecology; yet these applications of science are very different from the previous examples. It is worth examining how the relationships among land use planning, conservation biology, and ecology differ from the relationships between the previously mentioned applied and basic sciences.

First, there is the matter of goals. Highway bridges, automobiles, cookware, and pajamas must meet standards for safety, longevity, and efficiency that are set by governments and the marketplace. The goals of public health are more difficult to pin down, perhaps in part because there is no marketplace to set standards; instead, we depend on international bodies, governments, and nongovernmental agencies to set targets for lowered death or disease rates. Setting conservation goals is even more difficult, since they include targets such as: increased ecosystem health (if human health appears difficult to measure, ecosystem health is far worse); increased populations and augmented genetic diversity of endangered species; decreased populations of invasive species; improved management of disturbances (such as fire) throughout a region; increased public awareness and support; and improved public access to protected lands. In short, designing a highway bridge is in some ways far easier than designing a conservation plan, because there the goals can be relatively easily defined. Conservation planners face an additional problem: the ecosystems and human communities where they work frequently shift in fundamental ways, such that the conservation goals must shift as well.

Second, the underlying sciences of physics, chemistry, and biomedical studies differ greatly from ecology and conservation biology. Physics, chemistry, cell biology, and genetics all focus, by definition, on discovering universal understandings and general laws. In contrast, while ecologists and conservation biologists would like to uncover general laws, their sciences are among the most historical of all, since past ecological conditions place great constraints on the present and on future ecological possibilities. In fact, it is frequently stated that the First Law of Ecology is: "It Depends."

To highlight the difference among sciences, recall that in 1989, scientists at the University of Utah announced that they had achieved "cold fusion"—the release of large amounts of energy by fusing atoms at a relatively low temperature. Within months, labs around the world were attempting to duplicate these experiments, but none were able to replicate the findings. This pattern of attempting replication of results occurs in other laboratory sciences as well, when potentially important findings are reported. In ecology and conservation biology, however, stunning new reports do not lead to flurries of replication—in large part, because it is simply impossible to truly replicate a conservation biology or ecology study (see Figures 2.1-2.4).

For example, consider a recent study demonstrating that conservation corridors can be useful in linking subpopulations of Florida black bears (*Ursus americanus floridanus*) in the Osceola and Ocala National Forests.[1] This result, however, does not necessarily mean that a similar corridor between the Tensas and Atchafalaya river basins in Louisiana will help the threatened Louisiana black bear (*Ursus americanus luteolus*)—even though it is a closely related subspecies in a nearby region. If cold fusion works in Utah, it will work in New York. But if conservation corridors work for black bears in northern and central Florida, they may or may not be effective for black bears in Louisiana, or for Florida panthers in southern Florida, or for wolves in Montana. By definition, historical differences *always* exist between different populations, subspecies, and species—and the landscapes that they inhabit differ as well. If 1 lab claims that cold fusion works while 20 labs using the same procedures say that it does not work, we can be confident that we have discovered a universal truth about the functioning of the universe. But when 1 conservation biology study claims that a conservation corridor worked while 20 others disagree, all we can say is that historical conditions may have allowed the 1 to work.

There are surprisingly few universal truths in ecology and conservation biology. While engineers and materials scientists can turn to physics and

Figures 2.1–2.4. Ecological systems are ever-changing, often in ways that appear random over the short term. These four photographs were all taken on May 15 of consecutive years (2000-2003)—but note the striking variation in plant growth among the years.

chemistry for clear-cut universals, conservation biologists cannot lean on ecology in the same way. As a result, land use professionals looking for scientific input from conservation biologists and ecologists must recognize that they will get guidelines rather than clearly defined rules. Conservation biologists, too, must recognize the limits of what they can offer: while they have accumulated vast amounts of highly relevant information for land use planners, that information unfortunately cannot be distilled into easily and widely applicable rules.

In this essay, I first discuss several ways in which land use planners and regulators can make use of the findings of conservation biology to best improve the health of the land, both for the sake of native species and for humans. Then, I describe several key areas of conservation biology research that would be especially useful for improving the effectiveness of conservation efforts on the ground. Finally, I consider ways that conservation biologists and land use professionals can work more closely together.

What Are the Major Gaps in the Conservation Biology Research Agenda That Need to Be Filled to Improve Land Use and Conservation Planning?

Improving Priority-Setting Strategies

Conservation biologists all agree that there is too little money and too few human resources to address all of the world's conservation problems. As the first sentence of a recent article in *Nature* states: "One of the most pressing issues facing the global conservation community is how to distribute limited resources between regions identified as priorities for biodiversity conservation."[2] It is imperative that we set conservation priorities as effectively as possible, to avoid spending precious resources on less important problems. That said, several issues arise in attempting to set conservation priorities, because academic conservation biologists tend toward the following attitudes, as illustrated by the quotes from Kerrie Wilson and colleagues:

- *Viewing the setting of priorities as a technical problem to be addressed with scientific and technical solutions.* For example, "stochastic dynamic programming is used to find the optimal schedule of resource allocation for small problems but is intractable for large problems owing to the 'curse of dimensionality.' We identify two easy-to-use and easy-to-interpret heuristics that closely approximate the optimal solution."[3] My response: Conservation biology problems are not so easily defined that they have "optimal solutions"; they are very complex, and there is no single technical solution to any real-world conservation problem.
- *Assuming that a single set of goals is shared by all conservation practitioners (biologists and others).* "Our objective is to maximize the number of endemic species remaining across all regions when habitat conversion ceases because there is no unreserved or unconverted land . . . ."[4] My response: While protecting endemic species is certainly a very important objective, many other conservation objectives exist and must be included in setting priorities. For example, protection of widespread but rare species, or species that are culturally important, may be highly valued, even if the species are not endemic.
- *Assuming that conservation biologists are in charge of setting conservation priorities.* "Species richness, or endemic species richness, is typically used to estimate the biodiversity value of a region."[5] My response: The number of species (or of endemic species) is certainly used as a surrogate for biodiversity in many papers written by academic conservation biologists, in part because counting species is at least semi-feasible. But many other stakeholder groups have opinions about what kind of biodiversity is valuable in

a region, and their voices need to be heard. Species richness is by no means the single best measure of conservation value.

As my colleague Glenn Adelson and I have argued previously, the setting of conservation priorities is a multi-faceted interaction among many different stakeholder groups—only one of which is the conservation biologists.[6] While we are strongly in favor of protecting as many of the world's species as possible, and especially endemics, we believe that a wide variety of human values need to be brought to bear in selecting conservation targets, and that conservation biologists are not the sole arbiters of which targets to select. Given that resources are limited, an all-out effort to protect every one of the world's species, and a focus just on *species*, will mean that many worthy conservation efforts will not get much attention. On the other hand, some hands-on conservation groups do take a multi-faceted view of their conservation mission, focusing beyond individual species. For example, "The mission of The Nature Conservancy is to preserve the plants, animals and natural communities that represent the diversity of life on Earth by protecting the lands and waters they need to survive."[7]

Much of the conservation biology priority-setting literature has focused on finding the most efficient methods of getting complete coverage for a list of entities belonging to a single class—either all the species or all the different ecosystem types in a region.[8] In a different vein, however, Seth Guikema and Mark Milke have proposed using tools from the field of decision analysis to set priorities in multi-dimensional conservation problems.[9] Unfortunately, their paper has not been widely noticed in the conservation biology world; according to Web of Science, the paper has only been cited five times as of June 2006 (and two of those citations are in other papers by the two authors of the original paper).

I am convinced that aiming for optimal solutions using extensive but very narrowly focused data sets, e.g., focusing only on the presence/absence of species is not the most productive avenue we have for setting priorities among many potentially deserving conservation projects. I believe that the time is ripe to develop a wider range of priority-setting methods than conservation biologists have used to date.

Understanding the Needs of Native Organisms
and the Functioning of Native Ecosystems, Especially on Small Scales

In most western states, Alaska, and Canada, conservation work is being envisioned and performed on grand scales. In the Yellowstone-to-Yukon (Y2Y) project, for example, conservationists envision creating corridors 10- (or even) 20-miles wide in order to link existing reserves. To ensure that these proposed corridors fill the needs of the species being targeted, basic ecological studies continue to be performed on the dispersal patterns and habitat needs of large carnivores such as grizzly bears (*Ursus arctos horribilis*), wolves (*Canis lupus*), and wolverines (*Gulo gulo*). At these geographic scales, however, it is clear that if we effectively protect habitats for "umbrella species" such as these, many other species will also receive effective protection of their habitats.

In the East, however, and in more heavily populated areas of the West, conservation must be performed in relatively small regions at small scales. In Connecticut, 40 acres might contain an entire sub-development, instead of a single home, as might occur in Wyoming. At these small scales, planners do not have the luxury of assuming that the needs of hundreds of species will automatically be taken care of by planning for the needs of one or two species of large-bodied, wide-ranging carnivores. That said, careful understanding of the distribution and ecological needs of small-bodied plants and animals can lead to important protections, even if just a few dozen acres are conserved.

The Barton Springs salamander (*Eurycea sosorum*) is one of the most extreme examples of a vertebrate with a limited range.[10] This species is only known from a complex of springs found in Zilker Park in Austin, Texas, in or beside a natural public swimming pool. According to a map in the recovery plan for the salamander, these four springs are located in an area approximately 500 yards by 40 yards in extent (about four acres). Given that the fate of an entire species rests on the management of a heavily used municipal swimming pool, conservation biologists must learn all they can about the ecology of this (and other) species, and must communicate this knowledge to relevant government authorities (Figures 2.5-2.6).

Calibrating Our Research to Focus on What Is Important;
the Conservation Corridor Issue

Performing conservation biology research is fundamentally different from performing most other types of scientific research, including basic ecological research. As I described earlier, it is hard to come up with universal scientific truths in conservation biology. The problem is compounded by the fact that so many of the biodiversity elements on which we focus are in very delicate situations. When there are just a couple of dozen California condors (*Gymnogyps californianus*) or whooping cranes (*Grus americana*) left in the world,

Figures 2.5–2.6. Barton Springs Pool in Austin, Texas. Nearly all of the world's population of the Barton Springs salamander (*Eurycea sosorum*) lives in this public swimming pool; the others live in within sight of the pool in tiny springs.

it is extremely difficult to perform rigorous studies on their breeding biology— especially if those studies carry a risk of decreasing the reproductive output of even a single mated pair. Luckily, there were other, more common cranes and condors in the world that conservation biologists could study in an attempt to learn more about increasing the population of these endangered species. But if there are key aspects of the species' biology that must be studied, such as their migration or dispersal behavior, there is no substitute for studying actual whooping cranes and California condors. Similarly, if one is interested in the effects of fragmentation on the species and ecosystem functioning of old growth redwood forests, there really is no substitute for studying these specific ecosystems.

An ecologist interested in the annual movement patterns of salamanders could choose to study any of the 44 species of lungless salamanders in the genus *Plethodon*.[11] But the conservation biologist interested in protecting federally listed *Plethodon* species would focus on just two of these: (1) the Cheat Mountain salamander (*P. nettingi*); and (2) the Shenandoah salamander (*P. shenandoah*), which are listed as "threatened" and "endangered" respectively. It is certainly possible that a closely related (but not endangered) species from the same region, living in similar habitats, could give some useful comparison information on the salamanders' behavior, but if we are considering where to site a road near a known population of Cheat Mountain salamanders, we really need to know the movement patterns of this species.

This problem of needing to focus on specifics rather than generally applicable rules becomes especially acute in the case of conservation corridors. Conservation biologists agree that before humans had major impact on landscapes, the natural world had more "connectivity"; organisms could move fairly freely from one location to another. As humans have divided up the landscape, we have decreased connectivity by destroying habitats and creating roads, making movement significantly more difficult and dangerous for native species. The way to restore connectivity, according to many conservationists and conservation groups is to create corridors. Unfortunately, an effective corridor for one species, say the gray catbird (*Dumetella carolinensis*), may be a deathtrap for another, such as the endangered Key Largo cotton mouse (*Peromyscus gossypinus allapaticola*) when it exposes them to the depredations of domestic pets. Once again, it is the particulars of the ecology of each species that makes the difference.

Like all conservation biologists, I believe strongly that protecting large areas of quality habitat is the gold standard of conservation practice. I also believe that a truly "connected" landscape will be better than a fragmented landscape of disjointed habitats. That said, while maintaining high-quality corridors is essential, there is no one-size-fits-all corridor. Unfortunately, I do not see any way around specifying which organisms are the focus of a specific corridor, and then trying to accumulate the best research possible on the costs and benefits of the type of corridor being proposed for that specific organism. As conservation biologist Andy Dobson and 14 co-authors wrote: "[T]he first step in the analysis of corridor capability [should be] the selection of target species . . . the idea of a generic landscape corridor—connectivity for the sake of connectivity—is more aesthetic than scientific and will generally be dismissed in the hard light of scientific review."[12]

What Can Land Use Planners and Regulators Do That Would Help Lead to the Conservation and Recovery of Biodiversity?

Think of the Landscape Context;
Plan Beyond the Edges of the Planning Site or Region

Very early in their careers, conservation biologists and ecologists learn that the boundaries of ecosystems are quite flexible and permeable. Even if one has a clearly demarcated study site like a pond, outside influences such as weather, disturbances, e.g., fire and flood, and immigrating organisms may drastically change events within the site.[13] Speaking from a conservation biologist's perspective, I would suggest that land use planners similarly adopt the habit of looking well beyond the boundaries of their official region of concern.

Given land use planners' focus on human health and safety, it is of course critical to consider ecological events that could impinge on the residents of a given area. But the converse is true as well: what happens within a given planning area can have major ecological effects that spill well beyond the boundaries of the site or region. In other words, what happens in Las Vegas does *not* stay in Las Vegas: local ecological events spill out to affect the ecology of the surrounding Clark County landscape, and extend far downstream along the Colorado River.

It is also critical to understand the context in which a specific conservation project sits. Imagine a 50-acre farm property that comes up for sale in your region. The site includes a little forest and some wetlands: should the property be purchased or not? This question can only be answered by understanding the context. The parcel would be valued quite differently if (1) it were one of a few ordinary farms in a forested landscape, or (2) the forest is part of a critical conservation corridor, or (3) if the wetlands are an especially vulnerable and important part of a complex that provides water for humans (see Figures 2.7-2.10).

When humans insert themselves into a landscape, they affect a number of processes—all of which change the ecology of the larger region. In general, it is useful for planners to think about *flows* across the landscape. Water is an obvious example; when we create large amounts of impermeable surface such as pavement and rooftops, we change the hydrology of a region, especially the recharging of groundwater. Humans also change natural disturbance regimes, altering the natural patterns of fire and flooding (both of which can be seen as flowing across landscapes).

As has become apparent in the aftermath of Hurricane Katrina, dams on the Mississippi and Missouri Rivers have greatly decreased the accumulation of

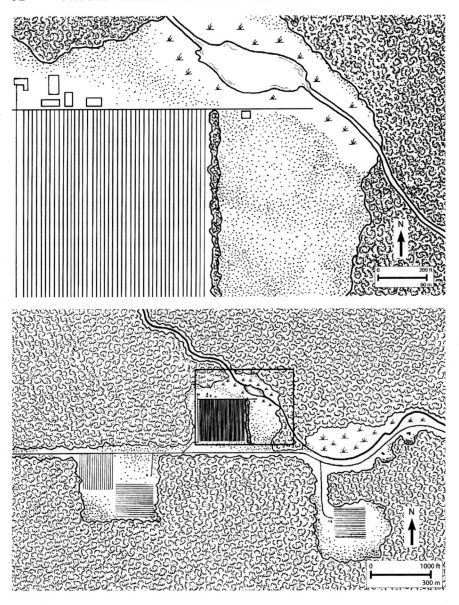

Figures 2.7–2.10. The conservation value of a given parcel depends heavily on its context. Figure 2.7 shows a hypothetical fifty-acre farm, that includes some forest and wetlands in addition to pasture and croplands. Figures 2.8–2.10 show this same farm in different contexts, to demonstrate that the site would have different types of conservation value depending

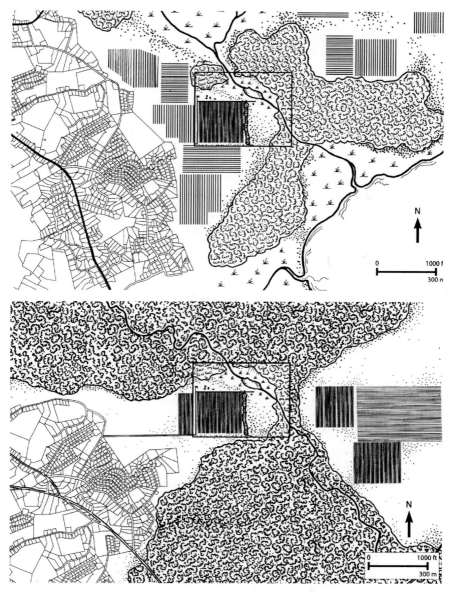

on where it is located. From *Practical Ecology for Planners, Developers, and Citizens* by Dan L. Perlman and Jeffrey C. Milder. Copyright © 2005 Lincoln Institute of Land Policy. Reproduced by permission of Island Press, Washington, D.C.

sediment in the Mississippi Delta, leading to a lowering of New Orleans and the surrounding area, which made the region more vulnerable to the effects of the hurricane. In addition, levees that straighten and speed the flow of the rivers—and that prevent flooding in one region—may have significant effects downstream, often leading to even worse flooding there. Regional planners in the upper Midwest may not regularly consider the needs of Louisiana residents, nor would Louisiana planners typically think about planning actions occurring in the upper Midwest; but actions upstream can have tremendous impacts on the people and native ecosystems downstream.

Understand the Geographic Scales Used by Specific Organisms

As a corollary of planning beyond the edges of a human-designated site or region, it is critical to know how organisms use the landscape. Consider a small pond, a vernal pool in New England, which might be home to the eggs and larvae of blue-spotted salamanders (*Ambystoma laterale*), a "species of special concern" in Massachusetts and New York. We now know that many invertebrate and amphibian species make use of vernal pools for breeding, and many of these are rare enough to be listed by their respective states. This basic ecological understanding has been written into laws and regulations across the United States, so that these temporary small ponds are protected in many jurisdictions. In Massachusetts, where I live, vernal pools that have been certified by the state are protected under the Massachusetts Wetlands Protection Act as well as several other state and federal laws.[14]

That said, we also know that many of the organisms breeding in vernal pools are not full-time residents, as they migrate away from the water for much or most of the year. In Massachusetts, vernal pools receive up to a 100-foot buffer around the pool's margin if there is wetland vegetation in the area, and this would certainly seem to be sufficient for the few-inch-long blue-spotted salamander. However, a recent study determined that these salamanders move quite a bit farther: conservation biologist Jon Regosin and his colleagues found that more than one-half of the salamanders in their study traveled more than 100 meters (over 300 feet) from the breeding pond.[15]

Consider this situation, then, in a typical development. If there were a vernal pool 100 feet in diameter, a required 100-foot buffer around the edge of the pool would mean setting aside 1.4 acres of land to remain undeveloped. Establishing a 300-foot buffer—recalling that over one-half of the blue-spotted salamanders actually moved more than this distance each year—would require setting aside over 8 acres of land; and a 400-foot buffer would require more than 14 acres. The bottom line is that the 100-foot buffer, which is not even required by law in all cases, may be woefully inadequate—and once roads, homes, and driveways are spread around this area, there will be no opportunity to create a more appropriate buffer. Thus, we must understand the ecology of the organisms we hope to protect.

Make Nature Easily Available in Order to Build Long-Term Conservation Constituencies

Having large portions of the public be strongly supportive of conservation is critical for the long-term health of ecosystems and native species, so we need to continue to build an extensive and powerful conservation constituency. Clearly, the major conservation groups have this goal in mind, as they continually reach out to the public to raise awareness (and funds). I am a strong supporter of the efforts of these groups, having worked with staff and board members of The Nature Conservancy (TNC), World Wildlife Fund-U.S. (WWF-U.S.), and Conservation International (CI). That said, I feel that these groups (and others) are missing a key long-term piece of the conservation puzzle with their tight focus on saving critically imperiled biodiversity regions around the world.[16]

The national and international conservation organizations are so focused on biodiversity conservation in high-profile/high-reward sites that they do not spend a great deal of effort on small sites and local education initiatives. I believe it is critical that each child and adult have access to some tract of "nature" nearby, even if it is tiny. Unless people form direct and personal connections to nature, it will be difficult to enlist their aid in conservation efforts around the world. I think the only way to build long-term support for conservation is through long-term local connections to *some* piece of nature; if people cannot connect with and appreciate their local nature areas, I do not think they will be committed supporters of distant areas. I clearly remember hearing Madhav Gadgil, India's leading ecologist and conservation biologist, state at a nationwide conservation conference in India that every child in his country should be able to experience a little wilderness right near his or her home village.[17] This is what I would like for our nation, as well.

In order to make this a reality, I think we need to understand "park-sheds," the area over which people gravitate toward a given natural reserve area. We need to assemble a better understanding of how people get to the parks and reserves they visit, how often and how far they travel, what they do in the parks and how they affect the sites. I have not uncovered any significant research in this area as pertains to local neighborhood parks, although there is literature on the use of national parks and similar large reserves. Knowing how people use parks will help us know where to create them and what to include. Then, knowing the needs of human visitors, we can move on from there to consider the needs of native organisms.

If we are able to offer engaging nature experiences—locally—for a large portion of the population, there is a good chance of building a long-term nature conservation constituency. Even if these parks are small, isolated, and overrun by invasive non-native plants, they can serve a critical educational role. Creating and preserving small neighborhood parks is the responsibility of local and regional planners; without the specific efforts of planning professionals, parks full of nature will frequently be replaced by playing fields and housing. The future of the conservation-minded public gets played out in neighborhoods across the country each year, as local land use decisions create or destroy local parks.

Avoid Exacerbating Exotic Species Problems

As part of appreciating nature, people typically enjoy being surrounded by attractive landscaping, especially flowering plants. Unfortunately, it turns out that quite a large number of non-native plants grow well in gardens *and* in native ecosystems, where they have few predators and parasites to keep their populations in check. In some cases, these species can become invasive, overwhelming native species and even taking over entire habitats; some notorious examples include purple loosestrife (*Lythrum salicaria*), Norway maple (*Acer platanoides*), and kudzu (*Pueraria montana*).

All too often, it takes a long time for the information that a plant (or animal) species is invasive to get from the scientific community to the landscaping community and general population. Planners could play an especially important role by keeping track of invasives and working with designers and landscape architects to stop importing and using these ecologically dangerous species.

Planners can also help combat invasive species by avoiding habitat fragmentation wherever possible. Invasives typically enter native habitats from the edges or from trails, so planners can help protect native habitats in two ways: (1) reduce the amount of edge that the nature park possesses (that is, make parks plump rather than elongated); and (2) create fewer dissecting paths so that there is a larger, untouched interior patch of habitat.

What Practices Would Help Convey Science-Based Information to Land Use Planners?

Coordinate and Expand Current Clearinghouses of
Relevant Conservation Biology Information for Planners

Many government and nongovernmental organizations (NGOs) maintain extensive guidelines for the conservation of certain species and habitat types. While a tremendous amount of excellent information exists, no single resource I know of functions as a repository for this information. For example, in my home state of Massachusetts, the Natural Heritage and Endangered Species Program maintains a number of thoughtfully prepared data sheets on the needs of species that are state-listed in one category or another. For instance, the 13 pages of guidelines for Blanding's turtle (*Emydoidea blandingii*) include data on habitat requirements, distances moved, and much more relevant information, along with nearly 3 pages of references from the scientific literature.[18] Unfortunately, this wonderful information is not easy to find, even when looking at the program website. My sense is that there is a tremendous wealth of information like this that government agencies and NGOs have created, but that it is sprinkled far and wide and difficult to find.

On a much larger scale, NatureServe, an NGO spin-off of The Nature Conservancy and its network of natural heritage programs, has developed an extensive database of information on the plants and animals of North America (and a separate database for Latin America). NatureServe's databases contain large amounts of information on the biology of individual species and many references to the primary literature. They include rankings of conservation status, such as endangered species listings from the U.S. Fish and Wildlife Service, listings from Canada's Committee on the Status of Endangered Wildlife in Canada, rankings from the World Conservation Union, and NatureServe's own state and province rankings, although they do not give the official status of species as listed by individual states. NatureServe offers good information on taxonomy (including discussions of whether a taxon is a truly distinct species, a subspecies, or merely a disjunct population), threats, geographic range, and management concerns. The organization has devoted a tremendous amount of work to create accurate, well-researched write-ups for each species.

It appears that there are many great resources available, but most of them are quite difficult to find. It would be extremely useful to have central access to the high-quality detailed conservation materials that have been created by governmental and NGO groups. I would like to see a single repository with a solid core of information, supplemented by links to detailed documents produced by other organizations. If NatureServe were willing to serve this function, they already have a superb foundation of information on many thousands of species; adding links to other resources would certainly require a fair amount of vetting, but would be very worthwhile.

Producing Resource Materials on Conservation Topics

Conservation agencies, both governmental and NGO, are almost invariably understaffed. It appears that university students, when carefully supervised, represent a major resource that is just beginning to be tapped. Like a number of other institutions, Brandeis University, where I teach, has a very active environmental internship program that places advanced undergraduates with a variety of different environmental organizations, including conservation groups. In these positions (either summer or term-time) a number of interns have created excellently researched reports, including a major document on exotic species of Massachusetts that was sponsored by The Nature Conservancy.

As an alternative to placing interns individually with organizations, a couple of universities have students researching and writing standardized reports that are widely used. In the largest such program I know of, Phil Myers, a professor of ecology and evolutionary biology at the University of Michigan, has enlisted vast numbers of students in developing very solid, in-depth materials about the world's animals for his website, the "Animal Diversity Web."[19]

In a similar vein, my students have been producing extensive reports on ecoregions of Canada and the United States, plus a few overseas ecoregions. Based on the ecoregion boundaries delineated by the WWF-U.S., these 40-50 page reports give background on each region's biodiversity, threats to that biodiversity, and responses to those threats. I am in the process of making the best of these reports available on the Internet, to make them freely accessible. It is clear from projects such as Animal Diversity Web and my students' ecoregion reports that using bright undergraduates to perform careful library research and then create cleanly edited synthesis reports has tremendous potential. I believe that—when properly supervised—these students can produce reports of great value for conservation and planning organizations. I am beginning to explore having students create reports on demand, asking governmental agencies and NGOs about their needs and then creating solid reports for them. Any of these models have real potential for planners: interns to perform research on demand; teams that produce libraries of reports; or teams that create reports on demand.

Where Can Planners and Conservation Biologists Come Together and Work Jointly? Why Are the Basics of Each Field So Foreign to Each Other?

Conservation biology is a highly interdisciplinary field, yet all too many conservation biologists remain largely isolated from their colleagues in the planning field. I would not recommend creating yet another society and journal to bring these groups together—there are already too many journals and annual meetings to be kept up with. But we need to find mechanisms to bring these two groups together.

The workshop for which this publication was prepared is an excellent model for helping the two groups learn from each other. In the past I have offered courses in which I share my understanding of conservation biology with practicing planners, and these have been well received. Rather than working within a course framework, however, I would suggest creating workshops or charrettes that bring conservation biologists and planners together to jointly focus on current issues in their region. It is critical that both groups begin to learn the language and problems that the other group of professionals uses, and I believe that this will best be achieved by addressing real-world situations.

During the first such charrettes, it will be important to keep the stakes low—these should not be high-pressure situations from which a complete and detailed plan is expected to emerge, ready to be put into place on the landscape. Instead, if at all possible, the early charrettes should be an opportunity for disparate players to describe the questions that they would raise in working on a given problem, along with the tools that they would employ in attempting to tackle it. As the series of charrettes progresses, the situations being discussed can become more immediate so that the plans can have real impact.

If possible, it would be good for a regional planning board to convene these charrettes; they would have access to good data and would in many cases have the regulatory authority to put combined conservation/land use plans into action. My hope is that over time, with added experience, planners will begin to ask questions that conservation biologists might raise, and vice versa; each group will begin to think a little bit like the other.

Conclusion

Conservation biologists and ecologists are trained to think as scientists, and typically consider themselves scientists. Despite their strong backgrounds in ecology, and their understanding of the world's complexity and variability, it is difficult for them to avoid the underlying scientific mantra that society's problems have discrete technical solutions, and that science is the primary tool to help solve problems. Moreover, conservation biologists are passionate about their subject; they believe that the world's biodiversity is deeply threatened, and they want to do what they can to help. When approached by planners seeking guidance about how to effectively protect biodiversity, we conservation biologists would like to offer clear, explicit answers. Yet we cannot simply say: "Salamanders need 600 feet of upland buffer around their vernal pool breeding habitats," or "Conservation corridors should be at least 300 feet wide." Situations in nature are too variable (in space and time and especially between species) for conservation biologists to make such definitive statements.

Accumulating knowledge of the ecological needs of different organisms is a slow and labor-intensive process; in addition, as indicated earlier, there are no general rules for calculating the needs of organisms. In general, the recommendations that conservation biologists make to land use planners and regulators have to be based on empirical studies of specific organisms. Both conservation biologists and land use planners have to recognize the limits of science-based information. While I am a very strong believer in the importance of scientifically determining how to keep native species and ecosystems healthy, I also think that (1) land use planners have to acknowledge that conservation biology and ecology are among the very most historical and idiosyncratic of all sciences, so that findings in one region or from a certain time will not necessarily apply in other locations or times; and (2) conservation biologists have to acknowledge that the problems they are addressing are not purely scientific in nature, and that many stakeholders need to contribute goals and expertise. Equipped both with the tremendous knowledge that ecologists and conservation biologists have accumulated over recent decades and with recognition that conservation biology responses must almost always be tailored to the particulars of a specific situation, I believe that planners and biologists will be able to help protect our biodiversity heritage well into the future.

Notes

1. Jeremy D. Dixon et al., *Effectiveness of a Regional Corridor in Connecting Two Florida Black Bear Populations*, 20 Conservation Biology 155-62 (2006).

2. Kerrie A. Wilson et al., *Prioritizing Global Conservation Efforts*, 440 Nature 337-40 (2006).

3. *Id.* at 337.

4. *Id.* at 339.

5. *Id.* at 337.

6. Dan L. Perlman & Glenn Adelson, Biodiversity: Exploring Values and Priorities in Conservation (Blackwell Science 1997).

7. The Nature Conservancy (TNC), *About Us*, http://www.nature.org/aboutus/ (last visited July 23, 2008.)

8. Robert L. Pressey et al., *Beyond Opportunisms: Key Principles for Systematic Reserve Selection*, 8 Trends Ecology & Evolution 124-28 (1993).

9. Seth Guikema & Mark Milke, *Quantitative Decision Tools for Conservation Programme Planning: Practice, Theory, and Potential*, 26 Envtl. Conservation 179-89 (1999).

10. U.S. Fish & Wildlife Serv., *Barton Springs Salamander* (Eurycea sosorum) *Recovery Plan*, http://ecos.fws.gov/docs/recovery_plans/2005/050921.pdf (last visited Feb. 28, 2007).

11. NatureServe, *Plethodon*, http://www.natureserve.org/explorer/servlet/NatureServe? loadTemplate=tabular_report.wmt&paging=home&save=all&sourceTemplate=review Middle.wmt (last visited Oct. 3, 2008).

12. Andrew Dobson et al., *Corridors: Reconnecting Fragmented Landscapes, in* Continental Conservation: Scientific Foundations of Regional Reserve Networks 129-70 (Michael E. Soulé & John Terbough eds., Island Press 1999).

13. Dan L. Perlman & Jeffrey C. Milder, Practical Ecology for Planners, Developers, and Citizens (Island Press 2005).

14. Natural Heritage & Endangered Species Program, Massachusetts Division of Fisheries & Wildlife, *Guidelines for the Certification of Vernal Pool Habitat*, http://www.mass.gov/ vernal_poos/pdf/vpcert.pdf (last visited July 23, 2008).

15. Jonathan V. Regosin et al., *Variation in Terrestrial Habitat Use by Four Pool-Breeding Amphibian Species*, 69 J. Wildlife Mgmt. 1481-93 (2005).

16. *See* TNC, *The Last Great Places*, http:www.nature.org (last visited Oct. 3, 2008); WWF-U.S., *The Global 200*, http://www.worldwildlife.org (last visited Oct. 3, 2008); and CI, *Biodiversity Hotspots*, http://www.biodiversityhotspots.org/Pages/default.aspx (last visited Oct. 3, 2008).

17. Personal Communication with Madhav Gagdil, Biodiversity Conservation Prioritization Conference, in New Delhi (Apr. 1998).

18. Natural Heritage & Endangered Species Program, Massachusetts Division of Fisheries & Wildlife, *Guidelines for Protecting Blanding's Turtles and Their Habitats*, http:// www.mass.gov/dfwele/dfw/nhsep/nhspguid.htm (last visited July 23, 2008).

19. *See* Animal Diversity Web, University of Michigan Museum of Zoology, *Homepage*, http:// animaldiversity.ummz.umich.edu/site/index.html (last visited Oct. 3, 2008).

CHAPTER THREE

Bridging the Gap:
Incorporating Science-Based
Information Into Land Use Planning

Bruce A. Stein

Land use planning, in one form or another, has been occurring since the colonization and establishment of the United States. Historically, planning has tended to focus on the allocation of land and other resources in a way designed to balance the protection and advancement of societal values, such as community health and well being, with the rights of landowners to use and benefit from their holdings. Incorporating ecological considerations into this planning balance was a fairly late arrival on the scene, marked in a serious way by Ian McHarg's 1969 landmark book *Design With Nature.*[1] This generally coincided with the public's broader interest in environmental protection, resulting from such things as the broad indictment of pesticides contained in *Silent Spring,*[2] an oil spill dirtying beaches in Santa Barbara, smog enveloping the Los Angeles basin, and chemical pollutants igniting on the Cuyahoga River. The launch of the modern environmental era was subsequently formalized in public policy through passage of milestone federal legislation, such as the Clean Water Act, the Clean Air Act, and the Endangered Species Act (ESA).

While some in the scientific community had long been involved in studying the effects of land use and other human activities on what is now known as biological diversity, most scientific work hewed closely to traditional disciplinary lines. Ecological researchers often worked specifically to avoid human influences, seeking to examine organisms or ecosystems untainted by interference from people. As an example, the Ecological Society of America's Committee on the Preservation of Natural Conditions—the predecessor to The Nature Conservancy—was chartered originally to identify pristine areas where ecological research could be carried out unhindered by human influence. Indeed, a difference of views as to whether that committee should retain a strict focus on research, or become more involved in preservation efforts and environmental advocacy, was at the root of its split from the Ecological Society of America and the eventual formation of The Nature Conservancy.

During the 1970s, following the public's awakening to the environmental crisis, environmental science began to be recognized as a legitimate discipline in the nation's colleges and universities. It was not for another decade, however, that the discipline of conservation biology was formalized.[3] Unfortunately, academic traditions, at least in the life sciences, tended to discourage students and faculty from entering fields such as conservation biology that are perceived as having an "applied" rather than "basic" science focus. Work with practical applications often held a stigma that was not helpful for academic career advancement. As a result, conservation-oriented biologists often carried out their work as an addendum to a more mainstream research agenda, or left academia to work in government agencies, nonprofit organizations, or private consulting firms.

The pendulum is now swinging in favor of recognizing the academic value of scientific research that has applied conservation value. The Society for Conservation Biology is now one of the fastest-growing professional societies, with more than 10,000 members around the world. Even the National Science Foundation, the primary federal funding source for non-medical life-science research, has adopted new proposal review guidelines that both recognize and encourage the broader impact of research, including its use for informing environmental protection and conservation efforts.

Despite the convergence in ecological interests over the past few decades between the land use planning community and the conservation science community, a considerable gulf still exists between the two groups. Many land use planning decisions still only incorporate ecological principles and biodiversity considerations in a cursory way, if at all. And many conservation scientists are still largely disconnected with how their research could have real-world application. What are the reasons for this continued disconnect, and what barriers exist that inhibit better integration of science-based information into the land use planning process? Conversely, where is the process working, and what opportunities are available for broadening such interaction and integration?

What Are the Most Significant Barriers to the Integration of Science-Based Information Into Land Use Planning?

At the heart of this disconnect are different cultural norms that characterize the two communities, exacerbated by differing communications styles. Land use planning involves the identification and balancing of multiple values—social, economic, and environmental—and usually takes place within a political framework where compromise is the norm. The scientific method places a premium on objective facts, and while a given hypothesis technically can only be disproved rather than proved, the focus is generally on identifying the "right" answer. Ideas and analyses are expected to stand or fall on their merits, and compromise is not a part of the scientific tradition. As a result, many natural scientists engaged in environmental management or planning processes are surprised (and often offended) when their fact-based "solution" is modified or ignored altogether.

In part, this is a result of different views of the role of science in public policy. Despite the popular notion that science drives decisionmaking, it is clear that even under the best circumstances science informs but does not dictate policy. Rather, scientific evidence serves as one of several inputs. This is most evident in the field of risk assessment, where scientific studies may quantify environmental degradation or human health effects, e.g., number of deaths, but these factors are weighed against economic cost and other social values in the development and adoption of policies and regulations. And ultimately, these factors are balanced within a political context.

Differing Values

In many ways, the issue is less about the role of science, and more about conflicts, real or perceived, among values. For instance, while there is an emerging body of knowledge that demonstrates that healthy ecosystems are important to long-term sustainability and economic prosperity, e.g., Millennium Ecosystem Assessment 2005, the classic clash among values gets simplistically articulated as "jobs versus environment."[4] A more nuanced conflict in values is even emerging within the smart-growth community. Smart growth is generally viewed as a more environmentally sustainable and socially responsible development style than traditional land use patterns. Nonetheless, different stakeholders within the broader smart-growth community may value different things—say, open space protection or affordable housing—which at times can represent conflicting goals.

Understanding the values that different parties bring to the table is not always straightforward, since people often are not clear or honest about their own underlying values. This lack of transparency can complicate efforts to better incorporate science-based information into planning processes, and can undermine trust relationships. Because many in the conservation biology field come to the profession out of a profound sense that too much of our natural world already has been lost, they often bring an implicit set of values that focuses on the protection or preservation of natural features. While this may be a perfectly rational (and indeed, laudable) set of values, working productively with planners who are attempting to balance a variety of values requires that at a minimum, this be made explicit. It also means that conservation scientists must be willing to constructively engage with parties that hold very different values in order to ensure that ecological considerations get incorporated into economic and social decisions.

Uncertainty and the Dynamic Nature of Ecosystems

The nature of scientific uncertainty creates another barrier to collaboration between planners and scientists. While uncertainty exists in all aspects of business, the development process thrives on certainty and tries to avoid surprises. Unfortunately, our scientific understanding of the natural world is imperfect, and even what we do know often comes with large caveats. Planners and other policymakers are often looking for definitive answers, when scientists can often only provide qualified guidance. Even the language used to describe uncertainties can be a major impediment to clear communication across communities. Expressing uncertainty and error bounds is good scientific practice, and is a means of quantifying the accuracy and reliability of information. To users in the planning and other communities, however, the focus on uncertainty can have the opposite effect, undermining rather than strengthening reliability, even when strong evidence exists.

A related barrier has to do with static versus dynamic notions of the natural world. Conservation scientists increasingly view natural processes as highly dynamic, responding not only to long-recognized ecological factors, such as succession, but to a host of new forces, including the spread of alien species and global climate change. And while biodiversity science historically has focused on documenting what exists, how species interact, and how ecosystems function, the science is actively moving toward a predictive and forecasting mode. As a result, conservation scientists generally have moved away from equilibrium-based models of natural stability, the so-called balance of nature, and are focusing more on understanding such things as natural ranges of variability and landscape-scale processes. Recognizing the dynamic nature of ecosystems is at the heart of the scientific communities' general unease with the "no surprises" policy for ESA implementation.

Most land use plans still have a fairly static view of the landscape, assuming that in the absence of direct human intervention, what currently exists on the landscape will continue to exist. Interestingly, incorporating dynamic change models into planning efforts is actually something that is routine. Traditionally, however, these models have focused on projections of such factors as population growth and economic performance, rather than ecosystem change. An example of how dynamic ecosystem processes are important for planning relates to vegetation dynamics and fire management in the so-called urban-wildland interface. As increasing numbers of homes are being built in and abutting naturally vegetated wildlands, long-term changes in vegetation structure have implications for such public safety issues as fire protection. Indeed, the very presence of homes in formerly unpopulated areas can constrain the use of fire management for vegetation maintenance, leading agencies instead to focus exclusively on fire suppression. In turn, such suppression efforts can lead to an unhealthy buildup of fuels, degraded wildlife habitat, and the potential for catastrophic conflagrations from both public safety, economic, and ecological perspectives.

Local Capacity

The scale at which most planning is carried out represents yet another challenge. Land use planning in the United States largely takes place at the local level, through county planning departments and city and township planning offices and commissions. While some of these planning offices are extremely sophisticated, particularly in large, wealthy jurisdictions, many local planning offices have small professional staffs or are run by volunteer commissioners. As a result, in many places planning staffs have relatively limited expertise in ecological sciences and limited capacity to maintain and run sophisticated software tools. The combination of a large number of such planning offices (there are more than 3,000 counties alone in the United States), and the small size and limited capacity in many of these creates an additional barrier to the incorporation of science-based information into the planning process.

Compounding this is the general lack of purpose-built tools and information products designed specifically to help planners understand and access relevant ecological information, and to analyze that information in a way that meets their specific needs. Many of the existing tools and scientific databases have been developed by scientists primarily for use by other scientists, and lack the type of cross-community translation and outreach functions needed to meet the needs of the planning community's large and geographically diffuse constituency. As a result, many planning offices rely on environmental consulting firms for the expertise to address ecological issues when the need arises. And while such firms may provide high-quality service, due to cost and other considerations they usually are only engaged in special circumstances, losing the opportunity for ongoing incorporation of biodiversity and ecological considerations into routine planning decisions.

What Are the Most Significant Opportunities for Advancing the Integration of Science-Based Information Across Communities?

Despite the barriers that exist, a great deal of progress is being made in increasing the degree to which ecological information is being incorporated into the land use planning process. The divide between the planning and conservation science communities increasingly is being bridged by individuals and projects that are committed to understanding the other's needs. In part, this reflects a maturing of the conservation science community, and a greater willingness of many scientists to get involved in the lengthy and often frustrating planning processes that end up shaping much of our natural landscape. It also reflects the planning community's response to an increasing interest among the public in open space, and its link to quality-of-life issues. Indeed, one of the most impressive political trends of the last decade has been the large number of bond issues passed at state and local levels, in which citizens are opting to increase taxes in order to protect habitat and preserve other open space.

Another major policy shift is at work that is encouraging greater collaboration and integration at the local level. The policy framework for conservation and environmental management is increasingly moving from the top-down, "command-and-control" regulatory approaches that were initially adopted to deal with such issues as water and air pollution, toward more flexible outcome- or incentive-based approaches that often include local involvement. Regulatory approaches have been extremely successful in dealing with certain types of problems, and will remain needed and relevant. Other problems, ranging from nonpoint source water pollution to the cumulative impacts of habitat fragmentation on wildlife, have proven to be resistant to top-down, command-and-control approaches. As a result, emphasis is now increasingly being given to empowering local communities to be creative about the way that they bring diverse stakeholders together and solve problems.

As an example of this approach, Washington State's Nisqually River is the focus of a locally based effort designed to sustain ecosystem health and promote economic vitality in the region. The Nisqually River Council has served as an umbrella for a host of watershed-based recovery activities, while local groups such as the Stewardship Partners have successfully enlisted broad-based landowner and citizen support for watershed activities. Such locally based efforts involving planners, scientists, farmers, ranchers, and environmentalists, among others, was at the heart of an August 2005 White House Conference on Cooperative Conservation.[5] A notable element of many of the successful initiatives highlighted at that conference was the close collaboration between scientists and planners, and the way in which scientific data, tools, and expertise were brought to bear in the planning and implementation of these efforts.

Data

The availability of reliable data is essential for helping to incorporate biodiversity considerations into planning processes. When dealing with a contentious project, clearly separating the fact base from the interpretation of those facts can help clarify where issues exist, and where they don't. Detailed mapping of a sensitive ecological feature, for example, will sometimes reveal that a potential conflict is not as serious as initially thought, providing more options for resolving the problem.

Basic types of data relevant to this need include information about the species and habitats that exist in a region, their condition or conservation status, the location of sensitive or other important features, and how these resources are likely to be affected by proposed activities. Fortunately, there are some excellent sources of data that are directly relevant to the needs of the planning and environmental management professions. For more than 30 years, state natural heritage programs have focused on gathering biological data for use in land planning and resource management. By carrying out inventories and managing their data according to consistent national standards, these programs offer planners a reliable source of detailed data on plants, animals, and ecological communities in each state, with particular focus on those of conservation concern.

NatureServe, a nonprofit organization that provides national coordination and technical support for these programs, integrates much of this data into a national view that can be accessed online through the NatureServe Explorer website.[6] Building on these core biodiversity databases, an increasing number of natural heritage programs are developing planner-friendly analytical products that map out environmentally sensitive areas. The Massachusetts BioMap project, for example, identifies sensitive biodiversity areas statewide, and has established a program designed to work with local planning offices in the application of these maps and the underlying data.[7]

State- and regional-scale conservation plans have been a particular focus of activity in recent years, and these plans provide important ecological context for planners. Federally funded State Wildlife Action Plans were completed for all states in 2005, and should serve to help chart the course of wildlife conservation efforts across the country. All of these plans identify animal species in need of special attention, and many include maps of priority habitats or areas for wildlife conservation. Another important effort has been The Nature Conservancy's work to identify and map out important biodiversity areas within each ecoregion of the country. These "ecoregional plans" offer another view of conservation priorities, and have the advantage of including both plants and animals of conservation concern. Still another regional planning approach focuses on what is variously termed green infrastructure, or green-printing. Such green-printing plans generally focus on identifying major remaining habitat areas, together with existing or potential connections among these core areas. Green prints can cover a single state, such as Maryland,[8] or can include multiple states, as in the case of the U.S. Environmental Protection Agency's (EPA's) Southeastern Ecological Framework.[9]

A variety of other data sources exist within individual states, although locating these sources can sometimes be difficult. Links to other state-based sources of information can be found through the NatureServe website,[10] Defenders of Wildlife's Biodiversity Partners website,[11] and through the U.S. Geological Survey-sponsored National Biological Information Infrastructure (NBII).[12]

Tools

A variety of technological tools now available to planners, some generic and some purpose-built, make ecological data, analyses, and expertise more accessible than ever before. It is hard to overstate how the Internet has revolutionized and democratized access to information in just over a decade. Not only is the Internet the primary means for scientists to communicate and share findings, but it provides planners in offices large and small with access to resources once available only to the privileged few. While the first generation of web-based resources took the form of static documents or information products, a new generation of mapping and visualization tools is now being deployed online. The current tools mostly provide opportunities to view the landscape, e.g., Google Earth®, as well as to add user-defined features. It will not be long, however, before fully web-enabled analytical geographic information system (GIS) packages are available through this medium. The Internet also has proven to be a social force, fueling the emergence of numerous virtual communities that address a variety of scientific- and planning-related issues, and providing unprecedented opportunities for citizen participation in scientific endeavors and planning processes.

Several important concepts emerge in considering how technology can enable the integration of scientific information into planning processes. Transparency and accountability are key for information and analyses to be credible, and to stand up to legal and political scrutiny. Such transparency is essential to create a trust relationship among parties that may have divergent and strongly held views and values; "black-box" solutions can undermine this trust. Because planning involves a balance among competing values, analytical tools should allow explicit recognition of the values underlying them, or accommodate different value sets. Finally, identifying alternative scenarios for meeting ecological needs, if possible, is preferable to producing a single "right" answer. Such alternatives allow planners flexibility where possible, and conversely show where there is little or no "wiggle room." A whole class of optimization techniques are becoming available to help evaluate the efficiency and effectiveness of these alternatives, and to help users decide among them.

NatureServe Vista is an example of a decision-support tool specifically designed to help incorporate biodiversity considerations into land use planning.[13] This GIS-based software allows a user to map out the biological features in their area of interest. Based on the condition and distribution of these features (and confidence in the source data), a "conservation value" landscape can be generated that displays areas of greater and lesser importance or sensitivity. In calculating this conservation value, the tool allows users to select and weigh different classes of features depending upon their particular interests, requirements, or values. For instance, a user may choose to limit the analysis to legally protected species, or might wish to include a fuller array of species and habitats of conservation interest. With a basic understanding of how these features are distributed across the landscape, a user can then evaluate how alternative plans or proposals would affect biological features of interest, or examine the relative significance of a given site or tract of land.

A number of more general land use planning decision tools are also available, such as CommunityViz® from the Orten Family Foundation.[14] This GIS-based tool provides a means to visualize analyses of land use alternatives, and to understand their potential impacts from environmental, economic, and social perspectives. Through the use of 3-D simulation, scenarios can be visualized from different angles, a feature that promotes citizen participation in planning processes. As with the Internet, this approach helps to realize the Jeffersonian ideal of participatory democracy by enabling broader understanding, dialogue, and participation.

Expertise

Despite the ever-increasing amounts of information and the analytical tools available to planners, putting these to work still fundamentally requires human interpretation and application. As a result, many of the solutions for breaking down barriers to the use of scientific information in land use planning must involve building human capacity and expertise. In fact, with the Internet providing a conduit for vast quantities of unfiltered information, the need for knowledgeable people to parse this into useful bits will only increase.

Development of a cadre of cross-trained conservation scientists and planners—individuals who are capable of bridging the divide between the two worlds—is a particular need. Scientists must learn to translate their concerns and findings into language that can be readily assimilated by non-specialists in the planning professions. This does not necessarily mean "dumbing down" such works, but rather taking the time to clearly express relevant information in a scientifically sound yet publicly accessible manner. The Environmental Law Institute's *Conservation Thresholds* publication, which gave rise to the present publication and conference, is an excellent example of translating research results into a form that is intelligible and meaningful for a planning audience.[15] Similarly, there is a need for planners to become more conversant in the language of the ecological sciences, both to help interpret and highlight important trends for their profession, and to provide input to the scientific community in terms of what would be useful for the planning profession.

Our experience at NatureServe over the years in providing biodiversity data to inform land use planning is that there is no substitute for one-on-one interaction with prospective users of the information. Often users know that they have an issue, but are unsure what the relevant questions are that they should be asking. Or they may know they have a need for data, but are either unaware of what exists, or what is appropriate for addressing their need. This is particularly true at the local level, where many planning offices are small, and staffed with individuals that must cover a wide range of activities. Several natural heritage programs, including those in Massachusetts and Virginia, have established local liaison offices to help such jurisdictions understand what is available and how to apply it to meet their local needs. Other programs, such as those in Colorado, Minnesota, and Pennsylvania, have county inventory programs underway that work with individual counties to map out sensitive ecological resources and provide specific information and advice.

Bridging the Gap

While barriers still exist between science and public policy, there are a number of developments that promise to bridge or shrink those gaps. Key to this is the growing public interest in maintaining quality of life, and the role that natural lands and open spaces play in this pursuit. To the degree that citizens have an expectation that wildlife conservation and open space preservation are a part of their communities, the planning profession is likely to respond to these desires. And fortunately, there is an expanding suite of data sources, tools, and expertise available to planners to help inform and guide land use and natural resource management decisionmaking.

Land use planning is a process that takes place in the context of strong political, economic, and social currents, and there will always be contentious issues that arise out of competing values. The role of science is not to provide *the* answer in these situations, but rather to ensure that the issues are addressed and decided on a fair and level playing field. Traditional planning processes have long focused on what is referred to as "gray infrastructure"—roads, sewers, and other aspects of the built environment. The challenge is to ensure that biodiversity and other components of "green infrastructure" are actively and routinely considered as part of this process. Nearly 40 years since the publication of *Design With Nature*, we are beginning to make real progress toward that goal.

Notes

1. Ian McHarg, Design With Nature (Natural History Press 1969).
2. Rachel Carson, Silent Spring (Houghton Mifflin 1962).
3. Michael E. Soulé & Bruce A. Wilcox, Conservation Biology: An Evolutionary-Ecological Perspective (Sinauer Associates, Inc. 1980).
4. Millennium Ecosystem Assessment, Ecosystems and Human Well-Being: Synthesis (Island Press 2005).
5. Council on Environmental Quality, Faces and Places of Cooperative Conservation: Profiles in Citizen Stewardship (2005).
6. NatureServe, *Explorer*, http://www.natureserve.org/explorer (last visited Oct. 4, 2008).
7. Natural Heritage & Endangered Species Program, BioMap: Guiding Land Conservation for Biodiversity in Massachusetts (2001).
8. Maryland's GreenPrint Program, *Homepage*, http://www.dnr.state.md.us/greenways/greenprint/ (last visited Oct. 4, 2008).
9. U.S. EPA, *EPA's Southeastern U.S. Ecological Framework Project*, http://www.geoplan.ufl.edu/epa/ (last visited Oct. 4, 2008).
10. NatureServe, *Homepage*, http://www.natureserve.org (last visited Oct. 4, 2008).
11. Defenders of Wildlife, *Biodiversity Partnership*, http://www.biodiversitypartners.org (last visited Oct. 4, 2008).
12. NBII, *Homepage*, http://www.nbii.gov (last visited Oct. 4, 2008).
13. NatureServe, *Products and Services*, http://www.natureserve.org/prodServices/vista/overview.jsp (last visited July 23, 2008.)
14. Orten Family Foundation, *CommunityViz®—GIS Decision Support for Planning and Resource Management*, http://www.communityviz.com/ (last visited Oct. 4, 2008).
15. Christina Kennedy et al., Conservation Thresholds for Land Use Planners (Envtl. L. Inst. 2003).

Private Developments Providing Conservation Benefits at Multiple Scales

The first set of case studies focus on private land developments that incorporate habitat conservation at the site level in ways that also support regional habitat needs. The three developments show how habitat conservation at multiple scales can be accomplished in sites of various sizes (640 to 20,000 acres) and types (New Urbanist to industrial to a luxury conservation development).

Chapter Four

Coffee Creek Center, Chesterton, Indiana:
Mixed Use New Urbanist Conservation Development (640 acres)

Coffee Creek Center is located on 640 acres in Chesterton, Indiana—50 miles southeast of Chicago, and directly south of the Indiana Dunes National Lakeshore in Porter County. The centerpiece of the ecologically minded, New Urbanist-style development is the 151-acre Coffee Creek Watershed Preserve (the Preserve)—managed by the Coffee Creek Watershed Conservancy (CCWC). The Coffee Creek Watershed Preserve not only serves central open space and stormwater management functions for the development but also as a riparian and wetland habitat for native wildlife. The CCWC, realizing that the environmental conditions affecting the Preserve cross property boundaries, quickly expanded its mission to include the protection, restoration, and enhancement of the entire Coffee Creek Watershed and developed the Coffee Creek Watershed Management Plan.

Chapter Five

General Motors, Lansing Delta Township, Michigan:
Corporate Lands Wildlife Habitat (1,100 acres)

The 1,100-acre General Motors Lansing Delta Township (LDT) site, a Leadership in Energy and Environmental Design (LEED) gold-rated assembly plant located in mid-Michigan, contains approximately 780 acres of undisturbed land including 75 acres of enhanced woodlands, prairie, and wetlands. The LDT Wildlife Habitat Team worked with wetland management and ecological restoration experts to create a plan for habitat preservation and environmental stewardship of the property. The LDT site is one example of the over 400 corporate habitats certified under the Corporate Wildlife Habitat Certification/International Accreditation Program implemented by the Wildlife Habitat Council (WHC). The WHC is a nonprofit, nonlobbying 501(c)(3) group of corporations, conservation organizations, and individuals dedicated to sustaining and enhancing wildlife habitat. Industrial and corporate lands, such as the LDT site, will be an important component of private land conservation and where these are administered and conceptualized in a regional context, they can offer a great potential habitat benefit.

Chapter Six

Santa Lucia Preserve, Monterey County, California:
Luxury Conservation Development/Preserve (20,000 acres)

The developers of the 20,000-acre Santa Lucia Preserve (the Preserve) constructed an upscale residential development while permanently protecting nearly 18,000 acres of the site as open space. The independently managed Santa Lucia Conservancy was established to manage the restoration and enhancement of the undeveloped 18,000 "Preserve Lands," and will preserve the land in perpetuity through fee ownership of nearly 12,000 acres and conservation easements on 6,000 acres. The conservancy, which operates as a Community Stewardship Organization in cooperation with the nonprofit Sonoran Institute, manages the Preserve through land protection, resource management, scientific research, and community education programs and ensures that the Preserve is linked in a meaningful way to regional biodiversity conservation efforts. The use of an approach that provides operating funds and institutional support for long-term conservation offers a model for future consideration in conservation developments in sensitive areas.

CHAPTER FOUR

Coffee Creek Center, Chesterton, Indiana: Mixed Use Residential Development

Chesterton, Indiana, in Porter County, is a rapidly growing community of about 12,000. Like the rest of Northwest Indiana, Porter County (also contains the town of Valparaiso) is experiencing increasing development as commuters move from the nearby Chicago metropolitan area.[1] Indiana has identified such commercial and residential development as one of the "top two reported threats to habitat."[2]

Coffee Creek Center (CCC), a New Urbanist-style development in Chesterton, has incorporated wildlife-friendly and ecologically minded development practices on-site while working to connect the site's open spaces to region conservation goals. Key among the design principles guiding the development of the site was the restoration of the native landscape—including restoration of the historical groundwater hydrology on-site and the restoration and protection of the region's native biodiversity. The centerpiece of the ecologically minded development is the 151-acre Coffee Creek Watershed Preserve (the Preserve). The Preserve not only serves central open space and stormwater management functions for the development but also as a riparian and wetland habitat for native wildlife. The Coffee Creek Watershed Conservancy (CCWC) was established to restore and conserve the Preserve.

The CCWC, realizing that the environmental conditions affecting the Preserve cross property boundaries, quickly expanded its mission to include the protection, restoration, and enhancement of the entire Coffee Creek Watershed and developed the Coffee Creek Watershed Management Plan. Over the past five years the CCWC has pursued opportunities to fund projects that meet its mission. The CCWC received a Clean Water Act §319 grant from the Indiana Department of Environmental Management to develop a watershed plan for the Coffee Creek Watershed in 2001,[3] funding from the Great Lakes Commission for a restoration project in 2003,[4] and funding from the Indiana Department of Natural Resources, Lake Michigan Coastal Management Program in 2004 to implement several tasks to help achieve the goals developed in the 2001 watershed management plan.[5]

The Lake Erie Land Company (LEL) acquired 640 acres in Chesterton for CCC in the mid-1990s. At the time of purchase, the former farmland had been zoned and entitlements had been put into place by a previous owner for a more conventional, mostly residential development.[6] In spring 1997, LEL brought together a team of experienced designers—including architects William McDonough + Partners, environmental consultants JFNew and Associates, and landscape architects and site planners Conservation Design Forum—to develop a new master plan for CCC. The new plan specified pedestrian streets and community transportation, advanced energy systems, and habitat restoration.[7] The CCC *Design Code Book*, developed by Conservation Design Forum and William McDonough + Partners, codified many of these design principles as a guide for on-site development.[8]

In 1997, the planning for CCC began with a natural inventory of the site. JFNew and Associates and Conservation Design Forum discovered a variety of unique habitats on-site including prairie, savanna, marsh, hillside fen, riparian forest, as well as Coffee Creek and its banks and floodplains.[9] The final master plan proposed the creation of several mixed use neighborhoods and commercial centers around a central watershed Preserve, which follows the course of Coffee Creek through the center of the development.[10] (See Fig. 4.1.) Although the site contained only 17 acres of nonbuildable area, the developers set aside 150 acres of high-quality habitat for the Preserve.[11] The original design for CCC also included plans for an additional 75 acres of parks and open space, residential neighborhoods, commercial and retail space, a downtown district, and civic and public facilities.

Construction on CCC began in 1998 with the restoration of the watershed areas designated as the Preserve. Conservation Design Forum and JFNew and Associates worked to develop, implement, and monitor the ecological restoration of the Preserve site. Restoration work involved over 3,000 linear feet of creek bank stabilization and revegetation; in-stream modification to support salmon, other native fishes, and macroinvertebrate populations; invasive species removal; and prairie and bottomland forest restoration.[12] In addition, native plants were restored to the prairies, savannahs, and open woodlands. Restoration efforts—such as brush clearing, erosion control, and burning—caused long-dormant native plants to reestablish populations in areas that were previously pastured and dominated by weeds.[13] Ecologists from Conservation Design Forum and JFNew and Associates conducted on-site monitoring to document the success of restoration activities and inform management decisions con-

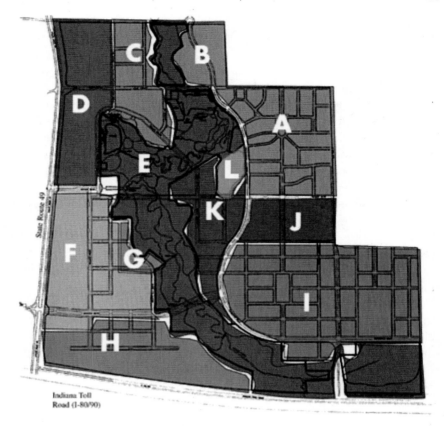

Fig. 4.1. The Coffee Creek Center. A. The Park Neighborhood (34 Acres/Underway); Mixed use area with approximately 190 multi-family and 250 single-family units currently underway and plans for a total of 490 residential units as well as corner office and store locations; B. Enclave Apartments at The Park Neighborhood (16 Acres/Underway); C. Village North (25 Acres/Underway): Mixed use, including single-family homes, townhomes, and apartments; D. The Village Green (14 Acres/Future Phase): Mixed use commercial/residential; E. Coffee Creek Watershed Preserve; F. Commercial Center: Includes the Hilton Garden Inn and plans for over one million square feet of commercial development as well as 750 residential units in multi-family buildings and some single-family; G. Multi-family, townhomes, and live-work neighborhood (9 Acres/Future Phase); H. Mixed use health care neighborhood (45 Acres/Underway): Includes Lakeshore Bone and Joint Institute, and plans for additional medical, retail, and residential use; I. Primary residential in scale mixed use area (78 Acres/Future Phase); J. Potential educational use and park/open space recreation (17 Acres/Future Phase); K. Future commercial office, conference center, with some residential (26 Acres/Future Phase); and L. The Conservancy Neighborhood: 10 homesites with direct access to the Coffee Creek Watershed Preserve. With permission from Tom Godfrey, Lake Erie Land Company.

cerning the Preserve. Data from 2002 indicate that restoration has resulted in improvements in the overall quality of the habitat.[14]

In addition to the restored habitats, a water plaza, an amphitheater, a pavilion, and a series of boardwalks and wetland overlooks were built within the Preserve. These structures, completed in 2000, serve meeting space, stormwater management, and recreation functions. Three miles of pathways made of durable concrete pavers connect the high use areas of the Preserve. Bridges were set by helicopter to avoid soil compaction, and pedestrian bridges and boardwalks were built from sustainably harvested California redwood.[15] The Preserve's restrooms have green roofs and adjacent wetland cells that clean wastewater naturally. And, four miles of crushed aggregate pathways in the more natural sections of the Preserve avoid root zones and hydrologically sensitive areas.

Although LEL made a large investment to get the infrastructure for CCC in place, residential development within CCC has been slow, and most of the planned neighborhoods remain unbuilt. LEL, after developing the master plan, sold parcels of land within CCC to other developers for subsequent construction. However, the model homes built did not attract buyers and one parcel of land sold in 1999 remains virtually undeveloped today. One reason for slow sales may be that CCC does not offer the large-lot, suburban style home that Chicago commuters may be looking for. However, a small number of houses, an apartment complex, a hotel, a medical center, and a number of retail shops and restaurants have now been built on the property,[16] and 250 houses are planned for the first phase of development.[17]

CCC has received a range of media attention,[18] and has received several awards including the ILASLA Merit Award of Design in 2001[19] and the Conservation and Native Landscaping Award from the U.S. Environmental Protection Agency (EPA) and Chicago Wilderness in 2003,[20] and was recognized as one of the Urban Land Institute's 26 Great Planned Communities.[21] LEL has since divested its interest in CCC,[22] and the property was purchased by another developer. The new developer has begun construction on the north side of the development, but not all of it has been in the spirit of the original master plan.[23] Build-out for CCC is anticipated in 2015.[24]

The Preserve

The 15.7-square mile Coffee Creek Watershed is located in the northeastern portion of Porter County, south of the Indiana Dunes National Lakeshore. Coffee Creek itself runs south to north and empties into the Little Calumet River, which flows into Lake Michigan about 10 miles west of its confluence with

Coffee Creek. The Preserve is located along a section of the creek in the lower one-third of the watershed.[25]

The Coffee Creek Watershed area was historically a cold water stream habitat with riparian corridor, open prairie, and open wetland habitats.[26] At the time of purchase by LEL, much of the site, with the exception of the main creek corridor, had been cropped or pastured. Coffee Creek itself had been deeply incised, and the water quality was poor.[27] The Preserve now includes diverse habitats such as riparian wetlands, hillside fens support populations of over 100 species of birds, 437 native plants, and several typical midwestern mammal species.[28] Coffee Creek supports a spawning population of salmon—especially in the restored areas—and 12 additional fish species. The Preserve is also home to two species of special concern to the state—the sharp-shined hawk and great blue heron—and two state-endangered bird species—the northern harrier and marsh wren.[29]

The Preserve is also now a well-used resource for the local community. The Pavilion Center and Chesterton Amphitheater are rented for local events and weddings, and the town of Chesterton now holds its annual picnic in the Preserve. The CCWC also coordinates hikes, field trips, and volunteer activities in the Preserve. An updated property management plan for the Preserve, completed in fall 2007, emphasizes long-term management objectives and strategies to maintain and enhance the natural area status along the riparian corridor. JFNew and Associates serves as the primary consultant for on-going management.[30]

Operation of the Development

The CCWC

The CCWC was created in 1998 by LEL out of a need to "restore and steward" the Preserve,[31] which was donated by LEL to the CCWC in 1999.[32] CCWC's mission to "identify, maintain, and enhance the remnant biodiversity that resides within the corridor" encompasses both the long-term management of the Preserve as well as the restoration of the entire watershed.[33]

CCWC is headed by a board consisting of representatives of local environmental groups including Save the Dunes Council, the Indiana Wildlife Federation, the Porter County Chapter of the Izaak Walton League, the Northwest Indiana Steelheaders, the Coffee Creek Life Center, and the Chesterton High School SAFE (Students Actions for the Environment) Club.[34] Currently, the CCWC is funded by LEL and the CCC property owners association to manage the Preserve, coordinate public activities and volunteer opportunities within the Preserve, and conduct educational outreach to the public.[35] The CCWC will also continue to receive small donations from the Friends of Coffee Creek Watershed Preserve[36] and will continue to pursue grants for management and restoration activities.[37]

Watershed Management Plan

Realizing that environmental concerns cross jurisdictional boundaries, the CCWC expanded its mission to include the protection, restoration, and enhancement of the entire Coffee Creek Watershed, which covers approximately 16 square miles in northeastern Porter County.[38] (See Fig. 4.2.) In 2001, CCWC received a Clean Water Act §319 grant from the Indiana Department of Environmental Management to fund the development of a watershed management plan to address water quality concerns related to Coffee Creek and its tributaries.[39] The CCWC encouraged stakeholder involvement in the development process, and over 50 community members participated in the 319 public meetings.[40] In addition, the CCWC invited local landowners and representatives from the local natural resources agencies to participate.

The watershed management plan outlines strategies, action items, methods for measuring success, and time frames for achieving the stakeholders' vision of Coffee Creek: "Coffee Creek supports a healthy cold water biological community and provides an attractive resource for citizens."[41] The goals outlined in the plan include: hiring a watershed coordinator; establishing permanently protected, vegetated streamside buffers along Coffee Creek and its tributaries; encouraging the conservation, management, and improvement of existing forested land in the upper portion of the watershed; educating and informing stakeholders of the value of Coffee Creek; gaining a better understanding of pathogenic contamination of Coffee Creek and educating stakeholders on management techniques; documenting and reducing the contribution of sediment, nutrients, and bacteria from surface and subsurface drains; and reducing the amount of sediment and nutrients reaching Coffee Creek via Pope O'Connor Ditch and Shooter Ditch.[42]

In 2004, CCWC received funding from the Indiana Department of Natural Resources Lake Michigan Coastal Management Program to implement several tasks to help achieve the goals developed in the watershed management plan.[43] The grant provided funding to hire a watershed coordinator to help manage and implement a range of priority projects. Initial projects to be completed under the grant included conducting landowner surveys of riparian buffers, educating local landowners with forested land on the importance of their land to

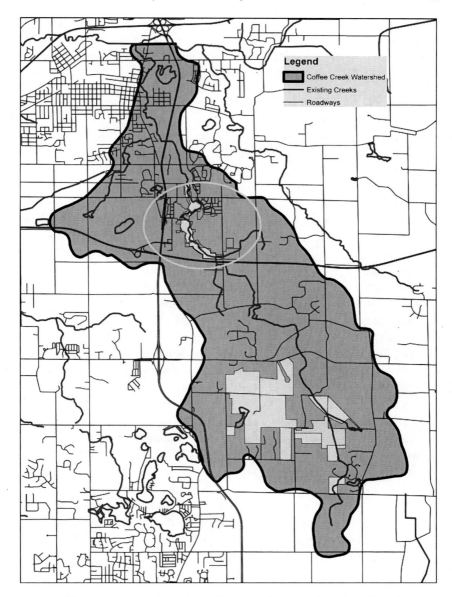

Fig. 4.2. Coffee Creek Watershed. The Coffee Creek Watershed Preserve is circled. With permission from the Coffee Creek Watershed Conservancy.

the quality of the creek, managing the volunteer Hoosier Riverwatch monitoring program,[44] and developing an agricultural best management practices (BMP) brochure specific to the Coffee Creek Watershed and working with local farmers to implement these methods on their land.

Shooter Ditch Restoration

In 2003, the CCWC received funds from the Great Lakes Commission for the restoration of Shooter Ditch, located at the southern end of the Preserve, with a goal of establishing a historic hydrological regime by creating a more functional wetland complex.[45] Despite being the smallest of the four major sub-watersheds of Coffee Creek, Shooter Ditch contributed the second highest amount of sediments (and attached pollutants) to the creek.[46] In 2004, CCWC purchased conservation easement rights from affected property owners and began restoration on the site. Restoration involved constructing a water control/weir structure, sediment trap, spillway, and earthen dam to better accommodate a 100-year flood, reduce sediment loads into the creek, and restore wetland hydrology and its associated habitat. In addition, 30 acres of native grasses, sedges, and forbs and 6 acres of native trees and shrubs were planted. The outcomes of the restoration were reduced sediment and nutrient loads, improved wildlife habitat and recreational use in open water; increased habitat connections between critical habitat in the Coffee Creek floodplain and wetlands in the upper watershed portion of shooter ditch; and improved relations among regulatory agencies, private property owners, and CCWC.[47] As a result of these restoration efforts, annual sediment savings are anticipated to exceed expectations and 30 acres of wildlife habitat were created and enhanced within the Preserve. Today, the site is covered by wetland vegetation, such as bulrushes, sedges, and other such emergent vegetation.[48]

Community Outreach

In an effort to implement the goals of the watershed management plan, CCWC works with local landowners to educate them about water quality and management issues affecting Coffee Creek. Throughout the year, CCWC conducts water quality monitoring, bird monitoring, educational tours, and exotic species control work days for community members. Volunteer opportunities at the Preserve include bird monitoring, flower hikes, garlic/mustard control and other invasive species control, creek water monitoring, and a frog hike. The CCWC also hosts the Hoosier Riverwatch Fun-Filled Field Day, where community members spend the day practicing monitoring techniques including measuring stream flow and habitat quality, trying chemical testing kits, and monitoring macroinvertebrate communities.[49] The CCWC also runs guided field trips through the Preserve; introducing participants to the plants and animals that live in the Preserve as well as the water management system.[50]

The Coffee Creek Center: Green Development

All construction in CCC is supposed to follow a set of rigorous site planning, materials, landscaping, and stormwater guidelines—codified in the CCC *Design Code Book*.[51] The developers were dedicated to designing a community that focuses on pedestrian streets and community transportation, generates no surface water runoff and no wastewater discharge of any kind, and is built with rigorous standards for green building materials, native landscaping, and energy efficiency. However, some of the early commercial development did not strictly adhere to the *Design Code Book* guidelines, including a 370,000-square foot shopping center built within CCC. Some of the more recent development projects, including the office and retail space in the Pavilion Center, better resembles the original New Urbanist-style intent of CCC.[52]

Stormwater and Wastewater Management

In putting together the master plan for CCC, the design team focused on restoring the historical groundwater-dominated hydrology to the site. The site contains no infrastructure for holding stormwater or removing it from the site. Instead, water flows underground through a distribution system and is then absorbed through restored swales and deep-rooted native prairie grasses. Stormwater is first directed to exfiltration manholes that direct water to distribution pipes that direct water to perforated detention pipes for storage and percolation. The water is then routed through the distribution system. Excess water is routed to Phillips Pond. Water in the distribution system is dispersed through a series of underground level spreaders, which allow water to percolate into the ground. The level spreaders are located on the descending hillside between the Weir Bridge and Coffee Creek in the Preserve. As the spreaders fill with water, the excess spills over and runs downhill to the next spreader. The water is filtered by the native prairie grasses as it runs downhill. The water that percolates through the spreaders is filtered underground and eventually reaches Coffee Creek.

In the main commercial areas of CCC, stormwater will flow into cisterns under the parking lots. When full, water will flow out of the cistern to the restored pond in the Preserve. Two small waterfalls will naturally aerate and cleanse water in the pond. Excess water from pond flows under the Weir Bridge into a vegetated swale for infiltration.[53] According to the *Design Code Book*, owners of industrial, civic, and commercial buildings and associated parking must ensure that stormwater runoff on developed land is at a level equal to or less than the respective 24-hour, 2- and 10-year pre-development peak discharge rates. Stormwater practices in the commercial areas of the development must control the volume and rate of flows, and lead to the infiltration or evaporation of retained stormwater.[54]

In keeping with LEL's commitment to treating all wastewater on-site, consultants JFNew and Associates designed a wastewater treatment master plan for CCC. The wastewater system includes the construction of subsurface wetlands and adsorption fields planted with native species selected for their effluent treatment and evapotransiration capabilities. Treated wastewater is pumped to an absorption area in the Preserve with deep-rooted native grasses and flowers.[55]

In addition, landscaping that encourages infiltration of rainfall and surface runoff from the roof and other impervious surfaces is encouraged whenever possible, e.g., the strategic location of grasses and other vegetation around and between impervious areas. And, subsurface irrigation, except for drip or delivery from a grey water source, is prohibited in CCC.[56]

Analysis

Nature-friendly developments can play a significant role in land conservation by preserving open space and protecting critical habitat within the boundaries of the site. More meaningful conservation contributions can be made by linking these open spaces to regional preserved land and habitat corridors and by establishing an entity dedicated to managing and preserving the land. The preservation of the Preserve has made it possible for CCWC to pursue larger watershed restoration and preservation goals including securing outside funding to develop a watershed plan, restoring habitat within and outside of the Preserve, and educating community members on a local and regional scale.

CCWC collaborates with the public, private landowners, the town of Chesterton, and Porter County agencies to carry out the goals of the regional watershed management plan. CCWC also collaborates with regional environmental organizations such as the Indiana Coastal Restoration Action Team, Save the Dunes, and the Northwest Indiana Invasive Plant Network on regional biodiversity conservation efforts.[57] For example, in 2001, CCWC and several other environmental organizations and government agencies[58] received a $1 million grant from the North American Wetlands Conservation Act Standard Grant Program to acquire 710 acres to help link existing habitat in the area, restore 399 acres of wetlands and associated uplands, and enhance 60 acres of wetlands.[59]

In addition, local environmental organizations and agencies manage several preserves within the Coffee Creek Watershed; offering opportunities to link conserved habitat in the area.[60] The Indiana Division of Nature Preserves manages the 950-acre Moraine Nature Preserve, which is located at the headwaters of Coffee Creek.[61] The agency recently acquired the University of Chicago Woods with money from the National Oceanic and Atmospheric Administration, and the 28-acre Chrisman Sand Track, which connect the 76-acre University of Chicago Woods site to the main body of preserve. The Coffee Creek area is also within the planning area of the regional "Chicago Wilderness" biodiversity program. Chicago Wilderness coordinates activities affecting a set of regional natural areas managed by various public and private entities. This includes more than 225,000 acres of protected natural lands stretching from southeastern Wisconsin, through northeastern Illinois, and into northwestern Indiana.[62]

Local governments can encourage such nature-friendly private developments through properly constructed laws and policies that provide a source of authority for forward-looking plans and developments. Forward-thinking private developers, in turn, can provide stimulus for local governments to adopt such progressive policies. The CCC design team met with local government officials early in the planning process to describe the underlying philosophy of the development. Many of the proposed site planning, stormwater and wastewater engineering, and development plans were outside the scope of Chesterton's existing codes and ordinances, thus requiring numerous zoning variances from the town. The community came to support CCC and facilitated the changes necessary to implement the final master plan.[63]

Although not in place at the time of planning for CCC, Porter County has since instituted some progressive land use policies. In 2001, the county adopted a Land Use and Thoroughfare Plan that stresses growth near cities and protection of rural areas.[64] In general, it encourages high-density housing closer to cities and towns and agriculture and low-density housing in the more rural areas, and provides recommendations to "preserve open space, agriculture and natural resources, provide recreation opportunities and ensure an efficient transportation and infrastructure network."[65] The land use plan recommends the protection of Porter County's significant environmental features through the use of an innovative subdivision design, which preserves open space, environmental features, and the general character of the area.[66] In 2006, Porter County drafted a Unified Development Ordinance, which brings the county's land use ordinances in line with the Land Use and Thoroughfare Plan.[67] In addition, Porter County passed an open space ordinance in 2004 that requires planned unit developments, multifamily developments, and residential subdivisions to set aside significant open space and to preserve 100% of designated priority areas within the site.[68]

Carefully planned private developments can provide for habitat corridors, adequate riparian buffers, and protected areas of core habitat. The developers of CCC considered the natural features and processes of the site when planning the development, and in establishing the CCWC allowed for the consideration of its regional ecological context as well.

Notes

1. U.S. EPA, *Building the Comprehensive Community: Traditional Neighborhood Development for Porter County, Indiana*, http://www.epa.gov/piedpage/pdf/portercounty.pdf
2. D.J. Case & Associates, Indiana Comprehensive Wildlife Strategy (2005), *available at* http://www.djcase.com/incws/manuscript/FINAL_CWS_MANUSCRIPT.pdf.
3. JFNew & Associates for the CCWC, *Coffee Creek Watershed Management Plan*, http://www.coffeecreekwc.org/media/mgmt_plan_docs/mgmt_plan_web.pdf (last visited Oct. 6, 2008).
4. Great Lakes Basin Program for Soil Erosion & Sediment Control, *Shooter Ditch Sedimentation Project*, http://www.glc.org/basin/project.html?id=217 (last visited Oct. 6, 2008).
5. Indiana Lake Michigan Coastal Program, *Projects Awarded 2003-2006*, http://www.in.gov/dnr/lakemich/grants/Projects%20Awarded%20to%20date.pdf (last visited Oct. 6, 2008).
6. Personal Communication with Jim Patchett and David Yocca, Conservation Design Forum (July 30, 2007) [hereinafter Patchett & Yocca Communication].
7. Coffee Creek Center Design Principles, http://www.coffeecreekcenter.com/pages/design-/design-principles.htm (last visited Oct. 6, 2008).
8. *See* Patchett & Yocca Communication, *supra* note 6. *See also* CCC, *Design Code Book*, http://www.coffeecreekcenter.com/media/mediaattn/CCC-Codebook_web.pdf (last visited Oct. 6, 2008).
9. Patchett & Yocca Communication, *supra* note 6.
10. CCC, *Development Opportunities*, http://www.coffeecreekcenter.com/pages/residential/development-opps.htm (last visited Oct. 6, 2008).
11. Urban Land Institute, *Great Planned Communities_Coffee Creek Center*, http://www.coffeecreekcenter.com/media/mediaattn/PRINT-COVERAGE/GPC.pdf (last visited Oct. 6, 2008).
12. Personal Communication with Steve Barker, CCWC (June 22, 2007) [hereinafter Barker Communication].
13. Patchett & Yocca Communication, *supra* note 6.
14. The Preserve, *Monitoring Reports*, http://www.coffeecreekwc.org/pages/reports/monitoring_splash.htm (last visited Oct. 6, 2008).
15. Adam R. Arvidson, *Selling Sustainable Development: This Indiana Subdivision Is a Model of Ecological Design. So Why Are Sales So Sluggish?*, 94 Landscape Architecture 100-11 (2004).
16. Personal communication with Tom Anderson, Save the Dunes (August 7, 2007).
17. CCC, *Building Opportunities Abound, Commercial/Retail*, http://www.coffeecreekcenter.com/ (last visited Oct. 6, 2008).
18. CCC, *Media Attention*, http://www.coffeecreekcenter.com/pages/media/media-list.htm (last visited Oct. 6, 2008).
19. LEL Press Release, Coffee Creek Center Wins the ILASLA Merit Award of Design, http://www.coffeecreekcenter.com/pages/media/documents/ILASLAMeritAwardofDesign.pdf (last visited Oct. 6, 2008).
20. LEL Press Release, Coffee Creek Watershed Conservancy Wins the U.S. EPA Conservation and Native Landscaping Award, http://www.coffeecreekcenter.com/pages/media/documents/EPAAward021304.pdf (last visited Oct. 6, 2008).

21. *See supra* note 11.
22. Patchett & Yocca Communication, *supra* note 6.
23. *Id.*
24. *See* Arvidson, *supra* note 15.
25. *See Coffee Creek Watershed Management Plan, supra* note 3.
26. *See supra* note 11.
27. Patchett & Yocca Communication, *supra* note 6.
28. Barker Communication, *supra* note 12.
29. *Id.*
30. E-mail from Steve Barker, Coffee Creek Watershed Conservancy, to authors (Sept. 28, 2007) [hereinafter Barker E-mail].
31. *See Coffee Creek Watershed Management Plan, supra* note 3.
32. The Preserve, *Our Mission*, http://www.coffeecreekwc.org/pages/mission.htm (last visited Oct. 6, 2008).
33. *Id.*
34. *Id.*
35. Barker Communication, *supra* note 12.
36. Friends of Coffee Creek Watershed Preserve, *Homepage*, http://www.coffeecreekwc.org/pages/friends.htm (last visited Oct. 6, 2008).
37. Barker Communication, *supra* note 12.
38. *See Coffee Creek Watershed Management Plan, supra* note 3.
39. The Indiana State Wildlife Action Plan identifies §319 grants as a potential source of funding to support the goals outlined in the plan. *See* Indiana Comprehensive Wildlife Strategy, *supra* note 2.
40. CCWC, *Coffee Creek Watershed Conservancy Continues 319 Grant Work*, http://www.coffeecreekwc.org/pages/319grant.htm (last visited Oct. 6, 2008).
41. *See Coffee Creek Watershed Management Plan, supra* note 3.
42. *Id.*
43. Indiana Lake Michigan Coastal Program, *supra* note 5.
44. Hoosier Riverwater, *Homepage*, http://www.hoosierriverwatch.com/ (last visited Oct. 6, 2008).
45. Great Lakes Basin Program for Soil Erosion & Sediment Control, *Shooter Ditch Sedimentation Project*, http://www.glc.org/basin/project.html?id=217 (last visited Oct. 6, 2008).
46. *Id.*
47. *Id.*
48. Barker E-mail, *supra* note 30.
49. CCWC, *Volunteer Opportunities*, http://www.coffeecreekwc.org/pages/events/volunteer.htm (last visited Oct. 6, 2008).
50. CCWC, *Field Trips*, http://www.coffeecreekwc.org/pages/events/fieldtrips.htm (last visited Oct. 6, 2008).
51. *Design Code Book, supra* note 8.
52. Patchett & Yocca Communication, *supra* note 6. *See also Design Code Book, supra* note 8.
53. CCWC, *Level Spreaders*, http://www.coffeecreekwc.org/media/pdf/Level_Spreader_brochure.pdf (last visited Oct. 6, 2008).
54. *Design Code Book, supra* note 8.

55. JFNew & Associates, *Conservation Design_Coffee Creek Center*, http://www.jfnew.com/conservative-design.asp (last visited Oct. 6, 2008).

56. *Design Code Book*, *supra* note 8.

57. Barker Communication, *supra* note 12.

58. Collaborating organizations included the Indiana Heritage Trust, The Nature Conservancy, Lake County Parks, Lake Heritage Parks Foundation, Indiana Department of Natural Resources, NiSource, Ducks Unlimited, Inc., Lake Erie Land Company, Marsh Transplant Aquatic Nursery, Indiana Dunes National Lakeshore, and CCWC.

59. U.S. Fish & Wildlife Serv., *North American Wetlands Conservation Act Standard Grant Program*, http://www.fws.gov/birdhabitat/Grants/NAWCA/Standard/US/2001_March.shtm# 1576 (last visited Oct. 6, 2008).

60. Barker Communication, *supra* note 12.

61. Personal Communication with John Ervin, Indiana Department of Natural Resources (July 12, 2007).

62. Chicago Wilderness, *A Regional Nature Preserve*, http://www.chicagowilderness.org/ (last visited Oct. 6, 2008).

63. Patchett & Yocca Communication, *supra* note 6.

64. Rich Jackson, *Tips for Making Porter County a Better Place*, Post-Trib. (Indiana), June 16, 2007, *available at* http://www.post-trib.com/news/opinion/430032,betterporter.article.

65. Vicki Urbanik, *County's New Zoning Ordinance Now Open for Public Review*, Chesterton Trib., Feb. 25, 2006, *available at* http://www.chestertontribune.com/PorterCounty/countys_new_zoning_ordinance_now.htm.

66. HNTB Corp., Porter County Land Use Thoroughfare Plan (2001), *available at* http://www.co.porter.in.us/assets/files/pdf/plcm/PLCM_LandUse.pdf.

67. GroundRules, Porter County Unified Development Ordinance (2008), *available at* http://www.co.porter.in.us/assets/files/pdf/plcm/Unified_Development_Ordinance.pdf.

68. Porter County Code ch. 17.108_Open Space.

General Motors Lansing Delta Township Assembly Center: Industrial Private Development

As the owner of millions of acres of land, U.S. corporations have the opportunity to establish and maintain habitats on their sites in ways that are beneficial to wildlife. Since 2002, the General Motors Corporation (GM) has established Wildlife Habitat-Certified habitat conservation programs for 10 of its more than 50 U.S. sites. The 75-acre Wildlife Habitat Area at its Lansing Delta Township (LDT) Assembly Center near Lansing, Michigan, was certified by the Wildlife Habitat Council (WHC) in 2006. WHC-certified programs are chosen by a panel of WHC wildlife biologists and staff using a set of stringent criteria. Certified sites must be active for at least one year and must develop a management plan that lists goals, objectives, and implementation policies.[1]

The LDT facilities were constructed on 320 acres of a 1,100-acre greenfield site—leaving 780 acres virtually undisturbed.[2] From the beginning, GM set out to "design and build the world's most environmentally advanced auto manu-facturing plant."[3] Development of the LDT site began in the late 1990s with the construction of the Lansing Regional Stamping plant, which started production in 2003.[4] Shortly after startup, the Michigan Department of Environmental Quality designated the stamping plant a Clean Corporate Citizen for demon-strating environmental stewardship and a strong environmental ethic.[5] The entire LDT site has since been recognized as a Clean Corporate Citizen.[6]

Site preparation and construction of the LDT assembly plant began in early 2004.[7] GM planned to have the LDT assembly operations and associated build-ings achieve Leadership in Energy and Environmental Design (LEED) certification, and hired St. Louis-based Vertegy Consultants to guide the sus-tainable design and construction of the site.[8] Compared to similar plants, the LDT plant was designed to realize significant energy and water savings over the life of the facility.[9] More than 25% of the construction materials used in plant construction were composed of recycled content and more than 60% of the construction materials were sourced through manufacturers located within 500 miles of the plant. In 2005, the plant received a LEED gold rating—the world's first for an automobile manufacturing plant.

In 2004, GM began the environmental planning for the 75-acre LDT Wildlife Habitat Area in a location which was slated for habitat conservation before construction began on the assembly plant.[10] The area was chosen for the diversity of habitat—including forest, wetland, and prairie—found on the site. In addition, prior studies highlighted the importance of conserving the wetland portion of the site.

In April 2004, a biologist from the WHC conducted an initial site visit to identify opportunities for enhancing natural habitat in the Wildlife Habitat Area.[11] Based on this visit, the WHC provided an *Opportunities for Wildlife Habitat Enhancement Report* to LDT in June 2004. LDT formed a Wildlife Habitat Steering Team (Steering Team) to assess the recommendations outlined in the report and develop a habitat management plan for the site. In fall 2004, the Steering Team hired wetland management and ecological restoration experts from a local consulting firm, Environmental Consulting and Technology, Inc. (ECT), to conduct a baseline ecological inventory of the site and assist in the development of a Wildlife Management Plan.[12] The final plan details five major habitat initiatives including wetland enhancements, wetland buffer enhancements, woodland enhancements, trail development, and wildlife curriculum development.

In 2005, LDT established a Wildlife Habitat Team (different from the above-mentioned Steering Team) to provide stewardship for the Wildlife Habitat Area, implement the restoration activities outlined in the Wildlife Management Plan, and coordinate public awareness of and community involvement at the site. Habitat Sub-Teams were created for each of the wildlife projects and monitoring programs outlined in the Wildlife Management Plan. Restoration of the Wildlife Habitat Area, which began in 2005, involved improving general food, water, cover, and habitat for the wildlife species identified on the site's wetland, wetland buffer, and woodland areas.[13] The Wildlife Habitat Team collaborated with local environmental organizations to build and install boulder mounds, floating nest platforms, wood duck boxes, songbird houses, and bat houses in the wetland areas; to place eastern bluebird nest boxes, a purple martin colony house, American kestrel nest boxes, raptor boxes, and bee blocks throughout the buffer site; and to conduct snag assessment and invasive species removal in the woodland areas of the site. Trees, shrubs, and native grasses were planted on the site and invasive, non-native species were removed. In 2006–2007, the Wildlife Habitat Team collaborated with Pheasants Forever and

Thornapple Grand Conservation District to plant 40 acres of trees, shrubs, and prairie plantings in the wetland buffer area.[14] The development of the prairie was a multi-year process consisting of site preparation, seeding with native prairie grasses and flowers, and maintenance.[15]

Production of vehicles at the LDT site began in November 2006. The plant is currently running at full capacity, producing approximately 1,023 vehicles per day for a total of nearly 180,000 vehicles per year.[16] In 2006, GM applied for WHC's Wildlife Habitat and Corporate Land for Learning Certification for the LDT Wildlife Habitat Area. The Wildlife Habitat certification process included a site visit from a WHC biologist, submission of an application form and community references, and submission of a completed management plan supported by photographs and documentation of program monitoring and maintenance.[17] In April 2006, the LDT site received Wildlife Habitat and Corporate Land for Learning Certification and was recognized by the WHC as "Rookie of the Year" for creating an exemplary wildlife habitat on the site.[18]

Operation of the Site

LDT Wildlife Habitat Area

The LDT Wildlife Habitat Area consists of 75 acres of woodlot, wetlands, and prairie located east of the LDT manufacturing site.[19] The site includes a diverse woodland area; a restored prairie area; a large detention basin that serves stormwater management functions while providing habitat; a pond that provides deeper water habitat for fish and waterfowl; and several types of wetlands including marshes, swamps, and vernal ponds that provide habitat for amphibians, reptiles, and a variety of waterfowl. A number of native species including at least 90 bird species, 12 species of reptiles and amphibians, and 19 species of mammals inhabit the site. In addition, more than 65 tree species and 125 species of groundcover are found throughout the site.[20] (See Fig. 5.1.)

A system of earthen and mowed trails provides public access to emergent wetland, woodlot, and prairie areas from the main trailhead located near the GM LDT Visitor Center. Wildlife observation blinds enable the public to view wildlife with minimal visual interference. Outside of the 75-acre Wildlife Habitat Area, approximately 700 acres of the 1,100-acre LDT site have been left virtually undisturbed (aside from a few residential properties and some farming activity) and unmanaged by GM. Although there are no immediate plans for additional habitat restoration projects on this property, the area contains woodlots, wetlands, and grasslands that could be restored for wildlife.[21] It is

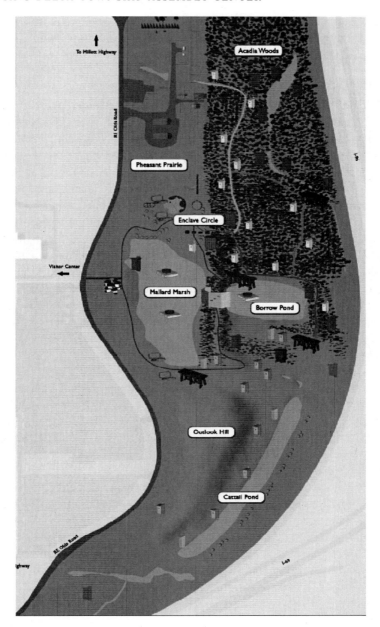

Fig. 5.1. General Motors Lansing Delta Township Wildlife Habitat Area. With permission from General Motors Corporation.

unlikely that the Wildlife Habitat Area will be able to be directly linked to this larger, currently unmanaged area because the Wildlife Habitat Area is isolated by roads and the assembly plant.

LDT Wildlife Habitat Team

LDT's Wildlife Habitat Team was created to provide stewardship for the Wildlife Habitat Area, implement the Wildlife Management Plan, and coordinate public awareness of and community involvement at the site. The Wildlife Habitat Team is led by one of LDT's senior environmental engineers who is also responsible for waste and water compliance at the LDT plant, including management of hazardous, universal, and industrial wastes, stormwater management, and waste water (sanitary and process) system management; management of the LDT's Resource Management Program; and other environmental program support.[22]

The LDT Wildlife Habitat Team is made up of the Steering Team, the Habitat Sub-Teams, and community partners who participate in habitat activities at the LDT site. The Steering Team consists of key LDT employees; including environmental and manufacturing engineers, facility maintenance personnel, and the conservation committee chair; and Habitat Sub-Team leaders. Habitat Sub-Teams, created for each of the wildlife projects and monitoring programs outlined in the Wildlife Management Plan, are led by an LDT employee (hourly or salary), and are made up of LDT employees and partners from the community and local organizations, such as Pheasants Forever, the Thornapple Grand Conservation District, and Prevention Through Experimental Education and Recreation (PEER), who volunteer their time at the LDT site.[23] Members of the Wildlife Habitat Team are volunteers, and there is no direct compensation for LDT employees who participate in habitat activities on site. However, employees occasionally participate in habitat management activities during work hours.

GM provides the Wildlife Habitat Team with an annual budget for its activities and projects. The budget varies from year to year depending on the projects planned for the upcoming year and state of the business within GM/LDT.[24] Volunteers and partners also occasionally donate time and materials for habitat projects. As resources can fluctuate, the long-term sustainability of the Wildlife Habitat Team depends upon the partnerships it has created with community volunteers and local conservation organizations.[25]

Wildlife Management Plan

LDT's Wildlife Management Plan outlines maintenance, monitoring, and outreach activities thought to be achievable in the first two years of implementation.[26]

The Wildlife Habitat Team "is responsible for ensuring that this [the management] plan is updated as programs evolve and the site changes."[27]

Five major habitat initiatives are detailed in the plan, including wetland enhancements, wetland buffer enhancements, woodland enhancements, trail development, and wildlife curriculum development. Goals, objectives, prescribed activities, and timelines for action are outlined for each of the focal habitat initiatives. Upon completion of a prescribed activity, a monitoring and maintenance plan that describes required actions, frequency, responsibility, and follow up is developed to monitor the progress of each activity and ensure the success of the project beyond implementation. The monitoring and maintenance plans are included as an appendix to the overall site management plan. The site management plan allows flexibility for project Habitat Sub-Teams to take on additional roles or change their focus in response to monitoring and species inventory results. The plan is updated at least annually as project Habitat Sub-Teams complete activities.

Over 18 Habitat Sub-Teams conduct the project, monitoring, and support activities outlined in the management plan.[28] Project Habitat Sub-Teams conduct activities such as improving food, water, cover, and habitat for on-site species, invasive species control, erosion control and water quality improvement through native plantings, and maintaining prairie groundcover. [29] Monitoring Habitat Sub-Teams conduct periodic inventory assessments of the types and quantities of flora and fauna at the site. LDT's Support Habitat Sub-Teams focus on activities such as trails and signs maintenance, communications, and education; addressing the last two plan initiatives (trail development and wildlife curriculum development).

Based on WHC and ECT site visits, a baseline species inventory for LDT's wildlife area was completed in 2004. This original inventory is updated annually based on the results of on-site monitoring by LDT's Monitoring Habitat Sub-Teams and of other monitoring initiatives. The management plan outlines seven Monitoring Habitat Sub-Teams, including bird, fish, and mollusk; Michigan frog and toad; reptile and amphibian; and insect, vegetation, and mammal, which conduct monitoring activities throughout the year.[30] Monitoring Habitat Sub-Team leaders are responsible for maintaining records of the monitoring events and for reporting their results to the Wildlife Habitat Team. Monitoring data is used to assess the condition of the site, to assess changes in the species observed and impacts of programs activities, and to update management plans for the site.

Potential future wildlife programs or projects are considered by the Wildlife Habitat Team during annual planning and budgeting.[31] Among other projects, the Wildlife Habitat Team is currently considering the installation of an educational greenhouse, construction of a pavilion to host student events, installation of a butterfly garden on-site, development of additional invasive species control implementation Habitat Sub-Teams, and development of an advisory team led by Michigan State University and the Thornapple Grand Conservation District to assist the Wildlife Habitat Team in planning future projects. Potential activities are considered by the Steering Team based on an evaluation of the overall site objectives, budget, and feasibility.

Community Education Efforts

The Wildlife Habitat Team's education programs encourage the public to visit the site. For example, the team, in partnership with Michigan State University and the Thornapple Grand Conservation District, conducted the first Bio-Blitz— a 24-hour snapshot species inventory of the LDT wildlife site—in August 2007.[32] The event had two primary goals: (1) to produce a snapshot species inventory list of the flora and fauna at the site; and (2) to educate the public about the diverse natural habitat that exists at the site and the species native to Michigan. Educational displays, interactive wildlife displays, and expert-guided hikes were available for participants. The species inventories were led by local biologists and were designed to both get an up-to-date snapshot of the diversity on-site and to improve the management of the site.

In addition, the LDT site is certified under WHC's Corporate Lands for Learning program, which recognizes outstanding wildlife education programs at corporate sites.[33] In order to qualify for certification, education programs must be in place for at least one year, offer at least 10 hours of active learning, and be visited at least once by a representative of WHC's Education and Outreach Department.[34] LDT's Corporate Lands for Learning program features a curriculum designed by the Woldumar Nature Center.[35] Woldumar developed the curriculum, designed primarily for middle-schools students, around four site-specific program areas: (1) Forests Are Fabulous; (2) Prairie Partners; (3) Wetland Wonders; and (4) Habitat Hunters. This "field-trip" type program involves hands-on exploration and interactive games to further learning and understanding of habitats.[36] GM has also partnered with PEER, a program for at-risk youth, on educational programs at the site. PEER students were involved in the construction and installation of wood duck boxes and learned about the necessity and importance of habitat.[37] PEER has also donated blue bird nest boxes and partnered with GM in habitat education projects.

The Facility: LEED-Certified Gold

GM set out to design and build a LEED-certified plant, and made certification a requirement of the design bid for the plant.[38] Specifically, the company set stringent standards for energy efficiency, materials, and wastewater management. As a result, energy costs at the plant are 45% lower than industry standards—a projected annual savings of $1 million. Lighting energy for the plant was reduced by 20% (three million kilowatt hours annually) by installing bright task lighting where needed and low overhead lighting in other areas. In addition, the plant's roof (1.5 million square feet) is made of a special white polymer that reduces heat absorption and annual cooling costs.[39]

Sustainable construction materials and methods were used for the LDT assembly plant.[40] More than 25% of the construction materials for the plant were composed of recycled content, and 38% of the construction materials were made from raw materials extracted within 500 miles. In addition, close to 60% of the construction materials were sourced through manufacturers located within 500 miles of the plant; translating to a local infrastructure investment of $33.8 million. In addition, GM used no ozone-depleting substances in the construction of the plant, and paints, adhesives, sealants, carpets, and composite woods were selected to limit off-gassing of indoor chemicals. And, 80% of waste generated at the plant during demolition and construction (3,963 tons) was diverted from landfills and recycled.

The plant includes a number of features designed to improve water efficiency; reducing non-manufacturing water used at the plant by 45% compared to a similar sized facility (4.1 million gallons annually).[41] Rainwater is collected from the roof of the assembly plant using a roof drain system. The collected water is stored in cisterns and used to flush toilets. Waterless urinals and low-flow plumbing facilities are used throughout the facility; saving more than one million gallons of water annually. Municipal water used for sewage conveyance at the plant was decreased by 70%. The landscape around the facilities was planted exclusively with native or specially adapted drought-resistant plants, which eliminated the need for an irrigation system. And, stormwater on-site is managed through an innovative system of ditches and culverts planted with vegetation that helps filter out solids and phosphorous.[42]

Analysis

Preserving habitat on privately owned lands is playing an increasingly important role in the conservation of wildlife in the United States—both because private land is being developed rapidly and because it supports particularly high biological diversity.[43] In addition to providing wildlife habitat, LDT's Wildlife Habitat Area is designed to improve public environmental awareness and community involvement in habitat conservation. The LDT Wildlife Habitat Team collaborates with scout troops, schools, and local community organizations on environmental education programs on the LDT site.[44] Local organizations visit the site to learn about a variety of conservation and wildlife habitat topics in both a classroom setting and field experience.[45] The Wildlife Habitat Team also hosts events to educate GM employees and their families on species identification, construction of artificial nesting structures, and implementation of habitat projects.

The Wildlife Habitat Area at LDT is bordered by the interstate on the east, highways on the south and north, the LDT assembly plant on the west; making direct linkage to other habitat areas unlikely. However, the LDT Wildlife Habitat Team does coordinate with several regional and local habitat conservation and environmental initiatives. GM's LDT habitat area is certified under the WHC. WHC is a nonprofit, nonlobbying 501(c)(3) group of corporations, conservation organizations, and individuals dedicated to sustaining and enhancing wildlife habitats. Since 1990, the WHC has recognized 408 corporate habitat programs, which manage a total of 2.4 million acres of land in 46 states, the District of Columbia, Puerto Rico, and 16 other countries.[46]

In 1992, the WHC initiated the *Waterways for Wildlife* program, which promotes voluntary corporate and private-sector programs in the development of comprehensive, regional wildlife management programs.[47] The program aims to "expand habitat acreage by linking private and public lands into integrated corridors" used by wildlife in riparian areas and watersheds. The Huron to Erie *Waterways for Wildlife* program engages an international coalition to enhance habitat for wildlife in the Lake Huron to Lake Erie corridor. Although the LDT site is not a member of the Huron to Erie program, over 30 corporations, several of which are located in Michigan, have enrolled habitats in the Huron to Erie program. As one of the founding members of the Huron to Erie program, DTE Energy has nine wildlife-certified facilities throughout Michigan, demonstrating the potential for regional conservation on corporate lands.[48] For example, DTE's Monroe Power Plant received a $5,000 Challenge Cost Share grant from the U.S. Fish and Wildlife Service to restore several wetlands on its site, which is located on the western Lake Erie shoreline within the boundaries of the Detroit River International Wildlife Refuge.

GM's Wildlife Habitat Team also collaborates with local environmental organizations and wildlife agencies to support regional conservation efforts.

Currently, the Eaton County Drain Commission is coordinating The Carrier Creek Stormwater Management and Restoration Project, "to address the increasing stormwater demands in the area, while also enhancing the natural resources of the corridor."[49] The restoration of Carrier Creek, which receives runoff from GM's LDT site, involves installation of water retention and control structures and stream bank restoration to improve water quality and wildlife habitat. As part of the overall restoration effort, the Eaton County Drain Commission is building a large wetland retention area on the LDT property (north of the Wildlife Habitat Area) to "improve water quality, assist in stabilizing downstream restoration efforts, and increase habitat for wildlife" in the area. The wetland retention area is not directly linked to the Wildlife Habitat Area. GM's Wildlife Habitat Team also collaborates with the Thornapple Grand Conservation District, which conducts habitat and wildlife restoration projects in the area of the LDT site, and Friends of Carrier Creek, a local community organization interested in the creek.

GM has realized significant financial benefit through the plant's LEED-certified design, which is independent of its wildlife habitat conservation expenditures. Sustainable energy measures, such as low overhead lighting and a unique white roof, save GM an estimated $1 million annually. In addition, LDT uses 4.1 million fewer gallons of non-manufacturing water and 70% less municipal water for sewage conveyance than comparable plants.

In addition, LDT's Wildlife Habitat Team gives the company a chance to establish partnerships with the community. GM has made a commitment to involve the community in habitat restoration and environmental education programs at the site. GM has taken advantage of this opportunity to show the community that the company "is not just making cars, we want to be community partners and help sustain and enhance where we can."[50] WHC certification of the site gives third-party recognition to the conservation efforts conducted on-site, and LDT's designation as "Rookie of the Year" gives the company an opportunity to promote these efforts. The WHC emphasizes that "employing exemplary practices and approaches to protecting natural resources and environment also promotes significant economic benefits."[51]

Notes

1. WHC, *Registry of Certified Programs*, http://www.wildlifehc.org/Registry_CertifiedSites/ index.cfm (last visited July 23, 2008) [hereinafter WHC, Registry of Certified Programs].

2. Personal Communication with Bridget Burnell, Senior Environmental Engineer, GM LDT (July 27, 2007) [hereinafter Burnell Communication, July].

3. Elizabeth Lowery, *GM Lansing Delta Township Is Wildlife Habitat Council's "Rookie of the Year,"* http://www.gm.com/company/gmability/environment/news_issues/news/conserva- tion_lt_112706.html (last visited July 23, 2008).

4. *See* Burnell Communication, July, *supra* note 2.

5. Michigan Department of Environmental Quality, *Meet Michigan's Clean Corporate Citizens*, http://www.deq.state.mi.us/documents/deq-ess-p2tas-c3-c3report2003.pdf (last visited July 23, 2008).

6. Personal Communication with Bridget Burnell, Senior Environmental Engineer, GM LDT (Sept. 13, 2007) [hereinafter Burnell Communication, Sept.].

7. *See* Burnell Communication, July, *supra* note 2.

8. Vertegy   Consultants,   *General   Motors   Assembly   Complex*,   http:// www.vertegyconsultants.com/project.cfm?project_id=5 (last visited July 23, 2008) [here- inafter Vertegy Consultants, *General Motors Assembly Complex*].

9. GM, *GMability Environment, GM Opens First-Ever LEED-Gold Certified Automobile Man- ufacturing   Facility*,   http://www.gm.com/company/gmability/environment/ news_issues/news/leed-cert_080406.html (last visited July 23, 2008) [hereinafter GM, *GMa- bility Environment*].

10. *See* Burnell Communication, July, *supra* note 2.

11. GM, General Motors Lansing Delta Township Wildlife Habitat Management Plan (issued June 13, 2005 and updated May 14, 2007) (on file with authors) [hereinafter GM, *GM LDT Wildlife Habitat Management Plan*].

12. *See* Burnell Communication, July, *supra* note 2.

13. *Id.*

14. WHC, *Registry of Certified Programs: General Motors Corporation Lansing Delta Town- ship Assembly Center*, http://www.wildlifehc.org/registry_certifiedsites/cert_sites_detail2 .cfm?LinkAdvID=77881 (last visited July 23, 2008) [hereinafter WHC, *Registry of Certified Programs: GM LDT Assembly Center*].

15. Personal Communication with Paul Morrow, Pheasants Forever (July 12, 2007).

16. GM, Video: GM's Lansing Delta Township Plan at NextGear, http://www.nextgearshow.com/ 1783/gms-lansing-delta-township-plant (last visited July 23, 2008).

17. *See* WHC, *Registry of Certified Programs*, *supra* note 1.

18. WHC, *Rookie of the Year General Motors Corporation Lansing Delta Township Assembly Center*, http://www.wildlifehc.org/awards/award_detail.cfm?LinkAdvID=75087 (last visited July 23, 2008).

19. *See* GM, *GM LDT Wildlife Habitat Management Plan*, *supra* note 11.

20. *See* Burnell Communication, Sept., *supra* note 6.

21. Personal Communication with Bridget Burnell, Senior Environmental Engineer, GM LDT (Aug. 22, 2007) [hereinafter Burnell Communication, Aug.].

22. *Id.*

23. *See* Burnell Communication, July, *supra* note 2.

24. *See* Burnell Communication, Aug., *supra* note 21.
25. *Id.*
26. *See* GM, *GM LDT Wildlife Habitat Management Plan, supra* note 11.
27. *Id.*
28. *See* Burnell Communication, July, *supra* note 2.
29. *See* GM, *GM LDT Wildlife Habitat Management Plan, supra* note 11.
30. *Id.*
31. *Id.*
32. *See* Burnell Communication, July, *supra* note 2.
33. *See* WHC, *Registry of Certified Programs: GM LDT Assembly Center, supra* note 14.
34. WHC, *Corporate Lands for Learning,* http://www.wildlifehc.org/corporatelands/index.cfm (last visited July 23, 2008).
35. *See* WHC, *Registry of Certified Programs: GM LDT Assembly Center, supra* note 14.
36. Personal Communication with Holly Vaughn, Woldumar Nature Center (July 13, 2007).
37. *See* WHC, *Registry of Certified Programs: GM LDT Assembly Center, supra* note 14.
38. *See* Vertegy Consultants, *General Motors Assembly Complex, supra* note 8.
39. *See* GM, *GMability Environment, supra* note 9.
40. *Id.*
41. *Id.*
42. *Id.*
43. David M. Theobald & N. Thompson Hobbs, *A Framework for Evaluating Land Use Planning Alternatives: Protecting Biodiversity on Private Land,* 6 Conservation Ecology 5 (2002), *available at* http://www.ecologyandsociety.org/vol6/iss1/art5.
44. *See* WHC, *Registry of Certified Programs: GM LDT Assembly Center, supra* note 14.
45. *Id.*
46. *See* WHC, *Registry of Certified Programs, supra* note 1.
47. WHC, *Waterways for Wildlife,* http://www.wildlifehc.org/waterways/index.cfm (last visited July 23, 2008).
48. Huron to Erie Waterways for Wildlife, *DTE Energy,* http://www.wildlifehc.org/stclairwaterways/corporate_habitats/dteenergy.cfm (last visited July 23, 2008).
49. Carrier Creek, *Carrier Creek Stormwater Management and Restoration Project,* http://www.carriercreek.com/about.htm (last visited July 23, 2008).
50. *See* Burnell Communication, July, *supra* note 2.
51. WHC, *WHC Awards,* http://www.wildlifehc.org/awards/index.cfm (last visited July 23, 2008).

Santa Lucia Preserve, Carmel Valley, California: Luxury Conservation Development/Preserve

The owners of the 20,000-acre Santa Lucia Preserve (the Preserve) in Monterey County, California, developed and constructed an upscale residential development while permanently protecting nearly 18,000 acres of the site as open space. The remaining 2,000 acres, located on the least environmentally sensitive areas of the site, include a golf course, equestrian and recreational facilities, and 296 one and one-half- to five-acre homesites. The independently managed nonprofit Santa Lucia Conservancy was established to manage the restoration and enhancement of the undeveloped 18,000 "Preserve Lands," and will protect the land in perpetuity through fee ownership of nearly 12,000 acres and conservation easements on an additional 6,000 acres. Funding for management activities is guaranteed through a $25 million endowment generated from a dedicated portion of the sales price of each homesite. The Santa Lucia Conservancy, which operates as a Community Stewardship Organization in cooperation with the nonprofit Sonoran Institute, manages the Preserve through land protection, resource management, scientific research, and community education programs.

The Preserve rests in the Carmel Valley on the central California coast. Over 50 habitat types and an assortment of species have been identified within the Preserve, a diversity that can be attributed to the variation in altitude, temperature, and rainfall.[1] Much of the land in the Preserve consists of oak woodlands and savannas, but coastal shrub and chaparral, grasslands, redwood forests, mixed evergreen forests, Monterey Pine forests, and riparian lands also span the Preserve, providing numerous niches for wildlife. (See Fig. 6.1.) Nearly 600 species of plants and over 160 species of birds have been identified.[2]

Archaeological records have traced settlement patterns back to 500 A.D., when Costanoan-speaking Rumsen Indians settled the land.[3] Europeans first came in contact with the indigenous peoples in 1770, after which the land underwent a number of exchanges, transactions, and occupations.[4] In the mid-1800s, the land was converted to a cattle ranch known as Rancho San Carlos. The ranch

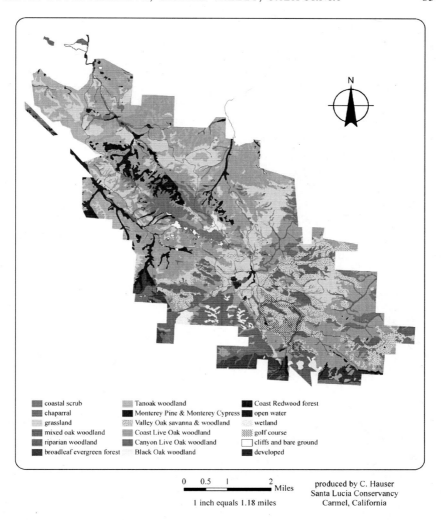

coastal scrub | Tanoak woodland | Coast Redwood forest
chaparral | Monterey Pine & Monterey Cypress | open water
grassland | Valley Oak savanna & woodland | wetland
mixed oak woodland | Coast Live Oak woodland | golf course
riparian woodland | Canyon Live Oak woodland | cliffs and bare ground
broadleaf evergreen forest | Black Oak woodland | developed

0   0.5   1   2
                     Miles
1 inch equals 1.18 miles

produced by C. Hauser
Santa Lucia Conservancy
Carmel, California

Figure 6.1. Santa Lucia Preserve Vegetation Cover. With permission from the Santa Lucia Conservancy.

was later converted in the 1920s by George Gordon Moore into a gentlemen's resort, with polo fields, an artificial lake (Moore's Lake), stables, and a 37-room hacienda called La Casa Grande, which today is utilized as the private Ranch Club on the Preserve.[5] The Great Depression forced Moore to sell his 20,000-acre estate to the Oppenheimer family of Piedmont, California, who worked the land as a cattle ranch for 50 years.[6]

The 20,000-acre site had been subject to several different zoning ordinances over its modern history. Monterey County zoning permitted 11,000 residential units in the 1960s, and 2,000 units (1 unit per 10 acres) in the 1980s. In 1982, when the county revised its General Plan, the Board of Supervisors downzoned the property to 1 unit per 160 acres. When the Oppenheimer family sued the county for taking action without an environmental impact report (EIR), the result was a "white hole" on the zoning map—20,000 acres with no clearly applicable land use designation or zoning ordinances.[7]

Tom Gray and the late Pete Stocker, lead partners of the Pacific Union Company, first visited the Rancho San Carlos property in February 1989 at the invitation of one of the Oppenheimer heirs. The partners were impressed by the scale, location, and natural diversity of the landscape, and agreed that the greatest value would come from maintaining the integrity of the landscape, rather than attempting to break it into numerous development properties.[8] Gray, Stocker, and an investment partner formed the Rancho San Carlos Partnership (the Partnership) and purchased the 20,000-acre property for $70 million in February 1990. Just three months later Stocker died in a helicopter accident on the property. Gray continued their vision for the property as a landscape-oriented conservation development.

The Partnership commenced what became a three-year study of the land. Using a geographic information system (GIS) mapping system, the team incorporated surveys of geology, hydrology, topography, conservation biology, and archaeology. With an interdisciplinary approach, Gray and his associates were able to examine habitat data and settlement patterns to protect the historical and natural resources of the landscape, including wetlands, riparian zones, and grounds with Native American remains, in order to avoid development in these areas.

Gray articulated three cornerstone principles for the project: (1) protect the landscape; (2) be forthcoming about plans and information; and (3) protect the cultural history of the land. According to Gray, the decision to preserve 90% of the land as open space was not only an effective means of protecting the cultural and natural resources, but was also politically smart: it appealed to environmentalists and county officials, as well as neighboring residents. With what he calls a "best for the land" strategy, Gray sought to pursue the value of the whole landscape over the value of its parts.[9]

During the planning process, the Partnership was required to adhere to the steps outlined by the California Environmental Quality Act (CEQA), which entailed collaborating with the California Department of Fish and Game (CDFG) and completing an EIR. The CDFG, which is only permitted to provide recommendations during the CEQA process, expressed some concerns about the adverse impact of the Preserve's water use—from stream removal and groundwater wells—on several species federally listed under the Endangered Species Act (ESA), as well as about the degree of parcel clustering.[10]

In addition to working with the CDFG, and conducting the environmental studies, Gray and his colleagues met with environmental organizations like the Audubon Society and neighborhood groups like the Carmel Valley Property Owners Association, which were willing to engage in dialogue about the plans for the site. The Partnership also completed several focus group studies in 1993. Input from these studies influenced the content of the product and overall design of the Preserve. For instance, market research revealed that over 30% of their target market audience would only live in a community that had a golf course. Many prospective consumers wanted to own between 5-40 acres, but only be responsible for 1-2 acres. From their market research results, the Partnership discerned that high-market consumers would pay for the certainty that their surroundings would be as beautiful in the future as they are today, particularly when thinking of the purchase as creating a family legacy. Consumers would pay for this certainty and the assurance that the land would not be further subdivided. The mechanism for providing this assurance was the creation of an independent land trust, the Santa Lucia Conservancy, which would maintain 18,000 acres as open space in perpetuity, via both ownership and management of conservation easements.[11]

In April 1994, the Partnership filed its application for approval with Monterey County. The county hired an independent environmental consulting firm, Jones and Stokes, to review the application. After 13 public hearings, the Board of Supervisors unanimously approved the application in February 1996. However, two lawsuits were filed in 1996 after the board's approval. The first contended that the development did not conform to the Monterey County General Plan or meet the CEQA requirements, in part because of a failure to cluster homesites. Opponents also sued the county to change the zoning. A ballot initiative was launched against the zoning of the project, which had included approval of the developers' plan for a resort/hotel. Controversy concerning whether the petitioners had met the number of required signatures to place the issue on the ballot in the county led to additional litigation. Subsequently, the California Superior Court placed the initiative challenging the decision to approve the development plan on the ballot, where the initiative was defeated. When the Partnership's appeal of the ruling to place the initiative on the ballot was heard, the California Court of Appeal ruled that the referendum petition contained insufficient signatures for placement on the ballot. The court further held that the controversy had become moot by virtue of the intervening election.[12] The end result of the two lawsuits was a rezoning of the property in 1998 to exclude the resort/hotel, which the Partnership was by that time prepared to forego based on additional market studies, and the elimination of 4 of the originally proposed 300 homesites that deviated from clustering requirements.[13] In March 1999, after nearly a decade of research, public hearings, litigation, a public vote, and final approval from Monterey County, the Preserve began selling parcels.

While a possible preference for "no development" of the Santa Lucia land might have maintained landscape ecological benefits in contrast with various possible development scenarios, there was in fact no guarantee of maintained ecological value in the absence of a management plan and funding, which was a consequence of the proposed and approved development. The approved development plan provides active rather than passive management, permanently protects resource lands and habitat areas on 90% of the site, and provides funding that can support connections to the wider landscape as well as within the 20,000-acre Preserve. Build-out will consist of 296 residential parcels located primarily on areas of prior disturbance or with fewer natural resource values than the conservation lands. Buyers have to comply with a list of over 200 Conditions for Approval from the county, Covenants, Conditions, and Restrictions (CC&Rs) created by the Preserve, and conservation easements deeded to and administered by the Santa Lucia Conservancy. "Homelands," what the Preserve calls building envelopes, are prescribed based on surveys of each parcel. The Homelands range from one to five acres, depending on the topography and surrounding habitat, and are designed to be concealed from outside the Preserve. The developers created a golf course and club house, equestrian center, and sports complex. These amenities, along with the 296 housing parcels, would comprise the 2,000-acre footprint for development. The rest is maintained in easements and fee title property owned by the Santa Lucia Conservancy, an independent nonprofit group that is partially funded by the initial real estate sales in the Preserve. As of July 2007, 55 homes have been completed and all but 22 parcels have been purchased.[14]

Operation of the Development

The Preserve Land

The Preserve land is classified into four categories: (1) Homelands; (2) Rancholands; (3) Openlands; and (4) Wildlands (together the Openlands and Wildlands are referred to as Settled Lands). (See Fig. 6.2.) Homelands refers

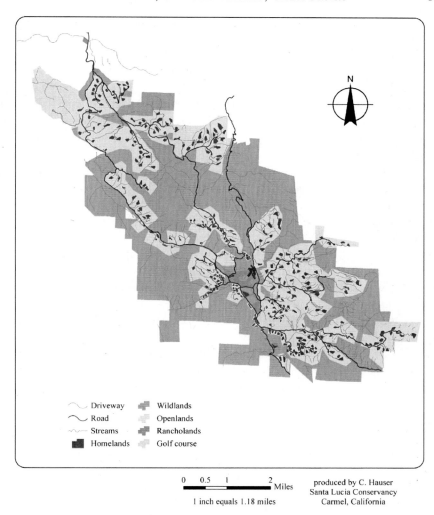

Figure 6.2. Santa Lucia Preserve Property Boundaries. With permission from the Santa Lucia Conservancy.

to the building envelopes on which residences are permitted. These are pre-scribed based on surveys of topography, visibility, and vegetation. While the Homelands vary from 1-5 acres, based on the suitability of each site, they gen-erally average 2-2.5 acres and comprise a total of 700 acres. The number of Homelands is limited to 296, all of which are subject to the CC&Rs, which permit measures like fire fuel management and equestrian use (on a limited number of sites), but restrict outside activities of household pets and prohibits temporary structures, trade and business, and an assortment of other activities. All Homeland owners must also employ "drought-tolerant native landscaping, water-efficient irrigation systems, low-flow shower heads, and water conserving toilets."[15]

Rancholands, the second category, refers to the 1,300 acres of amenities. An equestrian center offers barns, six irrigated acres of pasture, an exercise track, and arenas; the sports center includes a weight room, aquatic facility, tennis courts, and croquet field; the hacienda provides a venue for social events and dining. The golf course is included in the 2,000-acre cap of development as well. The course has incorporated habitat-friendly features. It is one of the first courses to have created a system that using the topography and underlying layers of hard clay pan and sand, captures and reuses irrigation water on a large scale. One-third of the irrigation comes from re-circulated water that is captured by a drainage system that underlies the course; another one-third of the irrigation comes from treated effluents; and the last one-third comes from potable sources. The golf cart trails are designed to pick up surface runoff and revert it to its original path, and the roughs are restored native grasslands.[16]

The third category of land in the Preserve, Openlands, refers to land owned by the residents and protected under conservation easements held by the Santa Lucia Conservancy. The residents of the Preserve purchase 20-30 acres of predetermined Openland in addition to their Homeland building parcel. According to Monterey County: "In order to retain the [O]penlands in an undeveloped state in perpetuity, the subdivider shall grant conservation easements to the Santa Lucia Conservancy or other appropriate nonprofit land trust organization for Openland areas within each phase of the project."[17] Openlands comprise more than 6,000 acres of the Preserve. The CC&Rs prohibit subdivisions, developments, mineral exploration, dumping and disposal, motorized vehicles, agriculture, native vegetation removal, fences, and the planting of non-native vegetation on Openlands.[18] Permitted uses include: livestock management; fuel and fire management; equestrian use; native plant cultivation; wildlife and habitat management; recreation; research; education; and some infrastructure (roads, bridges, campsites, erosion control structures, etc.).[19] The final category, Wildlands, consists of nearly 12,000 acres owned by the Santa Lucia Conservancy in fee title. According to Monterey County's Conditions for Approval: "A minimum of 5,000 acres of Wildlands shall be conveyed to the Santa Lucia Conservancy or other nonprofit land trust organization."[20] The Partnership's Deed to the Santa Lucia Conservancy outlines the various uses that are permitted: research; education; resource management; ranching; recreation;

and fuel and fire management. All subdivisions, development, mineral exploration, and any other action or use that "threatens or compromises the Protected
Values" are prohibited.[21]

While 90% of the land is preserved as open space under the latter two categories, many wildlife-related restrictions are imposed on Homeland sites. Of
the 203 conditions for approval placed on the Preserve by the county, many
address the stewardship responsibilities of homeowners. A Riparian Vegetation
Management Plan must be prepared to monitor riparian vegetation, control
removal of such vegetation, and provide restoration under certain circumstances[22]; construction practices are limited to protect fish habitat; and removed
non-landmark trees must be replaced at a 3:1 ratio, while landmark trees must
be replaced at a 5:1 ratio.[23] Homeland owners must consult a biologist to conduct nesting surveys for Cooper's hawks and golden eagles, and if a nest is found,
construction must be delayed until the young have fledged.[24] Unless suitable
mitigation efforts are employed to prevent adverse impact, development must
be setback at least 100 feet from wetlands.[25] Development is also to be restricted
and delayed by indications of spotted owl reproductive activity.[26]

Prior to submitting a building permit application to the Monterey County
Department of Planning and Building Inspection, applicants must first address
the Santa Lucia Design Guidelines, which have been "created to ensure that
all improvements at the [Preserve maintain] the natural beauty of this coastal
California setting and maintain a unified design throughout the community."[27]
The guidelines establish different zoning requirements and recommendations
for Homelands based on three broad ecological components: (1) grasslands;
(2) woodlands; and (3) savannah zones. Each zoning category has its own
restrictions and requirements based on the surrounding vegetation and habitat
in order "to ensure that [improvements] are built in harmony with the natural
landscape."[28] While the guidelines principally address aesthetic design, they
also address some important environmental concerns: under planting guidelines, "landscape improvements are to incorporate, rehabilitate and enhance
existing vegetation, utilize indigenous drought/fire resistant species, and minimize areas of ornamental planting and intensive irrigation"; recommendations
are incorporated to conserve energy and resources, including the use of "thick,
well-insulated walls, broad overhangs to shade windows and walls, natural ven-
tilation, shielded solar panels, and low voltage lighting"; all damage to other
property—including trees, shrubs, grades, and pathways—must be restored at
the owner's expense; drainage and grading must be designed to control erosion and sediment transport; and exterior lighting must be kept to minimal
yields.[29] Compliance with the Santa Lucia Design Guidelines and CC&Rs typ-

ically takes applicants about a year to fulfill, and requires lot owners and their design teams to collaborate with the Preserve's Design Review Board that includes two state-licensed architects and an appointee from the Santa Lucia Conservancy. Ultimately two of the three Design Review Board appointments, as well as the responsibility for the board, will be the domain of the Preserve Association (homeowners association).[30]

The Santa Lucia Conservancy

The conservancy was established in 1995 "to ensure the presence of a strong, stable, independent resource protection organization, in perpetuity, for the Santa Lucia Preserve." With a $25 million endowment from the initial real estate sales, the Santa Lucia Conservancy conducts research, manages the landscape, and works with residents as well as the community beyond the preserve to pursue "a mission to conserve and sustain the unique Central Coast landscape, and its mandate to preserve and protect the species and sensitive resources."[31]

Community Stewardship Organization

As a 501(c)(3) nonprofit, by filing a Form 1023 with the Internal Revenue Service, the conservancy agreed to allocate assets from its real estate funding to a supported organization. The Santa Lucia Conservancy's supported organization has been the Sonoran Institute since 2001; prior to that it supported The Trust for Public Land. The Sonoran Institute is a nonprofit organization that works with local communities to conserve and restore the landscape. One of the means by which the institute has augmented communal conservation is with the concept of the Community Stewardship Organization (CSO). A CSO is "a nonprofit independent entity formed to institutionalize a long-term conservation and community-building commitment in a land development, funded in perpetuity by market-based mechanisms in the development process."[32]

While the preservation and stewardship of 18,000 acres of intact open space, particularly in a high-priced real estate market, may be rather difficult to replicate, the Preserve is one of the pioneer CSOs. It provides a first-rate example of the implementation of some of these important and replicable principles: practicing initial due diligence (with extensive GIS maps and environmental assessments); practicing community due diligence (meeting with county officials, members of the local homeowners association, and environmental groups); ensuring long-term financial support (with an endowment from real estate sales to the Santa Lucia Conservancy); and fostering stewardship (with resource management, education, conservation easements, and community outreach).[33] Kristine Bentz, the Program Director for Land Conservation and Development at the Sonoran Institute, asserts that the Santa Lucia Conservancy meets the underlying purpose of the CSO: to connect land and people. It manages land and recognizes the importance of the residents and incorporates them in its stewardship efforts.[34] As a member of the CSO Network, the Santa Lucia Conservancy interacts to share information with other CSOs, and educates other organizations about the CSO concept. The conservancy has participated in several workshops and hosted developers at the Preserve to share ideas. One CSO, La Semilla in Patagonia, Arizona, was in part modeled on the Preserve, after the developer visited the conservancy.[35]

Research Activities

Within the Preserve, the Santa Lucia Conservancy actively researches and monitors the ecology. The conservancy has focused much of its research on bird monitoring and Sudden Oak Death, a disease first documented in the United States in 1995. A pathogen called *Phytophthora ramorum* produces the disease, which has had virulent effects on oaks and several other trees found throughout the central coast and on the Preserve.[36] The conservancy has participated with researchers from the Urban Forest Ecosystems Institute, Natural Resources Management Department, and California Polytechnic Management Department to study the effects of thinning on the growth of residual trees and to monitor the spreading of Sudden Oak Death disease.[37] The Preserve also serves as a research station for investigators and researchers from both the University of California, Davis and Berkeley to study the ecology and treatment of Sudden Oak Death and related pathogens (the Preserve has proven an attractive research site not only because it has infected oak trees, but also because it provides a secure research opportunity where long-term, ongoing studies will not be manipulated inadvertently or deliberately by the public).[38] Additionally, the Santa Lucia Conservancy is a member of the California Oak Mortality Task Force, "a nonprofit organization, under the California Forest Pest Council, that brings together public agencies, other nonprofit organizations and private interests to address the issue of elevated levels of oak mortality."[39]

Research on bird populations has been another focus of the conservancy. Collaborating with the Ventana Wildlife Society (VWS)—a community-based private nonprofit group that focuses largely on environmental education, species rehabilitation, and habitat restoration—the conservancy has monitored the avian diversity on the Preserve.[40] The VWS is monitoring avian productivity and survivorship along the Carmel River riparian corridor, which transects the Preserve.[41] In past efforts with the VWS, the Santa Lucia Conservancy's conservation biologist has assisted with netting and monitoring efforts.[42]

Management Activities

The Santa Lucia Conservancy monitors the changes in the ecosystem of the landscape, particularly those that "are detrimental to the diversity and health of the ecosystem." Prioritizing these threats, the conservancy develops management strategies to abate or eliminate these undesirable changes.[43] While the conservancy prioritizes its funds to managing the Wildlands, it also facilitates management on Openlands and Settled Lands by providing landowners with management prescriptions that are consistent with its science-based protocols employed in the conservancy's Wildlands efforts.[44] Since 2006, the conservancy has managed noxious weeds by integrating mechanical and chemical methods. The conservancy is projected to spend over $70,000 in 2007 to control several species of invasive plants on the Wildlands of the Preserve. Based on their successes, the conservancy has created prescriptions and lists of contractors for residents to utilize. This year, residents are projected to spend between $100,000 and $120,000 on contractors to manage noxious weeds on their Openlands and Homelands, based on the conservancy's prescription.[45] The conservancy is also a member of the California Invasive Weeds Awareness Coalition, "a partnership of nonprofit and industry groups working together to enhance weed control efforts and promote public awareness of invasive weeds in California."[46]

As part of the county's conditions of approval, the Santa Lucia Conservancy in 2005 began the implementation of a county-approved ecological grazing plan in the Wildlands called the Revised Rancho San Carlos Cattle Grazing and Livestock Management Plan. While the program is not yet to scale, livestock are proving to be effective in controlling some of the invasive annual grasses that have out-competed some of the native perennial grasses on the Preserve.[47]

The Santa Lucia Conservancy, in conjunction with the Partnership, has also funded the development of a Preservewide fuel management plan that is designed to balance fire protection with habitat protection and landscape aesthetics. Collaborating with federal, state and local fire agencies, and key adjacent landowners, the conservancy's fire planning consultant has developed a fuel management plan that tailors fuel management actions to site-specific vegetation types, topographic conditions, and weather-related patterns. The implementation of the plan is the joint responsibility of the homeowners, the Santa Lucia Community Services District (owner and manager of roads and other community service infrastructure), and the Santa Lucia Conservancy. Based on vegetation type, topography, and habitat, homeowners must take measures to reduce the fuel around their homes. The conservancy may suggest, for example, lowering the canopy height and altering the density of chaparral, rather than simply eliminating habitat in the Homelands to reduce fuel. Completed in 2005 and revised in 2006, the plan and its implementation were presented at the Third International Fire Ecology and Management Congress in San Diego, California.[48]

One of the conservancy's continuous management efforts is the monitoring of tree removal and subsequent mitigation efforts. Per the Monterey County's Conditions of Approval, the Santa Lucia Conservancy documented and reported the oak trees removed during the Preserve's infrastructure development, collected acorns from the preserve (they have to be of the same genetic stock), and developed and maintains an ongoing nursery at the conservancy office to mitigate for removed trees. The Partnership has had the responsibility of planting mitigation trees consistent with the county conditions and the Forest Management Plan developed for the Preserve and approved by the county. When seedlings are planted, they must be inspected annually and maintain an overall success rate of 90% during the mandatory five-year monitoring stage. To date, the Santa Lucia Conservancy has planting records of nearly 3,800 five-gallon oak trees, and its nursery contains between 2,500-2,600 native oak seedlings.[49]

The Santa Lucia Conservancy collaborates with the U.S. Fish and Wildlife Service (FWS) and the CDFG on several management efforts. Feral pigs are not native to the region and can have detrimental effects on the native biota of the landscape. The conservancy and residents in the Preserve have worked with the CDFG periodically to manage feral pigs; in accordance with CDFG depredation permits, they have followed prescriptive harvest quotas to locally manage pig populations and their impacts.

Additionally, the CDFG, the Ventura Fish and Wildlife Office, and the National Marine Fisheries Service (NMFS) have worked with the Partnership and the Santa Lucia Conservancy for approximately seven years in developing a draft habitat conservation plan (HCP), particularly in developing long-term management practices that effectively address the threatened and endangered species that inhabit the Preserve. One such organism is the red-legged frog, which uses several of the Preserve's historic stock ponds and creeks for breeding. Red-legged frogs have survived a 70% reduction of their total habitat on the Pacific Coast—a loss caused largely by urban encroachment, invasive organisms, fragmentation, and livestock. Of the entire historic range of the California red-legged frog, only 3 sites are estimated to support more than 350 adults, 1 of which is the Preserve.[50] Another threatened organism, the Smith's blue butterfly, relies on buckwheat (*Eriogonum* sp.). Buckwheat is a larval host plant that grows on the Preserve. The above agencies, the Partnership, and the Conservancy are currently devising management plans for the HCP that will address overcompetitive bull frogs in the red-legged frog breeding ponds, restoration efforts to control noxious weeds and to plant buckwheat for the Smith's blue butterfly, and management of grassland to benefit golden eagles.[51] While the HCP has experienced some delays, the conservancy hopes to have addressed all the FWS' comments on its HCP draft by the end of summer 2007.[52]

Due to the presence of several federally listed threatened species on the Preserve, the conservancy has also worked with the FWS to implement management strategies that protect the viability of threatened species such as the California red-legged frog, California tiger salamander, Smith's blue butterfly, and the steelhead trout. Working with the FWS to enhance the tiger salamander's habitat, the conservancy has developed adaptive techniques to control invasive weeds that account for the salamander's life cycle, which includes a period of aestivation when the adults spend extensive periods of time underground in uplands habitat in the vicinity of known breeding ponds. The conservancy has created mechanical and chemical techniques that are conducive to the life cycles of the salamander to manage the upland habitat for invasive plants.[53]

The NMFS, part of the National Oceanic and Atmospheric Administration (NOAA), also participated in the development of the HCP. The Carmel River Steelhead Association and the local Ventana Chapter of the Sierra Club filed complaints with NOAA contending that well pumping on the Preserve has adversely affected creek flow and, therefore, steelhead habitat. NOAA has investigated these complaints, but no conclusive determinations have been made, in part because of the lack of historical data and the fractured bedrock of the waterways which causes inherent variations in flow. The final EIR for the Preserve had concluded that well water withdrawals would not adversely affect stream flow; and as a condition of the approval, the conservancy must monitor water levels, stream flow, and base-flow pools annually to assess impacts and provide these reports to Monterey County for review. An additional condition required that the operation of wells be managed by a computerized system that collects data from all wells and controls withdrawals to minimize impacts. NOAA continues to work with the Preserve to ensure that steelhead trout have suitable habitat, and that the Preserve does not violate the ESA with its use of water from Las Garzas Creek, a tributary of the Carmel River and important habitat for the threatened steelhead species.[54]

Because of the importance of water in this landscape, complaints were also filed at various times with the California State Water Resources Control Board, beginning right after active development commenced. In 1999, the California

Sportfishing Protection Alliance filed a public trust protest against the Partnership relating to the management of water in the operation of Moore's Lake, an existing impoundment in Las Garzas Creek.[55] Stop logs, which are placed on top of dams to maintain lake levels, are removed in the winter to prevent flooding and reinstated in the spring to sustain lake levels. The first petition occurred in 1999, which was a particularly wet year with high stream flows; the stop logs were overlooked until late summer, at which point they were put back in place. When the stop logs were finally reinstated, they allegedly forced the stream flow to a halt, killing an estimated 200 fish.[56] The California State Water Resources Control Board filed a civil liability complaint against the Partnership in 2000 seeking $20,000 in penalties and $2,300 in compensation for the fish loss. In settlement of the complaint, the Partnership paid $2,300 in compensation for fish loss without admission of fault and agreed to work further with the state and federal agencies to address the effects of its water use on aquatic biota. The case was closed by the state water board. The Partnership agreed to work with the three agencies—the FWS, the CDFG, and NOAA— on an adaptive management plan. As an outgrowth of the litigation, the Partnership developed a protocol to match inflows and outflows for Moore's Lake, the impoundment whose management was at the core of the controversy.[57] A second complaint, filed by a neighboring landowner, was resolved with increased dialogue between the Preserve and its neighbors.[58] The third petition was filed in September 2003 by the local Ventana Chapter of the Sierra Club and the Carmel River Steelhead Association. Their complaint with the California State Water Resources Control Board alleged that the Partnership is "(1) harming public trust resources, specifically steelhead and red-legged frogs, by unauthorized diversions from Garzas Creek; and (2) that Moore's Lake, owned by the [Partnership], is an unreasonable use of water."[59] The state water board closed the case because no new evidence was introduced, and because the FWS, the CDFG, and NOAA were already collaborating with the Preserve on management of the creek.[60] The Santa Lucia Conservancy continues to monitor the inflow and outflow on Las Garzas Creek per its condition of approval and reports its stream flow data to Monterey County and other water-related agencies.[61]

The Santa Lucia Conservancy also plays a key role in assuring that the private-property interests carry out their conservation and management obligations. The homesite purchasers essentially have invested in conservation easements to protect the land in perpetuity, work with the Santa Lucia Conservancy on management efforts on their properties like abating noxious weeds, and they must adhere to strict county conditions and preserve codes to prevent adverse impact on the landscape and to blend development into the natural landscape. While many conservation easements in California within privately managed developments often raise concerns for the CDFG about monitoring, the managerial efforts of the conservancy provide better mitigation than in other such developments.[62]

Outreach Activities

Education programs at the Preserve provide an opportunity for residents and the community outside the Preserve to learn about ongoing actions of the Santa Lucia Conservancy and the ecological phenomena of the landscape. The conservancy contracts two educators to develop a curriculum for students ranging from kindergarten to high school. These contract educators annually guide students on walking tours, where the Preserve is the classroom. Approximately 1,500 students are taken on these tours every year to learn about wildlife, natural history, invasive plants, and conservation.[63] Some of the classes offered include the following: (1) A Seasonal Nature Walk Along Potrero Canyon; (2) Natural History of Cavity Nesting Birds; (3) All About Butterflies; (4) The Santa Lucia Preserve and California History; (5) Bird Habitats; (6) Mammals and Their Tracks; (7) Owls in the Redwoods; (8) Salamanders in the Santa Lucia Preserve; (9) Art and Poetry in Nature; (10) The Riparian Ecosystem; and (11) All About Oaks."[64]

In addition to educating school children, the conservancy also offers quarterly tours to the public, brings in guest speakers, and consults landowners "to raise awareness and sensitivity" toward the landscape. When the conservancy hosts outside guest speakers, it frequently invites its conservation partners of the outside Preserve—from universities, the CDFG, the U.S. Bureau of Land Management, local land trust, regional park staff, The Nature Conservancy, and landowners—to these evening events not only to increase awareness, but also to augment its working partnerships.[65] The conservancy also provides a unique opportunity for graduate students. While only one to two graduate students per year have utilized the Preserve, the conservancy plans on creating a grant program and field station to facilitate more research.[66]

Analysis

Private development will have important implications for conservation efforts in North America, particularly as many hotspots for biological diversity and habitats for endangered species overlap private land.[67] On the coast of central California, the Carmel Valley is especially rich in natural resources due to abiotic factors like variation in altitude, rainfall, and temperature. The Preserve, located in the Carmel Valley, represents a private effort to maintain the biologically diverse landscape in perpetuity. Several proactive efforts by the developers and ongoing activities of the Santa Lucia Conservancy have enabled the Preserve to protect wholly that which may have otherwise been degraded in subdivision.

One of the most critical components of preserving the landscape of the Preserve was the extensive planning by the developers. By researching the ecology, biota, topography, archaeology, and development from previous owners, the Partnership was able to develop principally on areas that were previously disturbed while avoiding cultural resources and environmentally sensitive areas like wetlands, ponds, and riparian habitat.[68] According to Terry Palmisano, a biologist at the CDFG who was involved with the planning: "[I]t was an extremely good survey set of wildlife habitat."[69]

Additionally, the Partnership invested time to make specific prescriptions for individual Homelands. Assessments were based on an objective to protect view corridors, natural vegetation, ponds, streams, and the topography while blending improvements into the microclimate.[70] During the CEQA process, the CDFG expressed concerns about the ecological footprint. While some efforts were made to consolidate the Homelands, the CDFG did not consider the degree of consolidation sufficient, and had some difficulty urging the Preserve to decrease the infrastructural footprint of the high-end properties.[71] Thus, a strong result was obtained, but not one that fulfilled all the ideals of those concerned with habitat.Another attribute that helped in the planning and substance of the Preserve, and assuring its connection to the larger conservation landscape is the Santa Lucia Conservancy's Board of Governors. This body was constructed to integrate scientific, legal, and governmental expertise to protect the landscape. The current Chief of Natural Resources for the California State Parks, a board member of the Wildlife Trust, and environmental lawyers and scientists are among those on the board. The conservancy has seemingly balanced its primary ecological management responsibilities for management within the confines of the Preserve real estate with extensive outreach to students and the general public.

The Preserve design and management are linked in a meaningful way to regional biodiversity conservation efforts. Geographically, the Preserve is connected to Garrapata State Park, Joshua Creek Ecological Preserve, Mittledorf Preserve, Glen Deven Ranch, Point Lobos State Reserve, and the Ventana Wilderness by the Palo Corona Regional Park, a 10,000-acre former ranch that provides:

a critical environmental link in a protected [70-mile-long] wild land corridor that begins at the Carmel River and extends southward to the Hearst Ranch in San Luis Obispo County. The park includes the headwaters of [13] watersheds and protects significant habitat areas, wildlife corridors, wildlife, and endangered species.[72]

Such connectivity can enhance efforts for preserving threatened organisms like the red-legged frog, the tiger salamander, and the federally endangered Smith's blue butterfly, and provide important habitat for a diversity of organisms including peregrine falcons, deer, mountain lions, and golden eagles.

As a Natural Resources Partner to the California State Parks, the Santa Lucia Conservancy "work[s] with the department to identify and safeguard natural resources within the department's control." While following Natural Resources Partner guidelines of "preservation, advocacy, restoration and stewardship . . . the Conservancy shares natural resource management techniques and research results with State Park staff."[73] With the Chief of Natural Resources of the California State Parks on Santa Lucia Conservancy's Board of Governors, the conservancy has been able to make important contacts and meet with resource managers of state parks to compare conservation strategies.[74]

In addition to working with groups like the VWS on long-term avian monitoring projects and university researchers on Sudden Oak Death, the Santa Lucia Conservancy has also collaborated with the Monterey Peninsula Regional Parks District to develop a sustainable fuel management plan that balances conservation management strategies with wildfire-safety precautions.[75]

Important to regional ecological health is the health of the waterways and wetlands and associated riparian habitat within the Preserve. While this effort has not been without controversy, the Partnership spent three years investing in GIS mapping of wetlands, critical habitat, riparian areas, streams, creeks, and other environmentally sensitive areas to avoid during development, both to meet its own design goals and to satisfy county, CEQA, and other state and federal regulatory requirements. The Preserve, following Monterey County's conditions of approval, produced a Riparian Vegetation Management Plan that includes monitoring the health and distribution of riparian vegetation, limiting the removal of such vegetation, and restoring riparian vegetation if monitoring indicates at least a 5% decrease in vegetation in the project area.[76] Additionally, the Preserve must prevent the deposition of harmful substances into fish habitat; provide that landscaping be native, non-invasive, drought-tolerant plants; and it must submit regular assessments of groundwater levels and flow rates to the County Water Resources Agency and Environmental Health Department.[77] External scrutiny is matched with internal accountability by the Santa Lucia Conservancy as a management entity.

In sum, the Preserve maintains 18,000 acres of oaklands, savannas, forests, grasslands, chaparral, and wetlands in perpetuity via conservation easements and a $25 million endowment for the Santa Lucia Conservancy's management of the landscape—thus achieving site-level conservation at a set of homesites with associated privately owned lands that cannot be developed and that are subject to conservation restrictions, at a large-scale 20,000-acre development and conservation level, and as part of a managed, connected regional coastal habitat matrix with ongoing science and cooperation.

Notes

1. Santa Lucia Conservancy, *Homepage*, http://www.slconservancy.org/natural.asp# (last visited July 23, 2008) [hereinafter *Homepage*].
2. *Id.*
3. Four Directions Institute, *Homepage*, http://www.fourdir.com/costanoans.htm (last visited July 23, 2008).
4. Costanoan Rumsen Carmel Tribe, *Homepage*, http://www.costanoanrumsen.org/chanjayera.html (last visited July 23, 2008).
5. Homestyle by the Sea, *Lovely Land*, http://www.homestylebythesea.com/media/pdf/fall2005/lovelyland.pdf (last visited July 23, 2008).
6. *Id.*
7. Personal Communication with Tom Gray, Pacific Union Company (July 9, 2007) [hereinafter Gray Communication, July].
8. *Id.*
9. *Id.*
10. Personal Communication with Terry Palmisano, Supervising Biologist, CDFG (Aug. 15, 2007) [hereinafter Palmisano Communication].
11. *See* Gray Communication, July, *supra* note 7.
12. Brief of Appellant, Rancho San Carlos Partnership v. Superior Court of Monterey County, No. H015817 (M34796) (Cal. Ct. App. May 17, 1998).
13. Personal Communication with Tom Gray, Pacific Union Company (Aug. 16, 2007) [hereinafter Gray Communication, Aug.].
14. Personal Communication with Lisa Guthrie, Director of Clubs, Santa Lucia Preserve (Aug. 7, 2007).
15. Declaration of Protective Restrictions art. III. A. xviii.
16. *See* Gray Communication, July, *supra* note 7; Personal Communication and Interview with Jim Sulentich, Executive Director, Santa Lucia Conservancy (July 9, 2007) [hereinafter Sulentich Communication, July].
17. Conditions for Approval 109.
18. Declaration of Protective Restrictions arts. III. C. ii. a-k.
19. *Id.* arts. III. A., C. i.
20. Conditions for Approval 108b.
21. Rancho San Carlos Partnership Deed §§2.1, 2.2.
22. Conditions for Approval 16.
23. *Id.* 22, 24.
24. *Id.* 27.
25. *Id.* 121.
26. *Id.* 132.
27. Santa Lucia Guidelines Preface & §1.1.
28. *Id.* §2.4.
29. *Id.* §§2.5, 2.14, 2.15, 3.15, and 6.12.
     See Sulentich Communication, July, *supra* note 16; *see also* Santa Lucia Guidelines §§4.2.
        Homepage, *supra* note 1.
           Institute, *Conservation and Land Development*, http://sonoran.org (last visited July

33. CSO Network, Community Stewardship Organization Due Diligence/Checklist (2001).

34. Personal Communication with Kristine Bentz, Program Director for Land Conservation and Development, Sonoran Institute (Aug. 15, 2007).

35. Personal communication with John Shepard, Deputy Director of Strategic and Program Advancement, Sonoran Institute (Aug. 16, 2007).

36. U.S. Forest Serv., *Sudden Oak Death*, http://www.na.fs.fed.us/SOD/.

37. Norman H. Pillsbury et al., Long-Term Growth, Sudden Oak Death Assessment, and Economic Viability of Coast Live Oak in Three California Counties (2004), *available at* http://www.ufei.calpoly.edu/files/ufeipubs/TechReport12.pdf.

38. Personal Communication with Jim Sulentich, Executive Director, Santa Lucia Conservancy (Aug. 2, 2007) [hereinafter Sulentich Communication, Aug. 2].

39. California Oak Mortality Task Force, *Homepage*, http://nature.berkeley.edu/comtf/index.html (last visited July 23, 2008).

40. VWS, *Homepage*, http://www.ventanaws.org/ (last visited July 23, 2008).

41. VWS, *The Carmel River Riparian Corridor Avian Guild Census and Monitoring Avian Productivity and Survivorship (MAPS)*, http://www.mpwmd.dst.ca.us/asd/board/committees/admincomm/2007/20070409/02/item2_exh2a.htm (last visited July 23, 2008).

42. *See* Sulentich Communication, Aug. 2, *supra* note 38.

43. *See Homepage*, *supra* note 1.

44. Personal Communication with Jim Sulentich, Executive Director of Santa Lucia Conservancy (Aug. 7, 2007) [hereinafter Sulentich Communication, Aug. 7].

45. *See* Sulentich Communication, July, *supra* note 16.

46. Cal-IPC, *Homepage*, http://www.cal-ipc.org/policy/state/caliwac.php (last visited July 23, 2008).

47. *See* Sulentich Communication, Aug. 2, *supra* note 38.

48. *Id.*

49. *Id.*

50. U.S. FWS, *Endangered Species Program*, http://www.fws.gov/endangered/r/fr96583.html.

51. Personal Communication with Jacob Martin, Senior Biologist, FWS (Aug. 7, 2007).

52. Personal Communication with Jim Sulentich, Executive Director of Santa Lucia Conservancy (Aug. 8, 2007) [hereinafter Sulentich Communication, Aug. 8].

53. *See* Sulentich Communication, Aug. 2, *supra* note 38.

54. Personal Communication with Joyce Ambrosius, Team Leader for Central Coast, NOAA (Aug. 7, 2007); Personal Communication with Tom Gray, Pacific Union Company (Sept. 18, 2007).

55. In the Matter of State Water Resources Control Board Water Rights Application No. A029282, Petition No. T030980, Water Rights Application No. 29282, Rancho San Carlos Partnership, Applicant (Dec. 9, 1999) (public trust protest by the California Sportfishing Protection Alliance).

56. Personal Communication with Charles Rich, California State Water Resources Control Board (Aug. 20, 2007) [hereinafter Rich Communication].

57. *See* Gray Communication, Aug., *supra* note 13.

58. *See* Rich Communication, *supra* note 56.

59. Sierra Club Ventana Chapter and Carmel Rivers Steelhead Association, Formal Complaint filed with the State Water Resources Control Board (Sept. 8th 2003).

60. *See* Rich Communication, *supra* note 56.

61. *See* Sulentich Communication, Aug. 2, *supra* note 38.

62. *See* Palmisano Communication, *supra* note 10.

63. *See* Sulentich Communication, Aug. 2, *supra* note 38.

64. *See Homepage*, *supra* note 1.

65. *See* Sulentich Communication, Aug. 2, *supra* note 38.

66. *Id.*

67. David M. Theobald et al., *A Framework for Evaluating Land Use Planning Alternatives: Protecting Biodiversity on Private Land*, 6 Conservation Biology 5 (2002).

68. *See* Gray Communication, July, *supra* note 7.

69. *See* Palmisano Communication, *supra* note 10.

70. Santa Lucia Preserve Guidelines §§2.1.

71. *See* Palmisano Communication, *supra* note 10.

72. Monterey Peninsula Regional Park District, *Homepage*, http://www.mprpd.org/parks/palocorona.htm (last visited July 23, 2008).

73. California Department of Parks & Recreation, *Natural Resources Partners*, http://www.parks.ca.gov (last visited July 23, 2008).

74. *See* Sulentich Communication, Aug. 2, *supra* note 38.

75. *Id.*

76. Conditions for Approval §16a-c.

77. *Id.* §§11, 12, and 112.

County Plans and Regulations Providing Conservation Benefits at Multiple Scales

The second set of case studies focuses on local government land use planning and growth management actions. The three counties profiled here demonstrate the variety of tools—from comprehensive land use plans, zoning, and overlay zoning to Habitat Conservation Planning under the Endangered Species Act (ESA)—that can be employed to achieve habitat conservation objectives.

Chapter Seven

Eastern Contra Costa County, California: Habitat Conservation Planning for Future Development (174,000 acres)

Contra Costa County, California, is undergoing rapid development from the San Francisco Bay area, and has prepared a Habitat Conservation Plan (HCP)/Natural Community Conservation Plan for the eastern part of the county under the federal ESA, the California ESA, and the California Natural Community Conservation Planning Act. The plan aims to streamline the endangered species permitting process through the U.S. Fish and Wildlife Service and the California Department of Fish and Game, while providing a framework for making local development decisions in the context of a regional HCP for the county. The plan proposes to address approximately 13,000 acres of impacts to lands in a 174,000-acre planning area and identifies a preserve system of between 23,800 and 30,300 acres of land to be connected to regional conservation lands for the benefit of 28 special-status species. The permittees are also working with the relevant agencies to develop a regional permit for impacts to jurisdictional wetlands and waters.

Chapter Eight

Baltimore County, Maryland:
Integrated Land Use and Environmental Regulation (388,000 acres)

Baltimore County is a metropolitan county with 809,000 residents. It has experienced intense development pressures for decades. The county has used a broad array of integrated land use plans, environmental regulations, and funding and investment policies, to deal with this growth while maintaining and restoring stream corridors, conserving rural areas, and reducing impacts of development on the Chesapeake Bay. The county's use of an urban-rural line for infrastructure, its land use plans and land protection zoning, environmental criteria, mandatory watershed conservation and buffer requirements, stormwater management, forest conservation and mitigation requirements, green infrastructure guidelines for builders, and links to Maryland's broader conservation initiatives make the county a strong example of both site-level conservation and of landscape-scale conservation not driven by ESA concerns.

Chapter Nine

Summit County, Colorado:
Wildlife Habitat Overlay Zoning (396,000 acres including federal lands)

Summit County, Colorado, spans about 619 square miles, 80% of which is in public (mostly federal) ownership. The county, which ranges from 7,900 feet to over 14,000 feet in elevation, has a substantial ski resort economy and a year-round resident population of approximately 30,000. It has adopted a wildlife habitat overlay district that establishes a required development review procedure that uses regional- and state-based information to protect the wildlife habitat and species of the county from "significant adverse effects" resulting from development on the privately owned lands (<75,000 acres) in the county.

East Contra Costa County, California: Habitat Conservation Plan/Natural Community Conservation Plan

Contra Costa County is located just east of the San Francisco Bay and Oakland, California, and north of Alameda County. The county was historically agricultural and includes prominent publicly owned open space features such as Mount Diablo, but has experienced rapid development as population increased in the East Bay area. The county, with a 2000 population of 948,000, and including such population centers as Antioch, Concord, and Richmond, is expected to grow by 127,000 people by 2025.[1] Although 35% of Contra Costa County's potential conservation greenbelt lands are already permanently protected, 82,200 of the county's 462,400 acres currently have a high probability of development. A significant portion of this population growth is expected in the eastern portion of the county, currently characterized by rural land uses and substantial open space.

In response to a growing concern over the rapid pace of development, endangered species listings, and the cumulative loss of habitat for native species, the county and four of the eastern county cities began work on a habitat conservation plan/natural community conservation plan (HCP/NCCP) in 1999. (See Fig. 7.1.) The purpose of the plan is to provide a coordinated regional approach to regulatory requirements concerning the conservation of species listed as threatened or endangered under the California Endangered Species Act (CESA) and the federal Endangered Species Act (ESA) and the conservation of those species habitat as well. The plan aims to streamline the endangered species permitting process through the U.S. Fish and Wildlife Service (FWS) and California Department of Fish and Game (CDFG), while providing a framework for making local development decisions in the context of a regional HCP for the county.

The plan proposes to address approximately 13,000 acres of impacts to lands in a 174,000-acre planning area and identifies a preserve system of

107

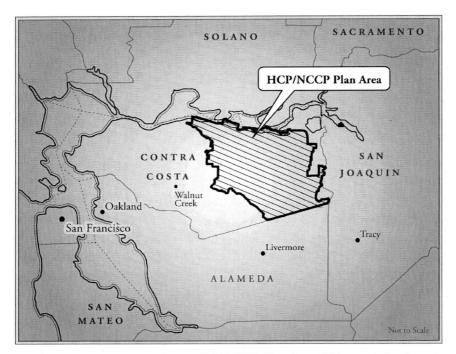

Figure 7.1 East Contra Costa County HCP/NCCP Plan Area. With permission from the Contra Costa County Community Development Department.

between 23,800 and 30,300 acres of land to be connected to regional conservation lands for the benefit of 28 special-status species. The permittees are also working with the relevant agencies to develop a regional permit for impacts to jurisdictional wetlands and waters.

HCPs

The ESA prohibits the "taking" (killing or harming) of species that are listed as "endangered" or "threatened" under the law or any activities that destroy the habitat necessary for their survival.[2] However, in 1982, Congress amended §10 of the Act to allow incidental take of species. The amendment allows the FWS and the National Oceanic and Atmospheric Administration's (NOAA's) National Marine Fisheries Service (NMFS) to permit in advance activities that may "take" protected species provided the taking is the result of otherwise lawful activity and that the impacts are minimized and mitigated to the maximum extent practicable.[3] In order to receive an incidental take permit, applicants must submit an HCP that specifies the impacts that are likely to result from the taking; the steps being taken to monitor, minimize, and mitigate such impacts; and the alternative activities that were considered but not adopted. The HCP planning process was intended "to integrate non-Federal development and land use activities with conservation goals, resolve conflicts between endangered species protection and economic activities on non-Federal lands, and create a climate of partnership and cooperation."[4]

Like the federal ESA, the CESA prohibits take of animals and plants that are listed as threatened or endangered by the CDFG.[5] The CESA also allows incidental take that occurs as the result of otherwise lawful activities provided the applicant submits an approved plan that minimizes and mitigates the impacts of the take. In 1991, California passed the NCCP Act to encourage "broad-based planning to provide for effective protection and conservation of the state's wildlife heritage while continuing to allow appropriate development and growth."[6] An approved NCCP allows for incidental take of the species covered by the plan. A revised NCCP Act, effective as of 2003, established rigorous standards for independent scientific input, public participation, biological goals that can be used in developing a monitoring and adaptive management program, interim project review, and approval criteria.[7]

Over the past 10 years, HCP efforts have largely evolved from small-scale, single development-focused plans to large-scale, multi-species plans that allow for a coordinated, proactive, and regional approach to conservation and regulation. Regional HCP/NCCPs allow local agencies to control endangered species permitting when making local development decisions. In addition, plans may encourage municipalities and counties to adopt regional habitat conservation priorities as a factor in local land use plans, ensure that species and their habitats are preserved in a regional context, facilitate preservation of habitat connectivity and wildlife corridors, and encourage private landowners to engage in habitat conservation—allowing a framework for local land use decisions to consider multiple spatial scales.[8] HCP efforts also enable local agencies to receive state and federal conservation funds that are reserved for HCPs and NCCPs.

Multi-species plans shift the focus from single-species to multi-species conservation and management by providing coverage for multiple species, including those listed under the ESA/CESA as well as species proposed for listing and other species not yet listed under the ESA. Multi-species planning can ensure that the plan will not have to be amended if covered species are listed under the ESA/CESA after the plan has been approved, and can provide advanced protection or may prevent subsequent decline for covered species that are not yet listed, provided that there is adequate scientific information about the species to provide for their conservation.

County Planning and the Urban Limit Line

In 1990, Contra Costa County voters passed Measure C, the 65/35 Land Preservation Plan, which limited urban development to no more than 35% of the land in the county and required that at least 65% of land be preserved for agriculture, open space, wetlands, parks, and other non-urban uses.[9] In order to enforce the 65/35 provision and ensure the preservation of open space, the measure created a countywide urban limit line (ULL), limiting urban land use designations to within a fixed boundary. The original ULL defined by Measure C encompassed 46% of the county land area, leaving only 54% of the county as open space outside of the ULL. However, unbuildable portions of each property within the ULL could be classified as open space to meet the 65% requirement.[10] In 2000, as citizen pressure to save open space grew, the county amended the ULL, reducing the area available for development by 14,000 acres.[11] The line was amended again in 2004, moving several incorporated areas of cities from the protected side of the line to within the ULL.[12] Measure C also required that the county and the cities in the county enter into agreements to preserve land for agriculture, open space, wetlands, and parks.

In 2004, county voters passed Measure J, linking transportation sales tax funding for a city to their acceptance of the county's ULL or adoption of their own ULL by 2009.[13] Voters in the California cities of Antioch and Pittsburg passed ULLs in 2005, which expanded their growth boundaries beyond the county's line.[14] The city of Brentwood rejected a similar measure, leaving the city to comply with the county's more restrictive boundary. The city of San Ramon passed a ULL in its 2001 General Plan.

Measure L, passed in 2006, updates the county's 2005-2020 general land use plan. Measure L also adopts a new ULL; extends the terms of the 65/35 Ordinance to December 31, 2026; requires approval by four-fifths of the county board and the majority of the votes to extend the ULL by more than 30 acres unless the board finds after a public hearing that there is substantial evidence in the record to show that the ULL expansion is necessary to avoid an unconstitutional taking of private property or is necessary to comply with state or federal law; provides for periodic review of the ULL and a comprehensive review in 2016; and retains protections for the county's prime agricultural land.[15] Cities in the county, except for Antioch, Pittsburg, and San Ramon, must now ratify the new ULL or pass their own in order to receive funding from the Measure J transportation sales tax.

Conservation Planning in East Contra Costa County

Regional conservation planning efforts in Contra Costa County began in 1995 with a mapping study, by the Alameda-Contra Costa Biodiversity Working Group, of the biological resources and conservation opportunities and constraints in the county.[16] The East County Pilot Study was designed to improve the information available for planning decisions relating to the conservation of biological diversity in eastern Alameda and Contra Costa counties, but met significant public opposition from landowners and others concerned with how maps of biological resources and conservation priorities would affect property values. As a result of the public concern, the focus of the effort changed from a mapping study to a stakeholder (conservation organizations, developers, agriculturalists, and agency staff) consensus process in 1997 to explore regional conservation planning concepts.[17]

At about the same time, the FWS and the CDFG approached Contra Costa County, the Contra Costa Water District, and the eastern county cities of Antioch, Brentwood, Clayton, and Pittsburg about the possibility of developing a regional HCP/NCCP. In 1999, the stakeholder consensus group released *East County Pilot Study Task Force Final Report: Consensus Recommendations for Improving Biological Resource Conservation*, which recommended the initiation of a regional conservation planning effort for the county.[18] Later that year, the four cities, the county, and the East Bay Regional Park District (EBRPD) (which owns 97,000 acres in Contra Costa and Alameda counties) began forming an HCP Association (HCPA) to begin the planning process. The County Board of Supervisors formally declared its intent to work with the agencies to develop an HCP/NCCP for eastern Contra Costa County in 2000.

In April 2000, the Contra Costa Water District (CCWD) agreed to work with and help fund the HCPA with the development of an HCP/NCCP as a condition for obtaining future water rights needed to serve the county's expanding population.[19] The CCWD's commitment was the result of a biological opinion (BO) issued by the FWS under §7 of the ESA,[20] at the request of the U.S. Bureau of Reclamation, concerning the CCWD's construction of a multipurpose pipeline and future water supply implementation program.[21] The BO suggested that a regional conservation plan would help offset any future impacts of development that could arise from future water deliveries and prohibited the CCWD from delivering more than 148,000 acre-feet of water per year until an HCP was approved and a §10 permit was issued for eastern Contra Costa County.

On June 30, 2000, the East Contra Costa County HCPA Agreement went into effect. The agreement formally established the East Contra Costa County

HCPA, a Joint Powers Authority consisting of the four cities (Brentwood, Clayton, Oakley, and Pittsburg), the CCWD, and the EBRPD. The city of Oakley, following its incorporation in 1999, opted to participate in the HCP effort. The county joined the HCPA in 2001. The city of Antioch, which is surrounded by Brentwood, Oakley, and Pittsburg, chose not to participate in the HCP. Consequently, future development in Antioch will require separate approval by state and federal regulatory agencies. However, the city of Antioch could choose to participate in the HCP following amendments to the HCP.[22] Contra Costa County Flood Control and the CCWD joined the effort in 2004.

Monthly planning meetings of the HCPA began in April 2002.[23] The HCPA was the lead agency in drafting the East Contra Costa County HCP/NCCP for submittal to the governing boards and member agencies and for supervising compliance with the CEQA and the National Environmental Policy Act (NEPA). In autumn 2001, the HCPA hired a local environmental consulting firm to help prepare the East Contra Costa County HCP/NCCP.

The planning process was informed by a science advisory panel, a stakeholder coordination group, and the public. The science advisory panel held four public meetings to provide scientific input on key issues related to the plan and to determine if the proposed conservation strategy was adequate for conservation of the 28 species included in the plan. The stakeholder coordination group, consisting of representatives from conservation organizations, businesses and development interests, landowners, state and federal regulatory agencies, local resource management agencies, and HCPA member agencies, was created in 2002.[24] The group held several public meetings, facilitated by the HCPA, to discuss key issues and review preliminary drafts of the plan. Staff members from the HCPA member agencies also met monthly to provide guidance on the development of the plan.

In June 2005, the HCPA released a draft HCP/NCCP and environmental impact report/environmental impact statement (EIR/EIS) for a six-month public review period. The final HCP/NCCP and EIS/EIR were released in October 2006 for approval by the permittees, and the parties signed an Implementation Agreement in December 2006. The City Councils of Brentwood, Clayton, and Oakley, the Contra Costa County Board of Supervisors, and the EBRPD Board of Directors approved the final HCP/NCCP in early 2007. The plan was approved by the Pittsburg City Council in June 2007. The plan has received unprecedented, nearly unanimous support from the eastern county cities and the county itself, with only 1 official voting "No" out of 32 elected officials. Further, local environmental organizations, development groups, and agencies strongly backed the plan.[25] The FWS and the CDFG issued permits in July 2007.

The requirements of the plan and implementation agreement will be carried out by the East Contra Costa County Habitat Conservancy (Conservancy).[26] The Conservancy is a joint powers authority formed by the county and the participating eastern county cities and consists of an executive director, governing board, and staff. One representative from each of the cities and the County Board of Supervisors serves on the governing board. The County Community Development Department will staff the Conservancy, at least initially.[27]

As part of the planning process, the HCPA is also working with the U.S. Army Corps of Engineers, the State Water Resources Control Board, the San Francisco Bay Regional and Central Valley Regional Water Quality Control Boards, and the U.S. Environmental Protection Agency to develop a regional wetlands permit program under the Clean Water Act §404 and §401, California's Porter-Cologne Water Quality Control Act, and §1602 of the California Fish and Game Code relating to Streambed Alteration Agreements.[28] If approved, the East Contra Costa County HCP/NCCP will be the first HCP/NCCP to incorporate wetlands permitting through a regional permit program.[29]

Operation of the Plan

Permitting

Contra Costa County, the Contra Costa County Flood Control and Water Conservation District, the cities of Brentwood, Clayton, Oakley, and Pittsburg, the EBRPD, and the Conservancy (the permittees) received a 30-year permit from the FWS and the CDFG that authorizes incidental takes under the ESA and the NCCP Act.[30] The local jurisdictions are able to extend the take authorization to cover local development and other projects that meet the specific terms of the HCP/NCCP. The covered activities are broadly defined to include all ground-disturbing activities within an urban development area (UDA), specific rural infrastructure projects outside the UDA, and management, restoration, and monitoring activities within the preserve system to be assembled under the HCP/NCCP. Two notable activities not provided for under the incidental take permits are minor subdivisions in unincorporated areas, i.e., "ranchette developments," and construction of new wind turbines, both of which would occur within the proposed preserve areas.[31]

The primary stated purpose of the East Contra Costa County HCP/NCCP is to "protect and enhance ecological diversity and function within the rapidly urbanizing region of eastern Contra Costa County."[32] Twenty-eight species are covered by the East Contra Costa County HCP/NCCP including 2 mammals,

4 birds, 4 reptiles, 3 amphibians, 4 invertebrates, and 11 plants. Each of the animal species is listed as endangered or threatened under the federal ESA, or is a California special-concern species, listed by the state as threatened, or fully protected by the state. All but one of the plant species is listed as rare or endangered in California and elsewhere by the California Native Plant Society.[33] Although included as covered species, no take of golden eagles or extremely rare plants is allowed under the plan.

To develop the list of covered species, information was compiled on 154 "special-status" species that were likely to occur in the inventory area. The final list of covered species includes those that occur within the inventory area, are listed under the ESA or the CESA or are likely to become listed within the 30-year term of the permit, and will likely be adversely affected by covered activities. In addition, sufficient data was available on each of the species to develop conservation measures for species recovery. It is expected that many other native species within the inventory area will benefit from the conservation strategy outlined in the plan.[34]

The Permit Area

The East Contra Costa County HCP/NCCP will cover up to 13,000 acres of projected impacts to specified land cover types within a 174,018-acre inventory area covering most of eastern Contra Costa County.[35] (See Fig. 7.2.) The permit area includes the UDA, the footprint of identified rural public infrastructure projects, and preserve lands that will be managed under the plan. The UDA includes either the area within the ULL of Contra Costa County or the city limits of Brentwood, Clayton, Oakley, and Pittsburg, whichever is larger.

One of the key considerations of the HCP process was the need to be flexible in identifying parcels for conservation and parcels for development in order to appeal to the broad range of stakeholders.[36] Therefore, there are no hard boundaries delineating where preservation or acquisition of specific parcels will occur under the plan, and the plan is not prescriptive of exactly where the development will occur within the UDA.[37] The plan is designed to have a flexible permit area to accommodate "reasonable and expected future growth" and local land use decisions based on the current general plans of the participating jurisdictions.[38]

To accommodate the uncertainty in future growth, two UDAs were defined by the plan. The initial UDA is most of the area within the current city limits and the county's ULL, while the maximum UDA is the "largest area to which urban development can expand under the terms of this HCP/NCCP" including potential future changes to city development limits.[39] A total of between 9,796

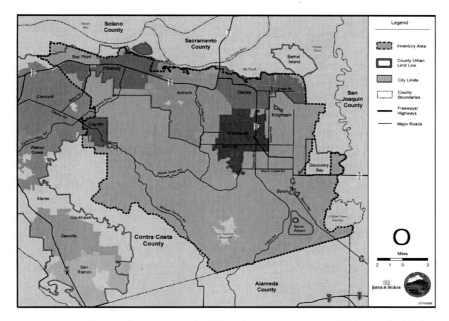

Figure 7.2 East Contra Costa County HCP/NCCP Inventory Area. With permission from the Contra Costa County Community Development Department.

and 13,029 acres of impacts to land cover types that may support covered species are allowed under the plan. These reflect, respectively, impacts within the initial and maximum UDAs and include 1,126 acres of impacts due to rural infrastructure projects.[40]

The plan permits development in the UDA, but does not *require* that development occur only with the UDA. An applicant can apply to develop outside of the UDA, but must apply individually to the FWS and the CDFG for endangered species permits for the project. Accordingly, developers have a major incentive to develop within the UDA.

Impacts to covered species and to each of the six broad land cover types addressed in the plan (wetlands, grasslands, alkali grassland, oak savanna, oak woodland, and chaparral/scrub), as well as cropland and pasture, were estimated using regional land cover data, species distribution data, species' habitat models developed for the HCP/NCCP, and a consolidated map of land use designations provided by the county that combines the land use designations identified in the General Plans of the county and the east county cities. Projected impacts were mapped and spatial analyses used to calculate the direct impacts of urban development on species and land cover types and the direct effects of covered activities on jurisdictional wetlands and waters.[41]

The Permit Process

The local jurisdictions are responsible for determining the completeness of each project application, applying the take authorization under the terms of the permit, reporting the relevant details of approved projects to the Conservancy, monitoring applicant compliance with the avoidance and minimization and other requirements of the plan, and calculating and collecting fees.[42] Each jurisdiction has adopted an implementation ordinance to outline the process by which the jurisdiction will review requests for third-party applicants, calculate mitigation fees, and extend take authorizations.[43]

The plan requires that all covered activities adhere to avoidance and minimization measures.[44] As a first step in avoidance, the permit area excludes most of the high-quality habitat for each covered species. Further, planning and preconstruction surveys must be submitted with each application.[45] *Planning surveys* must identify the natural resources affected by the proposed project, determine if any preconstruction species surveys are needed, and document actual impacts. *Preconstruction surveys* determine what species-specific avoidance and minimization measures are needed to ensure the project is in compliance with the plan. Any measures identified in the preconstruction survey must be included in the project design that is submitted with the application. The proper implementation of these avoidance and minimization measures is ensured by construction monitoring.

Mitigation Fees

Fees paid by developers for activities covered by the permit and for some temporary impacts will fund approximately 60% of the implementation of the plan.[46] The mitigation fees are designed to ensure that future development will pay a "fair share" of the costs of plan implementation proportional to its share of the overall impacts in the inventory area. The remaining implementation and land acquisition costs will be covered through new local, state, and federal contributions, maintenance of existing local, state, and federal conservation efforts, and from federal, state, and private competitive grants.[47]

Three fee zones are defined within the permit area: (1) zone 1—cultivated and disturbed lands; (2) zone 2—natural areas; and (3) zone 3—small vacant lots.[48] In 2008, fees on covered activities range from $6,039 per acre for infill projects of less than 10 acres to $24,155 for development on natural land cover types. Rural road projects are charged a greater per-acre fee because they fragment habitat, create barriers to wildlife movement, and induce growth. Additional wetland mitigation fees will be charged for applicants that fill, dredge, or remove jurisdictional wetlands or riparian woodland/scrub. Fees for impacts to wetlands and waters range from $46,748 to $183,731 per acre, and depend on wetland type.

The plan allows developers to pay for up to one-third of the permit fees through a real estate transfer fee (recurring tariff on home sales).[49] Developers also have the option of donating land in lieu of the permit fee, if the donated land supports plan requirements, has no property restrictions that conflict with the plan, is in an area designated as high or moderate priority for acquisition, and if the applicant will commit to funding the management and monitoring of the land.

Fees will be adjusted annually based on fee adjustment indices for land acquisition (based on Home Price Index for the Oakland-Fremont-Hayward, California Metropolitan Division) and for preserve system operation, restoration, and maintenance (based on the Consumer Price Index for the San Francisco-Oakland-San Jose Combined Statistical Area).[50] In addition, an independent fee audit will be conducted by March 15 of years 3, 6, 10, 15, 20, 25 to review the costs and the underlying assumptions used to generate the costs. Fees can be increased if they are found to be lower than needed to cover the mitigation fee share of the implementation costs, but not to make up for lower than expected state or federal funding.

During the development of the HCP/NCCP, interim developments paid mitigation fees into special holding accounts that will be used for HCP/NCCP implementation. The Conservancy has begun to collect funds, target land for restoration activities that can count towards plan requirements within the conservation area, and identify parcels for preservation in partnership with other agencies.[51]

Conservation Strategy

The conservation strategy of the East Contra Costa County HCP/NCCP is to "mitigate the impacts to covered species and contribute to the recovery of these species" through avoidance and minimization; habitat preservation, enhancement, restoration, and creation; and species population enhancement.[52] The East Contra Costa County HCP/NCCP distinguishes between mitigation and conservation components. Mitigation is required to offset covered activities, and conservation is required to contribute to the recovery of covered species. The two are distinguished because the FWS and the CDFG can only fund conservation activities that contribute to the recovery of covered species. A key goal of the conservation strategy is to link existing conservation efforts in the region with land acquisition and habitat restoration funded through mitigation fees collected under the plan (see Analysis section below).[53]

The conservation strategy is defined by conservation measures at multiple ecological scales:

- landscape (overall design, assembly, and management of a preserve system);
- natural community (vegetation management, habitat restoration, enhancement of ecosystem function, control of non-native species); and
- species (direct population management not covered by landscape- and community-level measures).[54]

The landscape-level conservation measures are designed to achieve 33 biological goals (broad, guiding principles) and 91 biological objectives (clear, succinct, and measurable efforts) for the benefit of covered species and natural communities.

Preserve System

The center of the conservation strategy is the assembly of a preserve system that is linked to regional protected lands. The goals of the preserve system are to conserve land, preserve major connections linking existing and future preserve lands, manage habitats to enhance populations of covered species, and compensate for lost habitat.[55] The amount of land to be preserved will be from 23,800-30,300 acres for the initial and maximum urban development area, respectively, and anticipates 424-586 acres of specific compensatory habitat restoration or creation in this preserve area.

Preserve design was guided by the plan's conservation goals and objectives as well as land use and economic factors. The process utilized a set of conservation science principles including acquiring the largest preserve possible and acquiring land in large blocks, preserving the highest quality communities, linking preserves, buffering urban impacts, minimizing edge habitats, fully representing environmental gradients, considering watersheds, considering full ecological diversity within communities, and considering management needs.[56] Regional land cover data, species distribution data, and species habitat models developed for the HCP/NCCP informed the preserve design process. Requirements for key covered species, such as the San Joaquin kit fox, were also taken into consideration when designing the preserve.

Like the definition of the permit area, acquisition priorities and potential locations were identified using a flexible map-based system. (See Fig. 7.3.) The East Contra Costa County HCP/NCCP habitat acquisition maps describe areas

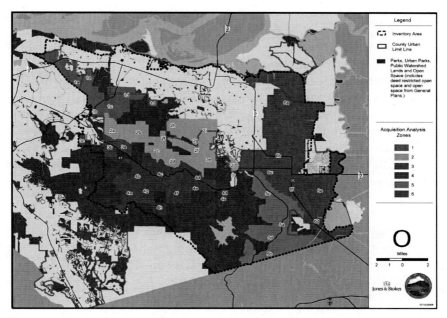

Figure. 7.3 Acquisition and Analysis Zones and Sub-Zones. With permission from the Contra Costa County Community Development Department.

in which land preservation should occur, without identifying specific parcels. Instead, the maps outline six *Acquisition Analysis Zones* that delineate acquisition priorities and "represent all undeveloped and unprotected land in the inventory area with regional conservation value and within which the preserve system can be designed."[57] Only high-quality habitat is identified in each zone. Acquisition priorities within each zone were identified based on ecological opportunities and constraints, and reflect land cover type, extent, and distribution; existing land use patterns and planned future land use activities; number of preserve design criteria met; and inclusion of habitat requirements for one or more covered species. The Conservancy will aim to acquire land under the greatest threat to development first.

This acquisition strategy allows the Conservancy some flexibility to choose appropriate parcels as they become available or are threatened by development, or to act in partnership with local conservation organizations opportunistically within the mapped areas. The HCPA considers this element of the plan to be essential to its success, but this strategy may place substantial burdens upon the Conservancy to continue to identify specific parcels as the plan is implemented and land is developed, and to ensure that each acquired parcel meets the conservation goals of the plan.

The HCP/NCCP requires the preservation of a minimum number of acres of each type of natural community to compensate for the projected impacts of covered activities on that community type.[58] In addition, buffers are required for land acquired adjacent to existing dense urban development to reduce fuel loads and minimize fire hazards. Minimum setbacks also were established for aquatic land cover types. Credit will only be given for an acquisition within a zone if it fulfills the land cover preservation requirements for the zone. However, under the HCP, the use of mitigation fees from impacts to specific land cover types will not be required to be used to preserve the same land cover types, but the assembly of the preserve is required to stay ahead of the impacts to covered species to ensure that conservation measures keep pace with development.[59]

The Stay-Ahead Provision requires that the ratio of land acquired to total land acquisition requirements exceeds the ratio of land impacted to land allowed to be impacted. Since the East Contra Costa County HCP/NCCP will conserve approximately 30,000 acres and impact about 13,000 acres, for every acre impacted a little less than 2.5 acres must be preserved.[60] To ensure that the preserve system meets the Stay-Ahead Provision at the beginning of implementation, the Conservancy is required to preserve at least 500 acres before a permit is issued (the Jump-Start Provision). The Conservancy has collected sufficient funds to acquire the necessary acres.[61] If the Conservancy determines that the plan is at risk of noncompliance with the Stay-Ahead Provision, the permittees must require that developers donate land in-lieu of paying a development fee. Implementation of the mitigation components of the plan must be also roughly proportional in time and extent to the impact on habitats or covered species.[62] Progress on the Stay-Ahead Provision and Rough-Proportionality Provision standards must be reported in each annual report.

Restoration, enhancement, and creation will be used to replace lost habitat types and supplement preservation within preserves. Habitat restoration at ratios of 1:1 to 2:1 is required for impacts to wetlands in order to meet the "no net loss" goal of wetlands. A total of 436-598 acres of restoration or creation will be accomplished under the plan. The Conservancy has just begun to study the restoration opportunities within the study area that may count toward plan requirements.[63]

Land Acquisition

The Conservancy will acquire land for the preserve system in any of six ways: (1) purchase land in fee title from willing sellers; (2) acquire conservation easements from willing sellers; (3) purchase land or conservation easements in partnership with other organizations; (4) accept land or easement dedication in lieu of fee payment under certain circumstances; (5) accept credits sold in private mitigation banks under special circumstances; and (6) accept land or easement dedication as a gift or charitable donation.[64] Land cannot be acquired by eminent domain using HCP/NCCP funding.[65] The Conservancy is likely to partner with local land conservation organizations on land acquisitions within the inventory area if the land is consistent with the goals of the HCP/NCCP, contains a conservation easement or equivalent real estate agreement, and will be protected in perpetuity under a Preserve Management Plan.[66] In addition, the regulatory agencies have agreed to help the implementation entity raise funds to acquire 8,700 acres. The plan also allows some flexibility to include mitigation and conservation banks within the inventory area if they are consistent with the conservation, monitoring, adaptive management, and other relevant provisions of the plan.[67]

Management of Preserve Lands

Each parcel acquired within the preserve is required to have a management plan.[68] All plans are reviewed and approved by the wildlife agencies, and updated and revised as part of the adaptive management plan. Individual preserve management plans must be completed within two years of acquisition of the property and cover necessary management or enhancement of habitat and species. Plans must include objectives of the conservation area, a vegetation management plan, a fire management plan, a plan for maintenance of infrastructure, monitoring requirements, and an adaptive management plan. Plans will be evaluated at least every five years during preserve acquisition and every five years after the preserve system has been completed. A systemwide management plan also will be developed to address exotic species and manage recreational uses.

The Conservancy will hold title to or conservation easements for the land it manages for the preserve system, and will also oversee agreements with land trusts or other land conservation organizations that own or manage lands as part of the preserve system.[69] Lands owned by partner organizations will be required to have conservation easements. Conservation easements will be tailored to each parcel, but allowable uses on all conservation easements will be limited to those that ensure the preservation or enhancement of conservation values consistent with the plan.[70] These lands will be managed by the Conservancy or the land conservation organization. Lands acquired by the EBRPD will not be subject to a conservation easement, however a deed restriction may be required.[71]

Grazing, recreation, and some agriculture will be allowed within the preserve system, if the uses are consistent with the goals of the plan. Agricultural management plans must be completed for cultivated lands acquired for preservation, and must be completed within one year of acquisition. Grazing is considered a key management tool for the preserve system, and grazing leases will be allowed if they are consistent with the preserve or agricultural management plans.[72]

Tracking and Accountability

An implementation agreement that specifies each permittee's obligations under the HCP was signed by the Conservancy; Contra Costa County; the cities of Pittsburg, Clayton, Oakley, and Brentwood; the Contra Costa Flood Control and Water Conservation District, the EBRPD, the FWS, and the CDFG in December 2006.

The Conservancy will coordinate with science advisors, outside consultants, land management agencies, and other specialists (real estate, grant administration, scientific oversight, consultants, and legal) to ensure proper implementation of the plan.[73] A public advisory committee, a science advisory, and an Independent Conservation Assessment Team (a separate group of scientists) will provide input to the Conservancy on plan implementation. The regulatory agencies will also serve as advisors and provide guidance to ensure that the Conservancy and permittees fulfill the terms of the permit.

The duties of the Conservancy include, among others, developing and maintaining budgets; obtaining grants; overseeing assembly, management, and monitoring of the preserve system; developing the monitoring and adaptive management program; managing implementation fees and calculating fee increases; negotiating and approving in-lieu land contributions; ensuring mitigation and conservation measures are being implemented; providing support to permittees; and preparing preserve management plans and annual reports.[74] Some of these activities may be delegated to designated organizations such as contractors or land management agencies.

The Conservancy will develop a spatial data repository to track implementation of the HCP/NCCP. The data to be tracked include monitoring and research results; HCP/NCCP funding and expenditures; status of covered activities, conservation measures, and research; adopted changes to the plan; and all reports/documents generated by the Conservancy.[75] The Conservancy also will develop a separate database to track compliance with the terms and conditions of the permit and progress toward the biological goals and objectives of the plan. The data tracked will include assembly of the preserve system; descriptions of conservation agreements; and the location, extent, and timing of impacts and conservation measures.

The plan outlines several opportunities for public input on plan implementation.[76] The meetings of the Conservancy's governing board are open to the public and the public is encouraged to comment on plan implementation and view monitoring reports. In addition, the governing board will hold annual public workshops to report on the progress of implementation directly to the public.

A public advisory committee will be established to solicit input from stakeholders on plan implementation.[77] The committee will consist of three conservation advocates, three private landowners or agriculturalists, three people representing suburban and rural residents, three private permit seekers, and public agency staff with direct interests in plan implementation. The committee will report to the governing board on its assessment of expenditure of funds for conservation measures, the general permit issuance process, operation of preserves and adaptive management, and adherence to plan commitments. The committee meetings will be open to the public.

Long-Term Funding

The implementation costs for the HCP/NCCP are expected to be between $297.090 million and $350.040 million for the initial and maximum UDA, respectively.[78] The costs include program administration, land acquisition, plan administration, environmental compliance, habitat management, habitat restoration, biological monitoring and adaptive management, remedial measures, and research on covered species. A provision for a contingency fund to temporarily cover land management or monitoring costs that are higher than the predicted costs is also included in the cost estimates.[79]

Funding sources for plan implementation include mitigation fees and in-lieu land contributions; local, state, and federal contributions; maintenance of existing local, state, and federal conservation efforts; and federal, state, and private competitive grants.[80] Local funding will include conservation expenditures by the EBRPD and local land trusts, mitigation funding derived from activities not covered under the plan, and potential open space ballot measures. State and federal funding contributions may include funds to acquire 8,700 acres from the CDFG and the FWS, and potential land acquisitions or expenditures by the California Coastal Conservancy and the California Department of Parks and Recreation. If the state and federal agencies are unable to contribute at this level then the Conservancy will work with the agencies to adjust plan implementation. Other state and federal funding sources may include federal ESA §6 Grants Program, state ballot propositions and bond measures for open space preservation and management, the state Wildlife Conservation Board, CalFed Bay-Delta Program, and the California Department of Parks and Recreation.

The Conservancy will develop and implement a plan for long-term funding of the preserve system, however long-term funding is not yet established. The plan requires that commitments for long-term funding must be secured before either 7,259 acres (50% of the authorized take) are developed or within 15 years of plan implementation. If the long-term management funds are not secured within the specified time frame, then the Conservancy and permittees must work with the CDFG and the FWS to consider slowing or stopping local permit issuance; revoking or suspending take permits; reducing take authorization limits, covered activities, or permit duration; raising fees; or developing alternative strategies.

Potential long-term funding sources include partnerships with land conservation organizations to assist with the long-term management of preserve areas, an endowment from savings over estimate plan costs, local tax or ballot measures for maintenance of open space, real estate transfer fees, reductions in the monitoring and adaptive management activities, grazing fees, and recreational use fees.[81]

Monitoring and Adaptive Management

The quality of HCPs can vary and major concerns have been raised about the adequacy of the scientific information and public input used to develop some plans and the strength of some plans' long-term biological monitoring and adaptive management provisions.[82] In addition, the no-surprises policy, which assures landowners that they will not have to provide more land or money than called for in the plan even if the HCP has detrimental consequences,[83] can make HCPs difficult to modify even as species continue to decline. And, many plans do not include provisions to fund additional conservation measures or plan modifications that may be called for during implementation of the plan. There is also some uncertainty about whether the mitigation called for in a plan is enough to offset take or be consistent with species recovery, or whether endangered species populations can be maintained as the result of HCP conservation measures.[84]

The East Contra Costa County plan outlines a framework, guidelines, and specific suggestions for developing a monitoring and adaptive management program for the preserve system, but the program has yet to be developed by the Conservancy.[85] The monitoring and adaptive management program will provide information on the status of the covered species and natural communities in order to evaluate and revise management strategies as needed. The Conservancy is responsible for developing and implementing the program, with technical assistance from the science advisors and wildlife agencies.

The monitoring strategy will be developed in three phases: (1) the design phase; (2) the inventory phase; and (3) the long-term monitoring phase. The monitoring design phase will "lay the foundation" for the monitoring program.[86] During this phase, the Conservancy will develop management-oriented conceptual ecological models for covered species and natural community types, prioritize and implement projects, identify focal species for intensive monitoring, and select biotic and abiotic indicators of ecosystem condition. The conceptual models will serve as a framework to understand how species react to management actions and will help the Conservancy determine the attributes to monitor for each natural community type.

The inventory phase will consist of an inventory and assessment of the landscape, natural communities, and species for each parcel acquired as part of the preserve system. The information gathered in the inventory phase will build upon pre-acquisition surveys conducted for each acquired parcel. The long-term monitoring phase will help the Conservancy determine the status and trends of the natural communities and species in the preserve system and the overall effectiveness of management strategies. The long-term monitoring will utilize strategies developed from information gathered during the design and inventory phases.

The Conservancy will be required to submit publicly available annual reports that document permit compliance, management actions, monitoring results, and research to the governing board, the FWS, the CDFG, and other interested parties.[87] These reports will also be used by the science advisors to assess the progress of implementation activities toward achieving the biological goals and objectives of the plan.

Analysis

HCPs are increasingly large-scale, multi-species plans that allow for a coordinated approach to regional conservation that could include innovative integration with local land use planning and regulatory tools. Such an approach can provide a framework for local land use planners and decisionmakers to make site-level decisions within a regional ecosystem conservation context. For example, the East Contra Costa County HCP/NCCP was designed to have a flexible permit area that can allows the plan to respond to land use planning changes in the city and the county given the build-out forecast in current general plans. If one of the participating cities or the county amends its ULL then the HCP/NCCP permit area would automatically change to reflect the change in land use policy as long as the revised UDA and projected impacts from covered activities does not exceed the maximum land cover or total impact projections of the plan, the revised UDA excludes high-priority acquisition areas, and the revised UDA is consistent with the successful implementation of the HCP/NCCP conservation strategy.[88]

General planning and zoning ordinances within the county have not been influenced by the development of the HCP,[89] but changes to general plans, specific plans, and zoning or land use ordinances cannot alter or diminish the permittees' obligations under the HCP/NCCP. The county could choose to use regulatory tools outside UDA to discourage development in the preserve area, but the use of these tools is not under consideration at this time.[90] However, HCP efforts could provide a structure for local governments to regulate land use while considering multiple scales.

Maintaining continuing access to conservation science was a key component of both the design of the plan as well as its implementation. The conservation strategy was designed with assistance from the Science Advisory Committee, which met four times to review the plan, elaborate on key scientific issues, and answer questions from the HCPA.[91] The science advisory panel consisted of experts in ecology, conservation biology, population biology, and reserve design, and was involved with the plan from the beginning.[92] The science panel commented on uncertainty or gaps in the data, biological goals and objectives, preserve design principles, and monitoring and adaptive management strategies, among other issues. The advisory panel produced a report documenting its findings after each meeting.[93] At the request of the regulatory agencies, the advisory panel also produced a composite report that organized its findings by topic area rather than chronologically.

The advisory panel meetings were designed to encourage interaction between the science advisors, the consultants, and the HCPA. The meetings were open to the public, and public participants were given a chance to comment or pose questions at specific points in the agenda of each meeting. Although this format gave the science advisors real time feedback on the real world context for their recommendations, some of the regulatory agency staff expressed concern that the format may have compromised the independence of the science advisors.[94] In the final composite report, the scientists indicated that the presence of the public and the HCPA did not bias their judgments or hinder the science advisory process.[95]

The Conservancy's implementation of the plan will incorporate two levels of scientific oversight.[96] A science advisor will provide technical advice and help the Conservancy assemble the best available scientific data on the plan's preserve assembly, monitoring, and adaptive management program. A second group of scientists, the Independent Conservation Assessment Team, will convene periodically to provide outside review of the overall plan progress.

Stakeholders and members of the general public were encouraged to provide input on the development of the plan during quarterly public meetings of the HCPA Executive Governing Committee, monthly public meetings of the HCPA Coordination Group, periodic public meetings of the HCP/NCCP Science Advisors, during the CEQA/NEPA public review process, and periodic presentations by the HCPA to the official governing bodies of participating agencies.[97] The public was encouraged to comment on draft versions of the HCP/NCCP and EIR/EIS and on the final plan. This commitment to public participation helped to ensure local stakeholders remained interested in preserving a network of open space lands in a rapidly developing area.

One of the key principles guiding the design of the preserve system and the acquisition process is that the preserves are linked in a meaningful way—both inside and outside of the planning area. For example, the HCP is being used to conduct long range planning for the San Joaquin kit fox and to establish a movement corridor for the species that extends outside the inventory area. In addition, the proposed land acquisition will link to existing protected areas in the inventory area, such as the 20,000-acre Mt. Diablo State Park, Black Diamond Mines Regional Preserve, Morgan Territory Regional Preserve, Round Valley Regional Preserve, Los Vaqueros watershed lands, Cowell Ranch State Park, and Vasco Caves Regional Preserve.[98] The Conservancy will work with local land management agencies where HCP/NCCP preserves border existing parks or public lands to coordinate land management activities across the region.

In addition, ongoing regional conservation programs will be complemented and extended by the HCP preserve system. The EBRPD manages over 97,000 acres of scenic ridge lines and other open spaces and 29 regional inter-park trails in the Contra Costa County area.[99] Many of the areas proposed for acquisition under the HCP/NCCP are areas that have been previously identified for future preservation by the EBRPD. The EBRPD may acquire as many as 10,000 acres over the next 30 years under the HCP/NCCP conservation strategy. The San Joaquin Council of Governments has acquired conservation easements on agricultural land in the western part of the county as part of its Multi-Species Habitat Conservation and Open Space Plan. These easements may support conservation efforts with the East Contra Costa County HCP/NCCP inventory area, and vice versa.[100] Alameda County, to the south of Contra Costa County, contains the Brushy Peak Regional Preserve, which comes close to connecting with the proposed Preserve system. EBRPD, CDFG, and the Altamont Landfill Open Space Committee also acquire or fund acquisition of conservation lands within Alameda County and there may be opportunities to coordinate with these agencies on other regional projects.[101]

The Greenbelt Alliance, a contributor to the development of the ECCC HCP/NCCP, is engaged in regional conservation planning and visioning efforts in the San Francisco Bay Area. Since 1958, the Greenbelt Alliance "has been protecting the Bay Area's greenbelt of natural areas and farms, and making the region's cities better places to live" by working with "diverse coalitions on public policy development, advocacy and education."[102] The Greenbelt Alliance helps cities and counties prepare growth policies that ensure the protection of the greenbelt; endorses development projects that create walkable neighborhoods close to shops, jobs, and transit; educates and mobilizes local citizens to have a voice in their community's land use decisions; and publishes research on strategies for how to accommodate growth while protecting the greenbelt. The Greenbelt Alliance is also working on a vision for open space in the Bay Area.[103]

In addition, several regional efforts are underway to identify priority areas for conservation. The San Francisco Bay Area Upland Goals Project, conducted by the Coastal Conservancy, uses a science-based process to recommend the types, amounts, and distribution of upland habitats, linkages, compatible uses, and ecological processes that are needed to sustain diverse and healthy wildlife populations in the Bay Area.[104] The spatial data gathered for this project are used to support voluntary, nonregulatory protection strategies and management policies. The San Francisco Bay and Sacramento Joint Ventures also are identifying priority locations for conservation within their regions. The San Francisco Bay Joint Venture, working with Ducks Unlimited, created a habitat tracking system that holds information on habitat acquisition, restoration, and enhancement projects as well as associated education and outreach projects to track progress on regional conservation goals.[105]

As of spring 2008, over 500 HCPs had been approved by the FWS—from all parts of the country. Large-scale HCP efforts could represent not only an opportunity to identify regional conservation priorities, but also a mechanism for local governments to think regionally about their land use decisions.

Notes

1. Greenbelt Alliance, At Risk: The Bay Area Greenbelt (2006), *available at* http://www.greenbelt.org/resources/reports/atrisk_2006/index.html.
2. 16 U.S.C. §§1531-1544, ELR Stat. ESA §§2-18.
3. U.S. FWS, *Habitat Conservation Planning Handbook*, http://www.fws.gov/endangered/hcp/hcpbook.html. *See also* 16 U.S.C. §1539(a)(2)(B).
4. *See Habitat Conservation Planning Handbook, supra* note 3.
5. Cal. Fish & Game Code §§2080-2085 (West 1991).
6. *Id.* §§2800-2835.
7. *Id.*
8. *See Habitat Conservation Planning Handbook, supra* note 3.
9. County Ordinance Code ch. 82-1.
10. Contra Costa County, *General Plan 2005-2020*, http://www.co.contra-costa.ca.us/depart/cd/current/advance/GeneralPlan/CCCGeneralPlan.pdf (last visited Oct. 20, 2008).
11. East Contra Costa County HCP/NCCP, *Chapter 2: Land Use and Covered Activities*, http://www.cocohcp.org/final-hcp/pdfs/ch02land.pdf (last visited Oct. 20, 2008).
12. *Id.*
13. *Id.*
14. *See* Greenbelt Alliance, At Risk: The Bay Area Greenbelt, *supra* note 1.
15. Greenbelt Alliance, *Contra Costa Urban Limit Line*, http://www.greenbelt.org/regions/eastbay/camp_ull.html (last visited Oct. 20, 2008).
16. East Contra Costa County HCP/NCCP, *Chapter 1: Introduction*, http://www.cocohcp.org/final-hcp/pdfs/ch01intro.pdf (last visited Oct. 20, 2008).
17. Personal Communication with John Kopchik and Abby Fateman, Contra Costa County Community Development Department (July 13, 2007) [hereinafter Kopchik & Fateman].
18. *See Chapter 1: Introduction, supra* note 16.
19. *See* Kopchik & Fateman, *supra* note 17.
20. 16 U.S.C. §1536.
21. *See Chapter 1: Introduction, supra* note 16.
22. *See* Kopchik & Fateman, *supra* note 17.
23. *See Chapter 1: Introduction, supra* note 16.
24. *Id.*
25. Personal Communication with Brad Olson, EBRPD (July 17, 2007) [hereinafter Olson Communication, July].
26. East Contra Costa County HCP/NCCP, *Chapter 8: Plan Implementation*, http://www.cocohcp.org/final-hcp/pdfs/ch08imp.pdf (last visited Oct. 20, 2008) [hereinafter *Chapter 8: Plan Implementation*].
27. *See* Kopchik & Fateman, *supra* note 17.
28. *See Chapter 1: Introduction, supra* note 16.
29. *See* Kopchik & Fateman, *supra* note 17.
30. *See Chapter 1: Introduction, supra* note 16.
31. E-mail from Brad Olson, EBRPD (Sept. 4, 2007) [hereinafter Olson E-mail, Sept.].
32. *See Chapter 1: Introduction, supra* note 16.
33. East Contra Costa County HCP/NCCP, *Chapter 3: Physical and Biological Resources*, http://www.cocohcp.org/final-hcp/pdfs/ch03setting.pdf (last visited Oct. 20, 2008).

34. *Id.*
35. East Contra Costa County HCP/NCCP, *Chapter 4: Impact Assessment and Levels of Take*, http://www.cocohcp.org/final-hcp/pdfs/ch04impacts.pdf (last visited Oct. 20, 2008) [hereinafter *Chapter 4: Impact Assessment and Levels of Take*].
36. *See* Kopchik & Fateman, *supra* note 17.
37. *Id.*
38. East Contra Costa County HCP/NCCP, *Executive Summary*, http://www.cocohcp.org/final-hcp/pdfs/02execsum.pdf (last visited Oct. 20, 2008).
39. *Id.*
40. *See Chapter 4: Impact Assessment and Levels of Take, supra* note 35.
41. *Id.*
42. East Contra Costa County HCP/NCCP, *Chapter 6: Conditions on Covered Activities*, http://www.cocohcp.org/final-hcp/pdfs/Ch06conditions.pdf (last visited Oct. 20, 2008).
43. *See Chapter 8: Plan Implementation, supra* note 26.
44. East Contra Costa County HCP/NCCP, *Chapter 5: Conservation Strategy*, http://www.cocohcp.org/final-hcp/pdfs/ch05constrat.pdf (last visited Oct. 20, 2008) [hereinafter *Chapter 5: Conservation Strategy*].
45. *Id.*
46. East Contra Costa County HCP/NCCP, *Chapter 9: Funding*, http://www.cocohcp.org/final-hcp/pdfs/ch09funding.pdf (last visited Oct. 20, 2008) [hereinafter *Chapter 9: Funding*].
47. For example, the East Contra Costa County HCP/NCCP has already been awarded a $6.5 million land acquisition grant from the U.S. Department of the Interior. East Contra Costa County HCPA, *HCPA Coordination Group Meeting*, http://www.cocohcp.org/downloads/CG_mtg_packet_9-18-03.pdf (last visited Oct. 20, 2008).
48. *See Chapter 9: Funding, supra* note 46.
49. *See* Kopchik & Fateman, *supra* note 17.
50. *See Chapter 9: Funding, supra* note 46.
51. *See* Kopchik & Fateman, *supra* note 17. Interim developments are those that received take authorizations after November 2003.
52. *See Chapter 5: Conservation Strategy, supra* note 44.
53. *See* Kopchik & Fateman, *supra* note 17.
54. *See Chapter 5: Conservation Strategy, supra* note 44.
55. *Id.*
56. *Id.*
57. *Id.*
58. *Id.*
59. *Id.*
60. E-mail from John Kopchik, Contra Costa County Community Development Department (Aug. 16, 2007).
61. *See* Kopchik & Fateman, *supra* note 17.
62. *See Chapter 5: Conservation Strategy, supra* note 44.
63. *See* Kopchik & Fateman, *supra* note 17.
64. *See Chapter 5: Conservation Strategy, supra* note 44.
65. *See* Olson E-mail, Sept., *supra* note 31.
66. *See Chapter 5: Conservation Strategy, supra* note 44.

67. *See Chapter 8: Plan Implementation, supra* note 26. Projects outside of the inventory area and not covered by the permit may use the HCP/NCCP for mitigation if they impact covered species and meet the goals of the preserve system.
68. *See Chapter 5: Conservation Strategy, supra* note 44.
69. *Id.*
70. *Id.*
71. *See* Olson E-mail, Sept., *supra* note 31.
72. *See Chapter 5: Conservation Strategy, supra* note 44.
73. *See Chapter 8: Plan Implementation, supra* note 26.
74. *Id.*
75. *Id.*
76. *Id.*
77. *Id.*
78. *See Chapter 9: Funding, supra* note 46.
79. *Id.*
80. *Id.*
81. *Id.*
82. Defenders of Wildlife, *Frayed Safety Nets*, http://www.defenders.org/programs_and_policy/habitat_conservation/private_lands/habitat_conservation_plans.php (last visited Oct. 20, 2008) [hereinafter *Frayed Safety Nets*].
83. *See Habitat Conservation Planning Handbook, supra* note 3.
84. *See Frayed Safety Nets, supra* note 82.
85. East Contra Costa County HCP/NCCP, *Chapter 7: Monitoring and Adaptive Management Program*, http://www.cocohcp.org/final-hcp/pdfs/ch07mon.pdf (last visited Oct. 20, 2008).
86. *Id.*
87. *Id.*
88. *See Chapter 2: Land Use and Covered Activities, supra* note 11.
89. *See* Kopchik & Fateman, *supra* note 17.
90. *Id.*
91. *See Chapter 5: Conservation Strategy, supra* note 44.
92. Personal Communication with Erica Fleishman, East Contra Costa County HCP/NCCP Science Advisory Panel Facilitator (July 20, 2007) [hereinafter Fleishman Communication].
93. *See Chapter 1: Introduction, supra* note 16.
94. *See* Fleishman Communication, *supra* note 92.
95. *See id. See also* Science Advisory Panel for the East Contra Costa County HCP/NCCP, *Composite Report*, http://www.cocohcp.org/downloads/composite_ECCC_report.pdf (last visited Oct. 20, 2008).
96. *See Chapter 8: Plan Implementation, supra* note 26.
97. *See Chapter 1: Introduction, supra* note 16.
98. *See Chapter 5: Conservation Strategy, supra* note 44.
99. *See* Olson Communication, July, *supra* note 25.
100. *See Chapter 5: Conservation Strategy, supra* note 44.
101. *Id.*
102. Greenbelt Alliance, *About Greenbelt Alliance*, http://www.greenbelt.org/about/factsheet_aboutus.html (last visited Oct. 20, 2008).

103. *See* Olson Communication, July, *supra* note 25.
104. Bay Area Open Space Council, *Upland Habitat Goals Project*, http://openspacecouncil.org/projects/upland/upland-habitat-goals-project/ (last visited Oct. 20, 2008).
105. San Francisco Bay Joint Venture, *Habitat Acquisition, Restoration, and Enhancement Projects*, http://www.sfbayjv.org/projects.html (last visited Oct. 20, 2008).

Baltimore County, Maryland: Integrated Land Use Regulation, Resource Protection, and Public Facilities

Baltimore County, a suburban county surrounding the city of Baltimore, stretches from the borders of Baltimore City to the Pennsylvania border.[1] The 607-square mile county exercises land use planning and regulatory powers throughout its entire area, and there are no incorporated municipalities within the county. Baltimore County's population began to increase rapidly beginning in the 1950s as residents of Baltimore City began to follow suburban trends and move into the county, and it now has 809,000 residents.[2]

In the early 1960s, a citizens' association sponsored a planning study which resulted in the 1964 *Plan for the Valleys,* prepared under the direction of University of Pennsylvania Landscape Architect Ian McHarg, later the author of *Design With Nature.* The concepts in the 1964 plan led to the county's adoption in 1967 of the Urban-Rural Demarcation Line (URDL), an urban services boundary, and were later incorporated into the first master plan for the county in 1972. (See Fig. 8.1.)

Within the URDL, urban development was to be accommodated including public services, while outside the line, urban development was not envisioned. In 1975, the county down-zoned areas outside the URDL to reduce allowable development, and focused its substantial open space protection and farmland preservation and acquisition efforts in these areas in the following decades.

In the 1980s the county adopted a stringent set of environmental codes, and it has continually amended and updated these to improve protection of watersheds, Chesapeake Bay tributaries, open space, and forests. The combination of planning, rigorous adherence to the URDL (even as necessary amendments occurred), and the marshalling of other state and county programs prescribing environmental requirements for new development and protecting farmland and open space, have resulted in a county in which 87% of the population lives within the URDL on 32% of the land area. The 68% of the county not within

133

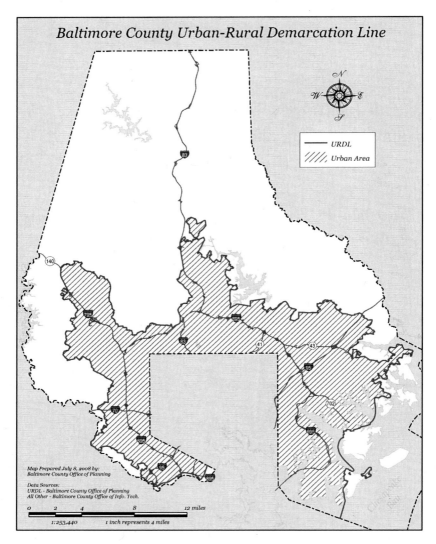

Figure 8.1. Baltimore County Urban-Rural Demarcation Line. With permission from the Baltimore County Office of Planning.

the URDL has retained its rural and open space character and its potential (at least) for supporting habitat goals. These policy tools also protect more than 90% of the watersheds of the several metropolitan reservoirs that today serve more than 1.8 million residents of the county and Baltimore City.

Baltimore County is economically diverse and contains housing of all types, with businesses located both in town centers and in newer suburban-style business parks located within the URDL. The county has retained over 800 working farms, and large open space areas especially along its major waterways, while managing to sustain economic development and substantially increasing its tax base within the URDL. It has provided for ecological functions by focusing on water, farms, and forests. The county addresses scale issues by imposing conservation requirements at the site level while steering both development and conservation decisions at the landscape level. It has maintained housing affordability and diversity in employment while managing conservation on a countywide scale.

Operation of the Programs

Urban-Rural Services Line and Land Use Regulation

Baltimore County's URDL defines for county officials and the public where urban growth is planned, and this determination is reinforced by a quasi-public corporation called the Metropolitan District. The Metropolitan District provides for the financing and management of public water and sewer services. Together the establishment of the line and the management mechanisms have determined to a substantial degree the density and level of development in different places in the county.[3]

Lands that are within the URDL are closest to Baltimore City and are served by the metropolitan water system that serves Baltimore City and by the sewage collection system and pumping facilities operated by the county and served by the city's sewage treatment plants. The Water Supply and Sewerage Plan is integrated with and consistent with the county's master plan for land use. Public water and sewer services may be extended to areas outside the Metropolitan District if the county approves and subject to concurrence by Baltimore City. The Metropolitan District service boundaries have been made substantially concurrent with Baltimore County's long-standing URDL. Areas within the URDL are also substantially the same as subsequently designated smart growth "priority funding areas" which since 1998 define where *state*-supported funding for growth and infrastructure may go.[4]

Land use regulation, and particularly zoning, has supported and sustained the effectiveness of the URDL in defining development and protecting watersheds and rural areas.[5] The URDL was established by the county in 1967, and was included in the county's first master plan adopted in 1972. Subsequent plans in 1975, 1979, 1989, and 2000 have reinforced the county's support for determining differing paths for growth in the rural and urban/suburban areas.[6] The county's 1975 master plan, which established different rural and urban zoning categories, was seen to result in large-lot sprawl in parts of the rural area. So in the 1979 master plan, implemented by 1980 zoning amendments, the county adopted agricultural lands zoning that specified a density of 1 dwelling unit/50 acres for parcels of land over 100 acres in the rural conservation areas, thus protecting areas large enough to support agricultural practices.

The 1979 Master Plan specifically designated two new growth areas for more intensive development, when the plan down zoned other areas of the rural county. In other areas the county allows cluster/conservation subdivision, allowing higher densities where a development places a substantial portion of a parcel in easement-protected open space. Recent years have seen a significant amount of redevelopment within older communities and the beginning of charrette-based new urbanism projects under the county's Renaissance Redevelopment program.[7]

The county also created two new resource conservation zones in the rural area, one of which was based on greenways and wildlife corridors. The resource conservation zones provide for conservation of larger parcels of land and contain their own stringent environmental criteria relating to development.[8] (See Fig. 8.2.)

The adoption of the URDL, mapped onto the landscape, is a form of spatially explicit planning, and the county has relied extensively on mapping during many decades of program implementation. The Chesapeake Bay critical areas and the priorities for land conservation and acquisition are also mapped and guided by science. Baltimore County's substantial investment in land preservation (discussed below) provides a basis for future wildlife habitat recovery that relies on assembling coherent linkages among parcels—and particularly focused on waterways and adjacent lands. Land preservation is focused in the northern two-thirds of the county outside the URDL and especially along waterways and riparian corridors (this is apart from preservation of agricultural lands, which is more widely dispersed).

Baltimore County's planning objectives are largely expressed in terms of quality of life and the protection of water resources, but the content of its programs reflects an ecological understanding that addresses landscape needs, and not just protection of specific species or specific habitat types. This means that the landscape is the relevant unit—but it also means that the success of the conservation programs are not measured in species richness or diversity, but rather in the protection of mapped areas of land through land use regulation and con-

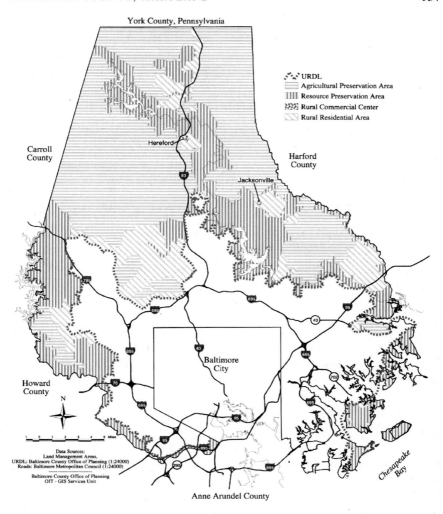

Figure 8.2. Baltimore County Rural Land Management Areas. With permission from the Baltimore County Office of Planning.

servation acquisitions. The county's most recent master plan, prepared in 2000, has the following language relevant to habitat:

Issue: Protecting Plant and Animal Habitats (Biological Diversity)
Many of the issues related to protecting plant and animal habitats have been discussed as important components of stream and forest preservation. Tra-

ditionally, another important habitat issue is the protection of rare, threatened, or endangered plants and animals. DEPRM [Baltimore County's Department of Environmental Protection and Resource Management, discussed below] takes a broad view in habitat preservation, including not only the protection of rare or significant species, but also assuring long-term conservation of the habitats for upland, forest, riparian, wetland and aquatic plants and animals. This broader concept is called biological diversity.

Actions
1. Continue to ensure that significant habitats are identified on development plans and continue to seek cooperation in protecting them through modification of site designs.
2. Seek to increase plant and animal habitat in conjunction with capital improvement projects for shore erosion control, stream restoration, wetland creation, and reforestation.
3. Work in cooperation with governmental and non-profit agencies to assess, protect, restore, and create habitats.[9]

County Environmental Regulations

The county code provides a very substantial set of mandatory environmental regulations relating to land development.[10] These provide for protection of riparian and wetland buffers, mandatory forest conservation on virtually all development sites (implementing Maryland's landmark Forest Conservation Act),[11] stormwater controls, and mitigation. Implementation of these requirements is overseen by the county's Department of Environmental Protection and Resource Management (DEPRM), created in 1987. The DEPRM's professional staff of over 100 is responsible for development reviews, environmental regulation, outreach, and voluntary and land protection programs. The unification of these functions in a single governmental organization keeps environmental issues at the forefront of implementation and maintains the landscape-scale focus of the county's efforts, instead of divorcing "environment" from land use regulation and subdivision. Environmental issues are reviewed on-site during the development review process. The county's separate Office of Planning, in contrast, handles the comprehensive plan and proposed zoning amendments, but not site plan and development review. The DEPRM's responsibilities include:

• Protection of streams, wetlands, and steep slopes, which must be identified on the development plan and protected in accordance with detailed county, state (and some federal) requirements.

- Enforcement of forest conservation requirements; these require any new development to reforest (or afforest) lands where forest is removed, and incentivize the retention of existing forest by prescribing a sliding scale of compensatory mitigation. Retained forest and reforested lands must be configured to maximize water quality and wildlife benefits.
- Enforcement of stormwater management and sediment and erosion control requirements designed to protect the Chesapeake Bay and its tributaries, and the waters of the county.
- Protection of groundwater through proper siting, design, and construction of water supply wells and on-site wastewater systems.
- Enforcement of development limits within the Chesapeake Bay critical area (within 1,000 feet of tidal waters).[12]

The county's critical areas provisions are laid out in detailed regulatory requirements that include requirements for permits, design standards, wetlands protections, buffers, "habitat protection areas," limited development areas, forestry requirements, and sediment controls.[13] These protected areas include requirements for "irrevocable offer[s] of dedication to the county of all habitat protection areas, buffers, wetland, forests and developed woodlands, afforestation and reforestation areas, wildlife corridors, and floodplains."[14] Development activities are prohibited altogether in habitat protection areas, unless the DEPRM certifies that the activities and restrictions will provide for the continuity of the wildlife habitat, no other physically feasible alternative exists for the location of a "road, trail, bridge or utility," the activities will not "alter the structure and species composition of natural heritage areas," comments from the state Department of Natural Resources are received and considered, restoration occurs for any disturbance allowed for a road, trail, bridge or utility, and on-site or off-site mitigation is required.[15]

Much of the county, including most of the northern area outside the URDL is not in a Chesapeake Bay critical area. However, many of Baltimore County's environmental regulations apply countywide. The protection of streams, wetlands, and floodplains, for example, is integrated into *all* development design, review, approval, and enforcement.[16] Developers, forest harvesters, etc. must submit a detailed plan identifying soils, natural resources, vegetation, historic resources, slopes, etc. Any plat submitted to the county must include irrevocable offers of dedication to the county of forest buffers to protect waterways and wetlands.[17] The code requires protection of forest buffers (measured from the centerline of first and second order streams, and from the bank of higher order streams). The buffer is 75-100 feet (depending on stream designation) or

25 feet from the outer wetland boundary, or 25 feet from the riverine flood-plain reservation, whichever is greatest; buffer restrictions are adjusted for greater stringency where slopes and erodible soils factors dictate. Residential dwellings must be set back 35 feet from the edge of the buffer, commercial and industrial buildings 25 feet, but appurtenant structures and driveways are allowed within the setback area.[18] Forest buffers, including wetlands and floodplains, must be managed "to enhance and maximize the unique value of these resources."[19] Variances from waters and wetland provisions may be granted under limited circumstances: for unreasonable hardship, for public improve-ments where there is no feasible alternative, for repair and maintenance of public improvements where avoidance and minimization of impacts have been addressed, and for developments that had stream buffers applied in accordance with prior county policies of the 1980s for which the potential for water qual-ity and aquatic resource degradation is minimal.[20] Approval of a variance may be conditioned on site design, landscape planting, best management practices, and other conditions.

Forest conservation and mitigation requirements also apply across the county for any development activities occurring on land of 40,000 square feet or more (slightly less than 1 acre). The ordinance requires assessment and mapping of existing forest cover, forest conservation planning, retention of forests, com-pensatory mitigation for removed forests either on-site or off-site via a county forest conservation fund paid into by developers, and long-term management and retention.[21] Forest and "tree cover" compose nearly 35% of the county's land area (132,500 acres); about 20% of this is in public ownership, the rest is on privately owned lands, mostly on small parcels of land.[22]

Environmental regulation has been thoroughly integrated into the devel-opment process, and more recently public-private voluntary efforts have arisen to define and promote environmentally sensitive best development practices. In 2006, a cooperative Baltimore County effort, the Builders for the Bay Pro-gram, published *Recommended Model Development Principles: Consensus of the Builders for the Bay Site Planning Roundtable*, integrating watershed and resource protection recommendations into guidelines for use by devel-opers and builders planning to undertake activities in the county. These include specific recommendations on natural areas, buffer management, tree conser-vation, maintenance of vegetation, land conservation, open space design, stormwater management, and other issues important for ecological and wildlife conservation.

Land Preservation

The county goal is to protect 80,000 acres (about 20% of the county's land area) by acquisition, a goal which has been halfway achieved.[23] In addition, private land trusts have protected over 12,000 acres in the county.[24] A number of state- and county-funded programs support land preservation. These goals serve both to help support Maryland's voluntary commitments under the 2000 Chesapeake Bay Agreement, and to meet county conservation objectives aimed at farming, forests, wildlife, water, and open space.

Scientific priority setting has been used to drive at least part of the land conservation agenda. Most recently, in 2006, the nonprofit Conservation Fund completed a "Baltimore County Land Preservation Model" based on scientific "green infrastructure" criteria, and followed that with a Water Quality Assessment to predict the impact of land conservation on water quality.[25] This built upon an earlier pilot study in which the Maryland Department of Natural Resources gave the Baltimore County DEPRM a grant in 1997 to develop a rapid assessment methodology for identifying high-quality resource lands for conservation. This methodology, in turn, became the basis for the state's statewide green infrastructure assessment technique. The approach used geographic information system (GIS) data layers on vegetation, streams, soils and the like to identify candidate protection lands for further field evaluation and prioritization. The Conservation Fund notes "the methodology provided the rapid assessment desired for identifying a connected system of forest resources that provide multiple ecological benefits, including water quality protection, biological diversity, and conservation or restoration of natural areas for both citizens and wildlife."[26] Watershed plans have been prepared for many of the watersheds in the county.

Agricultural lands preservation is a major focus for the county. Rural property owners engaged in agriculture or participating in U.S. Department of Agriculture agricultural conservation programs apply for designation of their property as an agricultural district; this then makes them eligible to sell conservation easements on the land to the Maryland Agricultural Lands Preservation Foundation (MALPF) or to the county itself, which can purchase easements under the county agricultural preservation program. The state and county programs both receive funds from the Maryland real property transfer tax on real estate transactions. These programs have protected about 18,000 acres of land in the county for agriculture.

Rural Legacy is a state-funded program enacted by the Maryland Legislature in 1997 as part of a package of smart growth laws.[27] The program targets the commitment of state open space acquisition funds to areas that are *outside* of designated "priority development areas"[28]—which in Baltimore County means areas outside the URDL. Baltimore County identified five areas to target rural legacy funds, in collaboration with private land trusts, and has conserved approximately 3,000 acres.[29]

GreenPrint was a state-funded program adopted in 2000 which was intended to use a statewide map of ecologically important hubs and corridors to guide acquisitions of land for conservation and preservation. GreenPrint funding was significantly reduced after its initial launch. Its focus and approach has largely been on forest and watershed lands.[30] (See Fig. 8.3.)

Additional lands, amounting to about 12,000 acres have been protected by conservation easements donated to the Maryland Environmental Trust.[31] Both state and county tax incentives, including county property tax credits and state income tax credits, stimulate donations of conservation easements.[32]

Stream Restoration

The county maintains an active stream and water quality restoration program funded primarily by county bonds and state and federal grants. In 2003, the county and Baltimore City signed a watershed agreement to address water quality issues in the watersheds that serve both jurisdictions. Substantial mapping of watersheds has been completed by the county, including buffers, critical areas for Chesapeake Bay tributaries, and other features. The county's Waterway Capital Improvement Program includes stream restoration, shoreline protection and enhancement, and stormwater retrofit activities.

The county identifies 14 "major" watersheds, of which 7 are part of the Gunpowder River Basin and 6 are part of the Patapsco River Basin.[33] The Gunpowder River Basin includes two major reservoirs (the Prettyboy and the Loch Raven), and the Patapsco River Basin includes the Liberty Reservoir. The three reservoirs, serving the water customers inside the URDL and in Baltimore City, lie outside the URDL so they can be protected; however, the Loch Raven Reservoir lies directly adjacent to the northern edge of the URDL. Baltimore City owns the reservoirs themselves and the water supply system, and owns and manages 17,200 acres of land directly around the reservoirs (albeit lying within the county). However, the watershed lands and the rivers and streams supplying the reservoir are the responsibility of the county—comprising 94% of the watershed areas supplying the three reservoirs. [34]

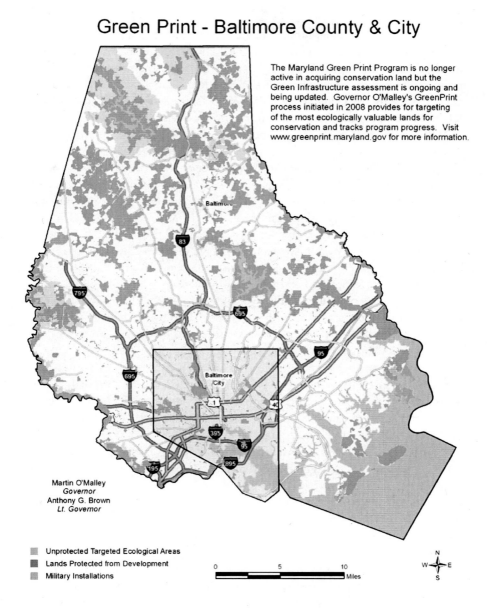

Green Print - Baltimore County & City

The Maryland Green Print Program is no longer active in acquiring conservation land but the Green Infrastructure assessment is ongoing and being updated. Governor O'Malley's GreenPrint process initiated in 2008 provides for targeting of the most ecologically valuable lands for conservation and tracks program progress. Visit www.greenprint.maryland.gov for more information.

Martin O'Malley
Governor
Anthony G. Brown
Lt. Governor

- Unprotected Targeted Ecological Areas
- Lands Protected from Development
- Military Installations

0   5   10 Miles

Figure 8.3. Maryland's GreenPrint Program: Targeting Funding for Key Ecological Lands

Analysis

Baltimore County's integration of its environmental standards into site-level decisionmaking, and its integration of the staff for site-level reviews and permitting with those responsible for voluntary- and landscape-scale conservation, provides an example showing that site-level regulations and actions can be designed and implemented to support broader landscape goals defined by both local government- and state-level information and science.

Baltimore County's landscape approach has achieved results that are relevant not only for its own 607 square miles (or even for just the area of the county outside the URDL where habitat and open space are best protected). By focusing on water supplies and watersheds initially, and by maintaining a compact and orderly development scheme in the face of rapid growth, the county has influenced some conservation results at a much larger scale. Indeed, it has responded to state laws and imperatives to protect the Chesapeake Bay and its tributaries. The county has also taken advantage of statewide opportunities to prioritize and identify its conservation lands. It has worked with Baltimore City on watersheds encompassed by both jurisdictions.

The county has not attempted to evaluate its conservation efforts or investments in terms of coordination with related decisions by adjacent counties, but has largely focused on its own and bay-watershed objectives. However, the county's 2010 Master Plan discusses the need for a regional framework. Specific coordination issues in Baltimore County's conservation area are discussed in the plan. These are coordination with Baltimore City on "interjurisdictional watershed management," desire to upgrade and protect Piney Run with Carroll County and the town of Hampstead in Carroll County, cooperation with Howard County on watershed management and reservoir protection through participation on the Patapsco Tributary Strategy Group, cooperation with Harford County in the management of the Deer Creek and Little Gunpowder watersheds, and cooperation with Harford County in future development of programs to "preserve large contiguous areas of farmland that cross jurisdictional boundaries" and also to "contain" the rural-residential development pattern that seems to be emerging in an area of Baltimore County/Harford County.[35]

Baltimore County has used a wide array of funding sources—taking advantage of state funding and grant programs, as well as using authority provided to the county by state laws involving counties in land conservation expenditures, tax incentives for easement dedications, and actions by developers. Funding has been adequate to support a robust DEPRM and, despite some ups and downs, a viable land conservation program. The organization of county government to include development review and environmental monitoring and implementation in the same unit of government along with land conservation planning and funding has benefitted the county greatly in terms of its on-the-ground effectiveness. It has also made possible the application of advances in conservation science to county regulations and initiatives. Because of these investments and staffing the county has been able to monitor some outcomes. It has been able to rely to a significant degree on state findings and Bay program models, while maintaining its ability to get staff into the field to monitor development. Adaptive management has been facilitated by regular updates to the county's Master Plan, and by the integration of science into its planning and regulatory processes. Baltimore County has also noted external awards for its work including a Source Water Protection Award from the U.S. Environmental Protection Agency, recognition for governance from *Governing Magazine*, and as a Nature-Friendly Community from the Consortium on Biodiversity and Land Use.

Notes

1. Baltimore City is not part of the county; the two are entirely separate, contiguous jurisdictions.
2. This history is briefly summarized in Christopher J. Duerksen & Cara Snyder, Nature-Friendly Communities: Habitat Protection and Land Use Planning ch. 4, at 152-55 (Island Press 2005). *See also* James M. McElfish Jr., Nature-Friendly Ordinances 100-01 (Environmental Law Inst. 2004).
3. *See* McElfish, *supra* note 2.
4. *See generally* Baltimore County, Master Plan 2010, at 99-103. Maryland's 1997 state "smart growth" legislation required its local governments to designate priority funding areas (PFAs), locations where the state, counties, and local governments would target their efforts to encourage and support economic development and growth. The state is prohibited from funding growth-related infrastructure outside of the PFAs. Md. Code Ann. State Fin. & Pro. §5-7B-01 (West 1998).
5. *See* Baltimore County Code art. 32, tit. 3 (Zoning), tit. 4 (Development), tit. 6 (Adequate Public Facilities), tit. 8 (Floodplain Management), tit. 9 (Growth Allocation).
6. *See generally* Baltimore County, Master Plan 2010, at 2-3.
7. *See* Duerksen & Snyder, *supra* note 2, at 162.
8. *See* McElfish, *supra* note 2, at 100; Baltimore County, Master Plan 2010, at 235-36.
9. Baltimore County, Master Plan 2010, at 133.
10. Baltimore County Code art. 33 (Environmental Protection and Resource Management). Article 32 (Planning, Zoning, and Subdivision Controls) also specifies design standards relating to open space, landscaping, grading and sediment control floodplain and wetland protection, slope protection and soils, preservation of natural or historic features, and scenic viewsheds. *Id.* §§32-4-411 to -417.
11. Md. Code Ann., Nat. Res. §5-1601 et seq. (West 1987).
12. *See generally* Baltimore County, *Environmental Protection and Resource Management: Land Development*, http://www.baltimorecountymd.gov/Agencies/environment/ep_highlights.html (last visited Oct. 23, 2008).
13. Baltimore County Code art. 33, tit. 2 (Chesapeake Bay Critical Areas Protection).
14. *Id.* §33-2-203.
15. *Id.* §33-2-501.
16. *Id.* art. 33, tit. 3 (Protection of Water Quality, Streams, Wetlands, and Floodplains).
17. *Id.* §33-3-110.
18. *Id.* §33-3-111.
19. *Id.* §33-3-112.
20. *Id.* §33-3-106.
21. *Id.* art. 33, tit. 6 (Forest Conservation), implementing Md. Code Ann., Nat. Res. art. §5-1601 et seq.
22. Baltimore County, Master Plan 2010, at 130.
23. *See* Duerksen & Snyder, *supra* note 2, at 157, 162.
24. *Id.* at 157.
25. *See* The Conservation Fund, *Baltimore County: Agricultural Preservation and Water Quality*, http://www.conservationfund.org/node/571 (last visited Oct. 23, 2008).
26. The Conservation Fund, Green Infrastructure: Linking Lands for Nature and People 4 (2004).

27. Md. Code Ann., Nat. Res. §5-9A-01.

28. Other laws in the state "smart growth" package deny state funding for infrastructure outside priority development areas, a concept drawing on the URDL approach pioneered by Baltimore County.

29. Duerksen & Snyder, *supra* note 2, at 163-64. *See generally* Baltimore County Code ch. 24 (Land Preservation), §24-5-101 (Rural Legacy).

30. Maryland's GreenPrint Program, *Homepage*, http://www.dnr.state.md.us/greenways/greenprint/ (last visited Oct. 23, 2008).

31. Md. Code Ann., Nat. Res. §3-201 (West 2000).

32. Md. Code Ann., Tax-Prop. §9-107 (West 2000), Md. Code Ann., Tax-Gen. §10-723 (West 2000).

33. Baltimore County, Master Plan 2010, at 123.

34. *Id.* at 127.

35. *Id.* at 33-37.

CHAPTER NINE

Summit County, Colorado:
Wildlife Habitat Overlay District

Many local governments in Colorado have adopted ordinances to protect wildlife. With express authority in state law to control development and land use that may threaten wildlife and other natural resources, some of these local governments have created strategies for protecting wildlife species and habitat. Local governments in Colorado have the "authority to plan for and regulate the use of land" by "[p]rotecting lands from activities which would cause immediate or foreseeable material danger to significant wildlife habitat and would endanger a wildlife species."[1] One such local government, Summit County, has adopted provisions in its Land Use and Development Code (Development Code) to control development, particularly a wildlife habitat overlay district that establishes a required development review procedure to protect the wildlife habitat and species of the county from the "significant adverse effects of development."[2] Summit County, located in central Colorado, ranges from 7,900 feet to over 14,000 feet in elevation, and spans about 619 square miles, 80% of which is publicly owned.[3] Today, the county has a year-round population of approximately 30,000,[4] which more than triples during the skiing season. The landscape of the county has a historic mining industry, several ski resorts, and a diversity of wildlife species and habitats.

In recent decades, residents, local policymakers, and Colorado Division of Wildlife (CDOW) officials in Summit County have expressed a mounting concern for protecting the open spaces—sage meadows, montane wetlands, coniferous forests, agricultural lands, and riparian areas—as well as their wild inhabitants—bald and golden eagles, mountain goats, bighorn sheep, deer, elk, and bear.[5] Accordingly, Summit County implemented its first wildlife policy in 1980.[6] This policy established a wildlife review process for proposed development, a process that largely relied on wildlife impact maps created by the CDOW. During public hearings held by the CDOW, citizens "identified species of local interest or value."[7] Based on the list of species identified by the public, the CDOW created wildlife impact maps that established areas of "potential impact on wildlife" that were classified as potentially high, moderate, or low.[8] The CDOW updated these wildlife impact maps in 1988 and 1989, based on knowledge gained from ongoing research. In 1990, the Summit County Board of County Commissioners (BOCC) adopted the new maps and requested that the CDOW provide assistance on how to strengthen the 1980 wildlife policy.[9]

Under the original wildlife policy, Resolution No. 80-1, implementation meant referring development proposals to the CDOW District Wildlife Manager, who worked with developers to incorporate revisions and mitigation efforts into their proposals. Private landowners, according to the policy, were "not obligated to furnish wildlife habitat for publicly-owned wildlife," and furthermore, "in the event an application for development is denied, wildlife or wildlife habitat shall not be used by the County Commissioners as the sole criterion" for the denial of any application.[10] In the early 1990s, the county began to work extensively with other counties, local residents, environmental consultants, and especially the CDOW to develop a more prescriptive approach that would be carried out in the Development Code, primarily in the form of the wildlife habitat overlay district, which was adopted in 1994. While the wildlife habitat overlay district section of the Development Code continued the procedure for development review established by the 1980 wildlife policy, it advanced the status of wildlife from the county's 1980 policy by allowing the denial of development proposals based solely on the value of wildlife species and their habitat.

In addition to creating a development review process using the overlay district, Summit County also adopted regulations to protect wetlands, incentives to control development in undeveloped areas, and programs to abate noxious weeds on private land. In 1998, the county adopted zoning regulations authorizing the Transfer of Development Rights (TDRs).[11]

Operation of the Program

Summit County's Countywide Comprehensive Plan, adopted in 2003, states: "The reason people live in or visit the County is largely due to the tremendous natural environment we enjoy. It is our responsibility to treat it with caring respect." The plan provides that land use codes and policies should demonstrate a respect for the landscape that prevents any "irreparable damage."[12] Many provisions incorporated into the Development Code as well as county-funded programs have been designed to avoid adverse impact to wildlife while enhancing wildlife habitat.

Wildlife Habitat Overlay District

The wildlife habitat overlay district establishes a procedure for development review, one aimed at "fully protect[ing] wildlife habitats within the wildlife overlay zone from the significant adverse effects of Development."[13] Much like the 1980 wildlife policy, the overlay district relies on a wildlife habitat map prepared by the CDOW to assess the potential impact of development proposals. Depicting land cover classifications based on vegetative habitats (conifer, aspen, willow, etc.), the wildlife habitat map creates the basis for the wildlife habitat overlay district, which includes "all lands within the unincorporated area of Summit County designated as wildlife habitat as identified by the official map."[14] The wildlife habitat map defines the bounds of the wildlife habitat overlay district and is intended "to protect the wildlife habitats necessary to support all wildlife species native to Summit County."[15] In addition to the wildlife habitat map, which the Planning Director is obligated to keep on file and accessible for public inspection, the overlay district requires the Planning Department and the CDOW to maintain an updated wildlife database for reference information.[16] The database "may be updated and revised . . . based on new information and knowledge about wildlife habitat and wildlife species."[17] Interestingly, the database, while not defining regulatory requirements or changing the overlay, may be used by the county to require a developer to prepare and submit a wildlife impact report.[18] (See Fig. 9.1.)

While the wildlife habitat map that defines the boundaries of the wildlife overlay is the one prepared by the CDOW in 1994,[19] the county has referred development proposals to the CDOW, which has dynamic maps that are updated every three years to depict the vegetative habitat, species distribution, and land use. The CDOW is able to use its more recent mapping information to submit comments and recommend mitigation and avoidance strategies.

When the Planning Department receives development proposals that will affect any of the land within the wildlife overlay district, the department must refer these proposals to the CDOW district wildlife manager.[20] Under §4204.01 of the Development Code, proposals subject to this review include: preliminary and final zoning; preliminary and final planned unit developments (PUDs); modifications to PUDs; conditional and temporary use permits; activities of state interest; preliminary plats; lot splits exempt from subdivision review; and rural land use subdivisions. The CDOW district wildlife manager is responsible for reviewing these proposals to identify "whether a proposal protects wildlife habitats and wildlife species from the significant adverse impacts."[21] Once the manager has referred to the wildlife habitat maps, databases, and other available knowledge, he must respond to the Planning Department as to whether

Figure 9.1. Map of Sensitive and Rare Species Habitat in Summit County, Colorado. From Theobald, D. M. and N. T. Hobbs. 2002. A framework for evaluating land use planning alternatives: protecting biodiversity on private land. *Conservation Ecology* 6(1): 5. Available at http://www.consecol.org/vol6/iss1/art5/. With permission from Dave Theobald, Colorado State University.

a significant adverse impact potentially exists, and identify methods of mitigation to abate or eliminate adverse impacts.[22]

According to the review process established by the wildlife habitat overlay district, after the CDOW provides comments and recommendations, the Planning Department is responsible for transmitting this material to the BOCC as well as to the applicable regional planning commission (Summit County is organized into four planning basins, each of which has its own master plan and planning commission).[23] The four regional planning commissions—the Lower Blue Basin, the Snake River Basin, the Ten Mile Basin, and the Upper Blue Basin—are oriented to "provide land use and development recommendations" specific to their basin to the BOCC.[24] The BOCC works closely with its four regional planning basins, which are all responsible for reviewing development proposals in the unincorporated lands of their respective regions. Every basin not only has a master plan to help it guide land use decisions, but is encouraged by the Development Code to review, modify, and readopt its master plan at least every five years. Requesting the planning basins to have master plans that are not only consistent with the County Comprehensive Plan, but also inherently capable of enduring frequent revision and re-adoption encourages the regional planning commissions to develop dynamic master plans that address new and local issues.[25] Regional master plans like that of the Snake River Basin address "unique land use issues." The relation of such plans with the Countywide Comprehensive Plan is as follows:

> The Countywide Comprehensive Plan is the county's overall guiding document that establishes the county's policies related to land use, growth, and other issues of importance to the community. The Countywide Comprehensive Plan provides direction to deal with issues of broad community interest or that are "countywide" in scope . . . . The heart of the Countywide Comprehensive Plan is the Land Use Element which directs the general location of where and how new growth will occur in the county. The Land Use Element establishes the county's overall direction on land use issues. For example, several policies focus on the need to identify urban areas and rural areas in the county. However, that specific identification is a task delegated to each basin master plan. Thus, basin or subbasin master plans continue to provide the primary guidance on the location of different types of land uses.[26]

After receiving staff reports from the Planning Department that include the CDOW recommendations, the relevant Planning Commission and BOCC are required to consider "whether the proposal protects the wildlife habitats and wildlife species from the significant adverse impacts of development."[27] The Planning Commission and the BOCC must "give special consideration to wildlife habitats that are determined by the Colorado DOW to be of critical or unique value."[28] Once the Planning Commission has considered the referral from the CDOW, it can either recommend revisions to the BOCC, or, when it has deemed that mitigation measures will fail to prevent a significant adverse impact, recommend denying the proposal.

If the Planning Commission or the BOCC are unable to determine, based on the CDOW response or the county's baseline wildlife information, whether adverse impacts will occur, either entity may require the developer to prepare a wildlife impact report.[29] Additionally, the Planning Director may require a wildlife impact report whenever, [30] based on the county's wildlife information database, "there is a potential for significant impact to wildlife habitat or wildlife species resulting from the development proposal." When a wildlife impact report is deemed necessary, the developer is required to hire a county-approved consultant to address the following in its wildlife report: total acreage of the project; total acreage of each habitat type; locations and total acreage of open space; known wildlife species in the project area; use patterns such as movement corridors and feeding areas within the site; relation with adjoining habitats outside project areas; potential impact on wildlife species and habitat; proposed list of mitigation methods; and other information deemed necessary by the CDOW and the BOCC to evaluate the impact of the proposal on wildlife.[31] The developer must then submit the report to both the county and the CDOW.

After considering all of this information and the recommendations of the planning commissions, the BOCC may "require special conditions or modifications of a proposal, or may deny a proposal in cases where the significant adverse impacts of a development cannot be adequately mitigated, resulting in a significant adverse impact on wildlife habitat and/or wildlife species in the County."[32]

The standard for evaluation is avoidance of a "significant adverse impact."[33] Much of the content of the wildlife habitat overlay ordinance outlines the factors that are used to determine a "significant adverse impact on wildlife habitat or wildlife species" in Summit County.[34] These are based substantially on recommendations and factors developed by the CDOW and reflect understanding of conservation biology and life cycle and habitat concerns.

In Sect. 4204.05 of the Development Code, five categories of analysis are defined to assess a possible significant adverse impact. The five categories are the following: (1) impact on wildlife species; (2) impact on wildlife habitat; (3) impact on wildlife movement patterns/displacement and adaptation of wildlife populations; (4) significance of habitat and species; and (5) cumulative impacts.

In regard to impact on wildlife species, assessments must factor in the following: acts of "humans, pets, and machines or equipment that disturb or harass an individual animal, group of animals or wildlife species"; site development or other acts, which may range from using fertilizers to producing excessive exterior lighting or introducing non-native vegetation, which disrupt behavior or extensively stress wildlife; the reliance of species on any unique habitat that may be affected; and proposed mitigation efforts.[35]

The second category that the overlay district requires the BOCC and Planning Commission to assess is the impact on wildlife habitat, which is determined by evaluating: the amount of habitat and vegetation removed and/or altered; the amount of contiguous habitat left intact within and adjacent to the site; existing and proposed amount of lot coverage; existence of contiguous adjacent habitat of similar type and quality; and proposed mitigation efforts to directly address negative habitat effects.[36]

The third category, which involves the impact on wildlife movement patterns/displacement and adaptation of wildlife populations, necessitates the consideration of the following: obstructing seasonal migration patterns; preventing wildlife from using a habitat they would normally use; increasing species' exposure to predation, human activity, and other conditions for which they may not be adapted; size of the affected habitat and the availability of similarly sized and quality habitat within the surrounding area; inability of the species to adapt to significant habitat alterations or to find a new long-term sustainable habitat; and consideration of proposed mitigation efforts that directly address the negative effects on movement patterns, adaptation, and displacement of wildlife.[37]

The next two categories for determining a potential significant adverse impact involve the consideration of the "elimination, reduction and/or fragmentation of wildlife habitat" and the effects of such land transformation on wildlife species.[38] The first of these, significance of habitat and species, is to be assessed by looking at the transformation or alteration of land that the CDOW or other state and federal agencies have classified as "unique or important" for its support of species "that do not commonly occur in or outside of Summit County."[39] The final category under which a significant adverse impact may be determined is cumulative impacts, which refers to cumulative impacts that may occur beyond the project site that may harm wildlife in the county.[40]

The wildlife habitat overlay district ordinance has only been amended twice since its implementation. In 1999, §4204.01, which explicitly lists the types of proposals that the county is required to refer to the CDOW, was amended to also include Rural Land Use Subdivisions. In May 2007, the county made mostly stylistic and editorial changes. Throughout the overlay code: Board of County Commissioners was abbreviated to the BOCC and the Colorado Division of Wildlife was abbreviated to the Colorado DOW; where appropriate, "which" was changed to "that"; and the list of adverse human related activities described under impact on wildlife species was qualified with the word "include" in order to make it clear that the list of impacts to be evaluated is not limited to those specifically enumerated.[41]

Over the past 13 years, the county has received on average between 6 and 12 proposals a year that require a referral to the CDOW. In most of these cases, the county incorporates input from the CDOW in its conditions for approval. Only a single proposal has been denied outright under the wildlife habitat overlay district.

Summit County has in substantial part funded the wildlife habitat overlay by (1) building the overlay review process into the normal planning, zoning, and development review process, (2) relying heavily on CDOW state-funded staff for expertise, and (3) retaining the option of requiring the developer to fund a wildlife impact report, but using a county-approved consultant and providing specifically-required information.

Jones Gulch Proposal

One of the most noteworthy applications of the wildlife habitat overlay district in recent years, which engaged the concept of "cumulative impacts" on a wildlife movement corridor, was a proposed subdivision plat by Keystone Real Estate Developments (KRED) in the Ski Tip Jones Gulch neighborhood. In 1998, KRED requested an approval from Summit County for 21 single-family lots and one tract for open space. The county Planning Department requested, per the wildlife habitat overlay district, that the CDOW comment on the proposal and that KRED hire an environmental consultant to produce a wildlife impact report. In fall 1998, representatives of the CDOW met with KRED's environmental consultant to discuss the proposal's impact on wildlife. While the CDOW acknowledged that the development would not on its own necessarily cause an adverse impact, its cumulative impact would cause great detriment to an important wildlife movement corridor.

Under §4204.05 of the county's wildlife overlay district ordinance, significant adverse impact can be determined if a development plan disrupts critical migration and movement patterns of wildlife. The BOCC consulted with the CDOW, the U.S. Fish and Wildlife Service (FWS), and the U.S. Forest Service (Forest Service), all of which expressed great concern for the preservation of the wildlife movement corridor that forest carnivores, including the threatened Canada lynx, utilize. Such wildlife species tend to avoid areas with human activity or disturbance, and rely on contiguous forested habitat for traveling, denning, and feeding. This particular corridor in Jones Gulch is one of only four such corridors west of the Continental Divide.

Past development, including the expansion of ski areas and Interstate 70, already presented obstacles to the corridor. After examining the proposal and the habitat potentially affected, the CDOW recommended several mitigation efforts, including TDRs away from the corridor, minimal outdoor lighting, wetland setbacks, and bear-proof receptacles.[42] The Planning Department sent this information in its staff report to the BOCC and regional planning commission—in this case, the Snake River Basin Planning Commission. After deliberating on these recommendations, the BOCC subsequently requested a wildlife impact report for the proposed subdivision. Once the report was conducted and reviewed, the Snake River Basin Planning Commission passed a motion in October 1999, to deny the KRED subdivision. The recommendation was not only based on the countywide conditions of significant adverse impact and cumulative impacts expressed in the wildlife habitat overlay district, but also on deviation from the wildlife goals and policies of the Snake River Basin Master Plan.[43] The commission noted the following: a lack of evidence indicating the prevention of a significant adverse impact; a failure to consider the cumulative effects as outlined in §4204.05(e); and a lack of general conformity with both the Snake River Basin Master Plan and the Countywide Comprehensive Plan. After further revisions, public hearings, and recommendations from both the Snake River Basin Planning Commission and the CDOW, the BOCC denied the preliminary plat in 2001.[44] The failure to comply with the Snake River Master Plan, which suggests the avoidance of development in areas "with wildlife impact potential" and "wildlife travel corridors," provided one of the county's grounds for denial.[45]

Complementary Programs

In addition to the wildlife habitat overlay, the county has implemented several other programs in accordance with the Environmental Element of the Countywide Comprehensive Plan, which states that the county's "natural setting is its greatest asset as it helps define and give character to the area."

Wetlands

One of the sensitive landscape types that "define[s] and give[s] character" to the county is wetlands, 7,000 acres of which exist on private land. In 1998, after the U.S. Army Corps of Engineers (the Corps) and the U.S. Environmental Protection Agency (EPA) expressed concerns about the cumulative loss of wetlands in the county, the BOCC adopted Resolution 99-46, "Conceptual Strategy for the Enhanced Management of Wetlands Within Summit County," to express its commitment to working with residents, private and local groups and federal agencies to achieve "no net loss" of wetlands. With a phased EPA wetland grant, the county commenced a multi-stage pilot study in 2000. Working with the Colorado Department of Natural Resources Wetland Protection Program, the Forest Service, EPA, and a consultant, the county sought to improve its management of the shrubbed, forested, and herbaceous montane wetlands of Summit County. In 2002, the Planning Commission evaluated the feedback from its consultant and a county wetland task force. One result of the pilot study was the establishment of wetland setbacks. Section 7105.01 of the Development Code states that "soil disturbance and structures are prohibited within 25 feet of a wetland area" for all multi-family residential and commercial development, as well as single-family and duplex developments platted after February 1996. The study also established a methodology for bioassessments that measures the health of wetlands and the effectiveness of current restoration activities. Since the completion of the pilot study, Summit County has completed 40 wetland assessments and the Forest Service has completed approximately 100 wetland assessments in the county. Incorporated towns like Breckenridge and Silverthorne have also utilized the assessments in their planning.[46]

TDRs

The four planning basins of Summit County have all implemented TDR programs. The Environment Element of the Countywide Comprehensive Plan suggests the use of innovative techniques like "TDRs, density bonuses, and incentives for voluntary practices to protect environmentally sensitive areas."[47] Designating sites as sending, receiving or neutral, TDRs manage the shape of growth by encouraging additional density in receiving areas that can sustain higher rates of density; these are often in urban areas with established infrastructure.[48]

The Development Code states that TDRs provide a means for "the protection of backcountry areas, rural areas, and land with development constraints."[49] Of the four planning basins, the Upper Blue Basin has been most successful in protecting open space and generating money for more open space purchase. With the revenue that is generated from selling development rights under the TDR program, the county has generated approximately $1.4 million to recycle into its open space acquisitions and protected over 930 acres of open space.[50]

Hundreds of private mining claims exist on the undeveloped mountainsides and in the valleys of the Upper Blue Basin. As these claims are permitted to be used for residential development, which would have adverse affects on the environmentally sensitive areas as well as the viewsheds of the basin, TDRs were developed to protect these backcountry areas. The TDR program allows property owners of parcels in undeveloped areas to voluntarily exchange their right to develop these backcountry parcels for monetary compensation and a transfer of their development right into a receiving area that is more suited for development. A market for TDRs exists because town and county policies in the Upper Blue Basin region "prohibit the upzoning of land (i.e., adding more units of density) unless TDRs are acquired." [51]

By rezoning the hundreds of mining claims in the basin to a backcountry zoning district,[52] the county sought to preserve the character of the undeveloped landscape by permitting "very low impact development" of the hundreds of private mining claims. The county has also created the Upper Blue Basin TDR Bank to facilitate transactions between buyers and sellers, where a TDR is equivalent "to 20 acres of backcountry and is sold by the County" for around $2,000 per acre.[53] The county puts these funds into its Open Space Protection Program, which uses "joint acquisitions and partnerships with towns, grants from Great Outdoors Colorado, land exchanges with the federal government, and donations from private landowners" to acquire open space from willing sellers.[54]

Due to its success in protecting backcountry, the Upper Blue Basin TDR has been used as a model by the other three planning basins. The Snake River Basin has had a TDR program since 1996. Prior to 2006, the Snake River Basin TDR program lacked the specificity to properly identify suitable sending and receiving areas.[55] Between 1996 and 2006, only 130 acres of open space were protected. At the time, several mining claims existed in the wildlife movement corridor utilized by the lynx and other forest carnivores. In an effort to protect the wildlife movement corridor in the Snake River Basin from existing mining claims and increased density, the TDR program was revised in 2006 to provide such development claims with a density bonus TDR value of 2-1 (2 development rights per 20 acres), encouraging the transfer of density away from the movement corridor.

The other two planning basins, the Lower Blue Basin and Ten Mile Basin, have fairly nascent programs. As of July 2007, the Lower Blue Basin continues to finalize its TDR regulations, and has had only one transfer.[56] The fourth basin, the Ten Mile Basin, adopted a TDR program in June 2006, and has not yet experienced any transfers.

Noxious Weed Program

One of the greatest threats to wildlife and wildlife habitat in the county is invasive plants. Non-native, noxious plants can out-compete native species and cause extensive devastation to an ecosystem. Summit County began addressing noxious weeds in the mid-1990s with a seasonal staff.[57] Today, the county has developed a Noxious Weed Program to abate these plants by using biological, chemical, cultural, and mechanical controls, as well as a cost-share program, which was developed in 2002, to allow landholders to apply for up to $500 from the county to control weeds on their property.[58] While most of the work is done in developed areas, as land disturbances facilitate the growth of noxious weeds, the county has collaborated with the Forest Service in backcountry areas like the Green Mountain and Dillon Reservoirs.

Analysis

The wildlife habitat overlay is not limited to particular species or ecosystem types, but reflects a range of wildlife species and their habitats based on the CDOW's mapping and data. In addition, the county and CDOW data are updated regularly. The overlay also helps to protect wildlife in the larger statewide and bioregional context.

The Colorado Natural Heritage Program (CNHP) identified "[m]ore than 80 rare or imperiled plant or animal species and significant plant communities" in Summit County. In 1997 it concluded: "Overall, the concentration of elements indicates that conservation in Summit County will have state-wide as well as global consequences."[59] The Development Code reflects a concern for protecting this broader scale biodiversity.[60] Several of the streams and rivers that transect the county provide critical habitat for imperiled fish species. The Colorado River cutthroat trout, which has remnant populations in Colorado, Utah, and Wyoming, has experienced declining populations due to competition with non-native fish species, hybridization with other trout species, and aquatic pathogens. The wetlands supported by the Blue River Basin in Summit County sustain the cutthroat population by "provid[ing] organic input as food, shelter from heat and predators, temperature regulation, and breeding habitat."[61] In a 2002 study examining land use in Summit County, David Theobald and N. Thompson Hobbs utilized more recent data from the CDOW and the CNHP to examine the distribution of sensitive and rare species. Wildlife habitat in the county continues to support bald eagle winter ranges, boreal toad breeding activity, critical cutthroat trout habitat, golden eagle nesting sites, winter ranges for elk and mule deer,[62] and potential linkage corridors for wolverine and lynx. The wildlife movement corridor in Jones Gulch "appears to be the last remnant of a naturally broad forested corridor through the Snake River Valley, connecting broad components of the ecosystem to the north and south . . .

if it is lost, all remaining potential for landscape connectivity from the Continental Divide to the Tenmile Range will be lost permanently."[63] It was protected on this basis through the overlay.

In preparing the wildlife overlay, Summit County developed, with help of consultants, factors to be applied when assessing a significant adverse impact. The firm recommended "more detailed substantive criteria," and a broader look "at the characteristics of the area's ecosystem."[64] The overlay district is important because it provides a way to review most development proposals of any size in the unincorporated portions of Summit County. The procedures ensure that sufficient data are generated in order to evaluate potential impacts, and the code allows sufficient discretion to support denial of development proposals on the basis of wildlife issues alone where the data support the decision. The careful definition of factors to be considered in assessing "significant adverse impact," including indirect and cumulative impacts, and impacts upon life cycle and habitat and potential alternative habitats, reflect a well-considered use of conservation biology concepts in a regulatory context.

Since its first wildlife policy in 1980, Summit County has worked extensively with and depended upon the CDOW. Under the first wildlife policy, implementation entailed submitting all subdivision and rezoning applications to the District Wildlife Manager, who worked with applicants to develop mitigation methods or revision when needed. In the early 1990s, when the county expressed an interest in strengthening its wildlife policy, the District Wildlife Manager assisted in developing the overlay district so that wildlife would be considered in all future development decisions.[65] Using the wildlife overlay procedure, the CDOW considers proposals sent by the county, meets with developers to discuss potential impact on the wildlife overlay, and makes comments to the Planning Department. One of the two District Wildlife Mangers in Summit County asserts that "the county has taken our recommendations very seriously." The other confirms this assertion, citing the county's involvement of the CDOW early in the planning and development review process, and its careful consideration and reliance on CDOW's specific comments.[66] As noted below, the CDOW has also conducted monitoring and information gathering that has assisted in applying current information to development proposals in the face of changing conditions and wildlife patterns.

As Summit County is an amalgamation of state, federal, municipal, and private land, the county Planning Department may confer with several parties when it receives development proposals. Often the county consults the Forest Service, the FWS, EPA, the CDOW, and the Corps with development proposals, especially with large-scale ski area projects. Representatives from these different federal bodies have met and worked well with the county on assessing several development proposals.[67] In the case of the Jones Gulch KRED proposal, the county Planning Department consulted the Dillon Ranger District of the Forest Service and the FWS—in addition to the CDOW—to coordinate "the management of intermingled ownership lands."[68] The FWS recommended "the elimination or movement of the development rights of this parcel to another location" away from the wildlife movement corridor,[69] and the Forest Service commented on the scientific information that the county provided. The opinion of the FWS and the CDOW—that the proposed subdivision would disrupt the movement patterns of forest carnivores to an extent that would threaten their health and viability, likely causing a significant adverse impact—was cited by the BOCC as a reason for denial of the proposed subdivision.[70]

While the master plans of the four regional planning commissions and the wildlife habitat overlay district only pertain to unincorporated areas within the county, the Planning Department has worked with incorporated towns on wetland bioassessments, management strategies for roadless areas, and various other habitat-related projects. When developing its TDR program for the Upper Blue Basin, the county collaborated with the town of Breckenridge and the town of Blue River to implement the program; densities may be transferred from unincorporated backcountry areas into either of these towns. Also, the town of Breckenridge is jointly responsible for administering the TDR Bank along with the county.[71]

As far as development matters that extend directly or indirectly beyond the county's borders, Summit County is a member of the Northwest Colorado Council of Governments, "a voluntary association of county and municipal governments who individually and collectively believes that working together on a regional basis provides benefits that could not be obtained without the association."[72] As a member of the council, Summit County adheres to a memorandum of understanding with its neighboring counties to refer all major development proposals to them for comments. One such proposal was a request for a large-scale development in the Copper Mountain ski resort that may affect traffic congestion in neighboring counties.[73] While wildlife habitat and species are not the focus of such referrals, the Northwest Colorado Council of Governments may provide an appropriate body for addressing future intercounty ecological matters.

Monitoring and adaptive management strategies are implied by the reliance on CDOW maps and continuous updating of wildlife data, as well as by the opportunity to require developers to submit a wildlife impact report, and to impose mitigation conditions. While the county has not updated its wildlife habitat map since the 1994 adoption of the wildlife habitat overlay district, the CDOW maintains its own maps that reflect indexes of natural diversity. These maps are updated every three years as part of a Gap Analysis Project, which is intended to "provide broad geographic information on the status of ordinary species (those not threatened with extinction or naturally rare) and their habitats in order to provide land managers, planners, scientists, and policy makers with the information they need to make better-informed decisions."[74] The CDOW maps reflect changes in the landscape, such as the encroachment of development on the winter ranges of deer and elk. The CDOW notes that "the text [of the wildlife habitat overlay district] is still very consistent with what we [the CDOW] are doing."[75] The CDOW continues to monitor the biotic community of Summit County. Using radio collars on indicator species like deer and elk, the CDOW is able to assess the viability of various wildlife movement corridors. Based on such monitoring, the county has not experienced any recent significant loss in these corridors.[76]

Notes

1. Colo. Rev. Stat. §29-20-104(b).
2. Summit County Land Use and Development Code §§4203.01, 4204 (West 2000) (the code says "affects" in one place and "impacts" in another).
3. Summit County, Colorado, *Planning: County Overview*, http://www.co.summit.co.us/Planning/index.htm (last visited Oct. 25, 2008).
4. Personal Communication with Jim Curnutte, Planning Director, Summit County (Sept. 4, 2007) [hereinafter Curnutte Communication].
5. Summit County Comprehensive Plan, "Environmental Element," at 31.
6. Letter from Brian Peters, Manager, Summit County Planning Division, to BOCC (Mar. 9, 1992) [hereinafter Peters Letter].
7. *Id.*
8. *Id.*
9. *Id.*
10. Summit County BOCC Resolution No. 80-1.
11. Summit County Land Use and Development Code §§3202.03 (West 2000).
12. Summit County Comprehensive Plan, "Environment Element," at 28.
13. Summit County Land Use and Development Code §§4203.01, 4204.
14. *Id.* §§4201, 4202.
15. *Id.* §4201.
16. *Id.* §§4203.01, 4203.02.
17. *Id.* §4203.02.
18. *Id.* §4204.02.
19. Section 4203.01 actually specifies that the overlay map is the "map of wildlife habitats prepared by the Colorado DOW and dated October 24, 1994."
20. *Id.* §§4202, 4204.01.
21. *Id.* §4204.01.
22. *Id.*
23. Summit County, Colorado, *Planning: Meeting Agendas*, http://www.co.summit.co.us/Agendas/meeting_Agendas.htm (last visited Oct. 25, 2008).
24. *Id.*
25. Lower Blue Planning Commission, *Summit County Lower Blue Master Plan*, http://www.co.summit.co.us/Planning/MasterPlans/PDFs/LowerBlueMasterPlan.pdf (last visited Oct. 25, 2008).
26. Summit County, Colorado, *Snake River Master Plan*, http://www.co.summit.co.us/Planning/MasterPlans/snakeRiver.html (last visited Oct. 25, 2008).
27. Summit County Land Use and Development Code §§4204.03, 4204.04.
28. *Id.*
29. *Id.*
30. *Id.* §4204.02.A.
31. *Id.* §4204.02.B1-9.
32. *Id.* §4204.04.
33. *Id.* §§4201, 4203.01, 4204.01, 4204.02B&, 4204.03, 4204.04, 4204.05.
34. *Id.* §4204.05.
35. *Id.* §4204.05A1-4.

36. *Id.* §4204.05B1-5.
37. *Id.* §4204.05C1-7.
38. *Id.* §4204.05D, E.
39. *Id.* §4204.05D.
40. *Id.* §4206.05E.
41. Summit County BOCC Resolution No. 07-44 (May 22, 2007); *see* E-mail from John Roberts, Planner, Summit County Planning Department, to author (July 20, 2007) (*Revisions to Summit County Land Use and Development Code*).
42. Letter from Tom Kroening, District Manager, CDOW, to Chris Hawkins, Manager, Current Planning, Summit County Planning Department (Sept. 8, 1999); Letter from Richard W. Thompson, Wildlife Biologist, Western Ecosystems, Inc., to Tom Kroening, District Manager, CDOW (Jan. 20, 1999).
43. Letter from Chris Hawkins, Manager, Current Planning, Summit County Planning Department, to BOCC (June 25, 2001).
44. Summit County BOCC Resolution No. 2001-77.
45. *Id.*
46. Summit County, Colorado, *Planning: Environmental Planning—Wetland Background*, http://www.co.summit.co.us/Planning/environmental.html#grant (last visited Oct. 25, 2008).
47. Summit County Comprehensive Plan, "Environment Element," at 36.
48. David M. Theobald & N. Thompson Hobbs, *A Framework for Evaluating Land Use Planning Alternatives: Protecting Biodiversity on Private Land*, 6 Conservation Biology 5 (2002).
49. Summit County Land Use and Development Code §§3202.03A.
50. *See supra* note 3.
51. *Id.*
52. *See* Curnutte Communication, *supra* note 4.
53. *See supra* note 3.
54. Summit County, Colorado, *Summit County Open Spaces and Trails Department*, http://www.co.summit.co.us/OpenSpace.htm (last visited Oct. 25, 2008).
55. Personal Communication with John Roberts, Planner, Summit County Planning Department (July 20, 2007).
56. *Id.*
57. Personal Communication with Lisa Taylor, Weed Coordinator, Summit County (July 23, 2007).
58. *Id.*
59. California Heritage Program, Summit County Conservation Inventory Volume I: A Natural Heritage Assessment 1997 Final Report (1997).
60. Summit County Land Use and Development Code §§4201.
61. *See* Final Report, *supra* note 59.
62. *See* Theobald & Hobbs, *supra* note 48.
63. Letter from LeRoy W. Carlson, Colorado Field Supervisor, FWS, to Chris Hawkins, Manager, Current Planning, Summit County Planning Department (Feb. 17, 1999).
64. Letter from Erin Johnson, Clarion Associates, to Summit County Planning Department (Oct. 5, 1994).
65. *See* Peters Letter, *supra* note 6. Interview with Tom Kroening, District Manager, CDOW (July 6, 2007).
66. Personal Communication with Shannon Schwab, District Wildlife Manager, CDOW (July 6, 2007).

67. Personal Communication with Tom Kroening, District Manager, CDOW (July 31, 2007) [hereinafter Kroening Communication].

68. Letter from Jamie Connell, District Ranger, Forest Service, to Summit County (Nov. 12, 1999).

69. Letter from Allan Pfiser, Assistant Colorado Field Supervisor, FWS, to Summit County Planning Department (May 2, 2001).

70. Summit County BOCC Resolution No. 2001-77.

71. *See supra* note 3.

72. Northern Colorado Council of Government, *About NWCCOG*, http://www.nwc.cog.co.us/ NWCCOG/about_nwccog.htm (last visited Oct. 25, 2008).

73. Personal Communication with Jim Curnutte, Planning Director, Summit County (July 24, 2007).

74. CDOW, *Colorado Gap Analysis Project*, http://ndis1.nrel.colostate.edu/cogap/ (last visited Oct. 25, 2008).

75. *See* Kroening Communication, *supra* note 67.

76. *Id.*

State/Federal Programs Administered for Conservation Benefits at Multiple Scales

The final set of case studies offers examples of ways to implement environmental and infrastructure programs aimed at other goals that can generate wildlife habitat conservation benefits and stimulate meaningful regional conservation benefits if managed to do so.

Chapter Ten

Fall River, Massachusetts:
Source Water Protection (14,000-acre focus area)

Fall River, an older industrial town in eastern Massachusetts, participated in a collaborative deal with state and conservation organizations to conserve thousands of acres of its reservoir protection lands and integrate them with other private and public conservation lands as part of the Southeastern Massachusetts Bioreserve. Drinking water is a critical natural resource protected by an interrelated set of federal and state laws, including the protection of watersheds for reservoirs and other waters under the Safe Drinking Water Act's Source Water Assessment Program. The effective melding of water protection, conservation, and biodiversity goals was facilitated by a statewide BioMap adopted by the commonwealth of Massachusetts to assist towns in identifying areas important for the conservation of state biodiversity resources.

Chapter Eleven

North Carolina:
Mitigation for Transportation Projects
(600,000 acres in watershed areas statewide)

North Carolina developed a program in 2003 to identify lands and waters important for wetland and stream conservation throughout the state, and to target wetland mitigation funding associated with the federal highway program on such lands and waters, implementing the compensatory mitigation provisions of §404 of the federal Clean Water Act. This program, the Ecosystem Enhancement Program, administered by the North Carolina Department of Environment and Natural Resources, provides an opportunity to pursue conservation and restoration of ecologically significant lands on a statewide basis, and within particular targeted watersheds.

CHAPTER TEN

Fall River, Massachusetts:
Source Water Protection

Fall River is a 34-square mile older industrial city in southeastern Massachusetts with a population in excess of 90,000. It draws its drinking water from the North Watuppa Pond and from the Copicut Reservoir to the east, the watershed of which is located partly within Fall River and partly within the neighboring towns of Freetown and Dartmouth. In the 19th century, the city began to acquire watershed lands in order to protect its drinking water supply, accumulating more than 3,300 acres of watershed lands by 1925, and additional lands for the Copicut Reservoir (created in 1970) later on. In 1988, the Fall River Water Department issued a development/service moratorium for the area east of North Watuppa Pond (between the pond and the Copicut) while studying the watershed.[1] The study led to adoption of watershed protection district zoning in this area. Some private homes are located on inholdings in both water supply areas, and there was development potential for some additional lands.[2] The city of Fall River ultimately owned and managed for water supply purposes approximately 7,000 acres of lands and surface waters.[3]

For more than 20 years, beginning in the 1930s, the commonwealth of Massachusetts also acquired lands in the vicinity to create the nearly 5,500-acre Freetown/Fall River State Forest.[4] In 1965, the Division of Fisheries and Wildlife established a wildlife management area within the forest and in 1989 and 1990 purchased additional lands for the Acushnet Wildlife Management Area. Thousands of additional acres of forest land in the Copicut and North Watuppa watersheds were owned by the Acushnet Saw Mills, and the company's owner, the Hawes family.[5]

In 1996, Congress adopted amendments to the Safe Drinking Water Act (SDWA), which, after required U.S. Environmental Protection Agency (EPA) action, directed states to develop and implement over the beginning years of the 21st century programs to assess the condition of watershed lands that provide "source water" for public drinking water supplies.[6] Water supply issues

169

are beginning to come to the forefront as population rises and development pressures begin to affect the lands that supply water resources to both developed and newly developing areas.

In 1997, Fall River completed its first "Open Space Plan." The plan called for acquiring remaining undeveloped lands in the Copicut and North Watuppa watersheds, and for enhancing the "quality of land stewardship" in existing water board properties. The plan also called for pursuing "statewide recognition" of the city's watershed lands as areas of critical environmental concern. The plan also identified the importance of the Copicut watershed for its future "aquifer yield" and noted the importance of protecting its recharge areas including the Copicut Swamp.[7]

In 1999, Massachusetts' Environment Secretary Bob Durand approached the city of Fall River. He proposed that the city participate in a new state-led conservation effort to assemble lands in southeastern Massachusetts to create a biologically meaningful and sustainable "bioreserve." The idea was to take advantage of the amount of land in various forms of public and private ownership that had high existing biodiversity and conservation potential and meld it into a unit appropriately managed for biodiversity.[8]

The scientific basis for the Secretary's initiative was provided by a project known as the "Massachusetts BioMap." The BioMap was a Massachusetts-initiated inventory of biodiversity throughout Massachusetts using Natural Heritage data in order to identify "core habitats" and "supporting landscapes," and to compare those lands with lands that were currently protected and other lands that could benefit from future protection and management.[9] One of the largest "core area" landscapes identified in the commonwealth was the area surrounding the Copicut Reservoir including Fall River's watershed lands.

Working with the city, the commonwealth, a statewide land trust known as The Trustees of Reservations, and the Hawes Family, the state and city agencies and trustees signed a Memorandum of Understanding to Create the Southeastern Massachusetts Bioreserve (MOU) on June 29, 2000. The MOU, subsequently implemented by legislation enacted August 10, 2002,[10] called for the commonwealth to convey 300 acres of excess forest land to the Fall River Redevelopment Authority for economic development purposes in Fall River and Freetown subject to a 43-acre natural buffer zone within the 300 acres, the city of Fall River through its water board to convey to the commonwealth a conservation easement on 4,300 acres of reservoir lands and $2.45 million to reimburse the commonwealth for the purchase of additional lands for the reserve, state funding for purchase of lands from the Hawes family, and transfer of commonwealth fish and wildlife lands (including land acquired from the

Hawes family) to the Department of Environmental Management (now Department of Conservation and Recreation).[11]

The result is a 13,600-acre bioreserve consisting of 5,150 acres of state forest lands, 360 acres of the Acushnet Wildlife Management Area, 4,300 acres of Fall River reservoir lands, and 3,800 acres of former Acushnet Saw Mills property—much of which was transferred to state ownership while approximately 500 acres is owned by the Trustees of Reservations as "Copicut Woods."[12] (See Fig. 10.1.) The bioreserve created by this transaction is not the only protected land. Just to the southeast of the bioreserve, the Dartmouth Natural Resources Trust owns another 210 protected acres, including a 52-acre parcel of forest land acquired in 2007 to connect its Ridge Hill Reserve lands to the bioreserve, including lands within 300 feet of the reservoir and identified as core habitat on the commonwealth's BioMap inventory of biodiversity lands.[13]

The Southeastern Massachusetts Bioreserve contains 16 species of conservation concern, Atlantic white cedar swamps, 17 ponds, at least 12 vernal pools, 92 bird species and 291 documented plant species, and protects the drinking water supply for Fall River.[14] The participating parties agreed to manage their lands consistent with a management plan for the bioreserve. The plan was completed in draft form in 2003, and final form a year later and presented to the parties but has not been formally adopted by the state agencies.[15] In July 2005, the Trustees of Reservations adopted their own detailed management plan for the 502-acre Copicut Woods parcel the Trustees own and manage.[16]

Operation of the Program

The lands must be managed for watershed and biodiversity purposes, consistent with the purposes for which they were acquired and assembled.

Source Water Assessment Program

Providing for safe drinking water at one time was primarily concerned with locating or developing water sources (rivers, lakes, reservoirs, aquifers) with reliable supplies and with providing chemically treated water to customers. Even in the earliest years, it was recognized that forested landscapes offered crucially important guarantees of both water supply and water quality, so water companies and municipal water suppliers in the 19th century acquired lands around reservoirs and water sources in order to maintain the integrity of these supplies. As water treatment became more prevalent into the 20th century, less attention was often paid to these landscape issues as water supplies could be drawn from less pristine sources and treated to a level of acceptability. But this

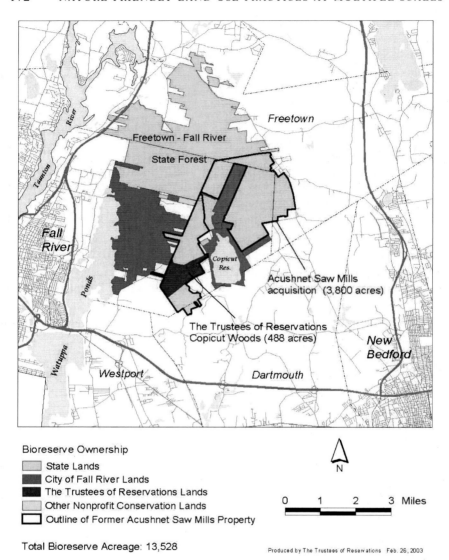

Figure 10.1. Southeastern Massachusetts Bioreserve. With permission from The Trustees of Reservations.

approach had serious limits, including cost, engineering feasibility, acceptability of the product to customers, and the fact that protecting water supplies at the source could guarantee both quantity and quality over the longer term. The federal SDWA was enacted in 1974 to provide a federal standard for the delivery of safe drinking water to the public.[17] The law, however, focused primarily on standards. In 1986, the Act added new provisions for identification of "sole source aquifers," creation of aquifer protection areas, and a wellhead protection program. In 1996, the Act was amended to include two new source protection programs: the Source Water Assessment Program[18] and a program for Source Water Quality Protection petitions to provide for voluntary incentive-based solutions aimed at specific contaminants.[19]

The Source Water Assessment Program was explained in a detailed EPA guidance document issued in 1997.[20] The 1996 Amendments required states to establish and implement Source Water Assessment Programs (SWAPs), which were to be submitted to EPA within 18 months after issuance of the EPA guidance document, with state implementation completed within 2 years after EPA approval of the programs (with an 18-month extension allowed). Essentially, this meant that the assessments were to have been completed in the 2002-2004 time frame. While protection of the watershed areas identified in the assessments was voluntary, EPA's guidance conditioned approval of state SWAPs upon a sufficient link to "ongoing or future" source water protection efforts.[21] The SWAP approach was to be consistent with EPA's prior approach to well-head protection for groundwater sources of drinking water under the 1986 SDWA, such that the surface water assessment would include "the entire watershed upstream of the [public water supply's] intake structure . . . up to the boundary of the state borders."[22] Source water protection then would be considered as a cost-effective alternative to "treatment or the development of new water supplies" in order to address problems or potential contamination.[23]

The potential usefulness of SWAP for land conservation was recognized almost immediately. In 1997, the Trust for Public Land (TPL) published a report entitled *Protecting the Source* in order to alert communities to these possibilities. In 2004, TPL and the American Water Works Association (AWWA) together published under the same title a much-expanded and more detailed look at "the case for land conservation as a source water protection strategy."[24] This guide for communities and water purveyors found that "land conservation work[s] best" as a water source protection tool where the drainage area is small (under 300,000 acres), where tracts of forest and grasslands are still in private ownership and may be vulnerable to conversion to other uses or development activities, and where overlapping benefits can be obtained for the conservation expenditure.[25]

The 2003 Massachusetts Department of Environmental Protection Source Water Assessment and Protection Report (SWAP Report) for the Fall River Water Department "commended" Fall River for "taking an active role in promoting source protection measures in the water supply protection areas."[26] The cumulative result of the bioreserve effort, together with prior actions, was to protect 92% of the Copicut Reservoir watershed and 86% of the North Watuppa Pond watershed.[27]

Bioreserve Management

In April 2001, the partners (the Management Planning Team) for the proposed bioreserve adopted a goals statement. The statement identified the mission of the Southeastern Massachusetts Bioreserve as:

> To protect, restore, and enhance the biological diversity and ecological integrity of a large-scale ecosystem with diverse natural communities representative of the region; to permanently protect public water supplies and cultural resources; to offer interpretive and education programs communicating the value and significance of the bioreserve; and to provide opportunities for appropriate public use and enjoyment of this natural environment.[28]

The goals statement identified a set of natural resource goals related to natural communities, hydrologic systems, habitat, restoration, rare species, forest resources, and wildlife and fisheries. It also identified the following water supply goals: "Permanently protect tributaries and watershed resources to ensure water quality in the Watuppa Ponds and Copicut Reservoir," and ensure that forestry and wildlife management practices and allowed uses of watershed lands "are compatible with water supply protection."[29]

Recreation was not previously allowed on the Fall River-owned lands subject to the conservation easements for the bioreserve. However the conservation restriction conveyed to the commonwealth provides for opening the watershed lands for passive recreational activities, while reserving to the city (through its water board) the right to close such access when, and for such time as may be, necessary to protect public health, safety, and the environment of the water supply.[30]

The Bioreserve Management Plan contains an extensive inventory of natural and cultural resources, and establishes resource management guidelines.[31] Specific goals are established for the forest mosaic, hydrological mosaic (including wetlands, surface waters, and groundwater), state-identified natural communities and others deemed to be regionally or locally significant, e.g., Atlantic white cedar swamps and bogs, state-listed species and priority habitats, inventory and control of invasive plant species, and cultural and other resources. The plan also identifies fundamental research needs for future management decisionmaking.

The Management Plan includes a chapter on management for visitor experiences, designed to be compatible with the resource goals.[32] A detailed matrix identifies each use, its potential impacts on bioreserve resources, and potential user conflicts. Visitor center locations have been identified—including a proposed visitor center to be managed by the Trustees of Reservations on the Copicut Woods parcel, and repurposing or expansion of existing facilities at the Freetown-Fall River State Forest headquarters and the Water Board headquarters.[33]

The management structure is outlined in the Management Plan, and is described as "collaborative." The partners will each manage their own lands, but will do so in accordance with the Management Plan and with their own more detailed "management and recreational plans" that are "to be consistent" with the Management Plan.[34] The project partners are to meet quarterly on operational issues and annually to review activities the previous year and to assess the needs for any changes. The annual meeting will include regional and senior managers from the partners.[35] Staff for the Bioreserve consists of the very small state forest professional staff, Fall River's existing watershed staff members, and staff for the Trustees of Reservations' Copicut Woods site. Primarily seasonal staffing is available. The plan recognizes that more staff will be needed to effectively manage the bioreserve.[36] The current superintendent for the Trustees of Reservations had previously served as a consulting forester for the city of Fall River in its management of the watershed lands, and as a forester for the Hawes family properties. His knowledge of the lands and their forest resources provided continuity in understanding of the landscape resources. [37]

The Southeastern Massachusetts Bioreserve represents a well-thought effort to bring together the goals of watershed protection and biodiversity conservation on a landscape basis using scientific information and management planning on a regional basis.

Analysis

Reliance on watershed lands and source water protection will be particularly important for biodiversity in heavily populated landscapes. Thus, finding opportunities to conserve biodiversity should be linked with watershed protection whenever scientific knowledge, funding, and management capabilities make this connection possible. The Southeastern Massachusetts Bioreserve protects substantial biodiversity lands within 10 miles of 400,000 current residents; the southeastern Massachusetts region is expected to grow by 200,000 residents in the next 20 years.[38]

Examining the Fall River case study to determine the ability of source water assessment and state and local public water supply programs to generate ancillary benefits for wildlife makes it clear that the outcome was dependent on several key factors.

State Development of Data and Support for Community Decisionmaking

GEOGRAPHICALLY SPECIFIC BIODIVERSITY INFORMATION

First, the project was made possible by the commonwealth of Massachusetts' initial investment in identifying areas important for biodiversity and providing the information on which decisions could be made. It was also made possible by the supporting state investments and land transfers that justified the participation of holders of resource lands including watershed lands. The BioMap project built on goals that had been articulated in an April 2000 *State of Our Environment* report, which articulated biodiversity as a resource of statewide importance and announced to the public statewide goals to "initiate the statewide biomapping project" and "create a statewide system of bioreserves, starting with ecoregions most under stress."[39]

The Fall River watershed lands and the other lands that became part of the bioreserve were the largest undeveloped privately owned conservation land area in Massachusetts, and presented a critical opportunity for conserving a large land assemblage. Interestingly, the same complex of lands had been identified nearly a century earlier on a statewide map, which had helped form the basis for the prior acquisitions early in the 20th century. [40]

The BioMap information was supplemented in 2003 by a study of Massachusetts lands and waters important for freshwater biodiversity.[41] Then in 2004, the commonwealth prepared specific reports and maps of "core habitats" for every Massachusetts town based on these data.[42] The reports identify rare and important species and natural communities, give a threat status, and indicate their prevalence; there are also descriptions of specific communities.

But Massachusetts did not map biological resources and lands alone. It also undertook complementary mapping and data efforts that could be important in other states looking to improve watershed conservation for multiple values including wildlife.

BUILD-OUT MAPS

Massachusetts also prepared a set of build-out maps for all of its towns in 2002, in order to enable them to assess future land use patterns and development impacts if development proceeded under current land use zoning and regulation. The Executive Office of Environmental Affairs prepared such a computerized analysis[43] as well as a *Build-Out Book* to explain the process.[44] TPL's and AWWA's *Source Protection Handbook* noted that the Massachusetts Executive Office of Environmental Affairs "build-out maps and analyses for all 351 cities and towns" enable local communities and water suppliers to determine future needs and identify currently developed and protected lands.[45]

The handbook also discusses how a "conservation priority index" can be constructed in order to prioritize properties for acquisition in a water resources context, to include consideration and advancement of multiple resource values.[46]

WATER ASSETS STUDY

In 2003, the commonwealth of Massachusetts launched the Water Assets Project, a series of studies to assess the resource conditions and needs of communities in rapidly developing eastern Massachusetts along the general corridor of the I-495 Beltway, and also launched a Drinking Water Supply Protection Grant Program to aid towns in acquiring lands to protect existing or future water supplies.[47] The commonwealth provided individual assets reports to each community in 2004 and then a regional report for each watershed in 2006 to supplement the build-out analysis and other planning data available to the towns and water suppliers. This study, too, helps make the water needs clear on a watershed as well as political jurisdictional basis—and such efforts could assist in building the case for land conservation elsewhere.

The Water Assets studies identified "Water Supply Protection Areas." These include not only lands overlying aquifers, but also the land within one-half mile of the upper boundary of the bank of a surface water source. The maps looked at currently undeveloped lands within water supply protection areas, and used these to identify for communities potential targets for protection.[48]

Management of Watershed Lands on a Collaborative Basis

Management on a collaborative basis was important to secure both watershed protection and habitat benefits, and to enhance the longer term stability of these lands as conservation lands. The city found it necessary to retain ownership and management responsibility for its watershed lands in order to be certain that water supply goals could be met. However, the partnership managing the larger land matrix of the bioreserve made it possible to achieve a more stable public identity and support and to meet multiple goals on different portions of the bioreserve lands. The partnership for the bioreserve "worked as well as could be expected."[49]

The city lands were already protected watershed lands, but the transaction for their inclusion in the bioreserve and the creation of an enforceable conservation restriction prevented the city from allowing development or divestiture of some lands in the future. It further gave the watershed lands a public identity that made it possible to build public awareness of the value of these lands, and created support that allowed the city to oppose incompatible activities on adjacent lands (such as residential development, re-zoning, or expansion of a nearby industrial landfill). That, in turn, created an opportunity for adjacent landowners with similar properties and potentially compatible conservation goals to talk about and pursue long-term management. [50]

The bioreserve also made it possible for others to pursue conservation on nearby lands that were not initially part of the bioreserve. This included the identification and purchase by others of adjacent parcels important for the conservation of the bioreserve and watershed lands. The Dartmouth Natural Resources Trust gained impetus for its own conservation purchases based on the conservation represented by the bioreserve transaction, and it participated in the bioreserve management planning team even though its lands lay outside the initial bioreserve assemblage.[51]

Including private partners, like the Trustees, helped to insulate the Bioreserve from the vagaries of political change. The BioMap and emphasis on creating bioreserves (products of the Celluci/Swift administration) were not priorities for the Romney administration that followed, but the relevant management activities were carried forward. As for the bioreserve lands themselves, under their original separate ownership, forest management had improved in the mid-1980s on both City and Acushnet Saw Mills lands, with a continuous forest management and stand quality improvement program.[52] But the future management of these lands was not guaranteed, just as prior lapses in management had occurred for more than a 20-year period prior to 1984. The Bioreserve places the conservation of these lands and their management on a more permanent footing, particularly because of the separate participating parties who can hold one another accountable, at least publicly and through meetings if not necessarily through mutually enforceable management instruments.[53]

Express Links to Other Identified Biodiversity and Conservation Lands

The project made explicit links between the bioreserve and other biodiversity lands. The BioMap and the Southeastern Massachusetts Bioreserve Management Plan both made explicit reference to identifying and protecting core landscapes and supporting landscapes—key concepts in biodiversity conservation on a landscape scale.

The Southeastern Massachusetts Bioreserve Management Plan notes that the commonwealth and its partners will seek to connect the bioreserve to other protected lands, and further notes that about 4,000 acres were protected by conservation restrictions in the Assawompsett Complex to the east of the Bioreserve—lands that form important parts of the watershed lands for Lakeville, New Bedford, and Taunton.[54]

The management plan also thoroughly discusses what conservation biology has to say about managing a dynamic landscape including a mosaic of habitats. The bioreserve itself is recognized as a "largely unfragmented, forested landscape within a rapidly developing region" with a limited set of potential corridors to other such landscapes.[55]

The management plan notes the utility of the BioMap in guiding additional connections, and also the Greenways vision developed by the Division of State Parks and Recreation as expressed in the plan "Commonwealth Connections." This plan identifies water trails and greenways both north and east—the Taunton River Greenway and the Buzzards Bay Greenway.[56] The Copicut Woods management plan notes that about 1,000 acres of "conservation lands not enrolled in the Bioreserve program" surround the bioreserve—primarily consisting of 736 acres of Fall River Water Department lands, but also including Fall River Conservation Commission lands (the Miller Brook Conservation Area, acquired after the formation of the Bioreserve), Dartmouth Natural Resources Trust lands, and a number of parcels owned by the Greater Fall River Land Conservancy.[57] The Copicut Woods plan prioritizes the potential acquisition of 11 identified parcels whose status is essential or important to the Copicut Woods portion of the reserve.[58]

Notes

1. Green Futures, *Facts about the Southeastern Massachusetts Bioreserve*, http://www.green-futures.org/projects/green/biofacts.html (last visited Oct. 26, 2008).

2. Southeastern Massachusetts Bioreserve Management Plan, at 3-3, 3-12.

3. *Id.* at 3-3.

4. The Wampanoag tribe has a cultural reservation within the state-owned forest.

5. *See* Green Futures, *supra* note 1.

6. 42 U.S.C. §300j-12 SDWA, ELR Stat. SDWA §1453. The Source Water Assessment Program is discussed *infra*.

7. Green Futures, *Fall River Open Space Plan—1997*, http://www.greenfutures.org/projects/osp/default.html#contents (last visited Oct. 28, 2008).

8. *See* Daniel Barbarisi, *Southeastern Massachusetts Bioreserve: Forest Will Become Parkland in "Bioreserve,"* Providence J., Oct. 23, 2002, *available at* http://www.fallriverma.org/pressarticles.asp?ID=74.

9. The BioMap was published in accessible booklet form as: Commonwealth of Massachusetts Executive Office of Envtl. Affairs, BioMap: Guiding Land Conservation for Biodiversity in Massachusetts (2001).

10. Mass. Gen. Laws ch. 266, Acts of 2002 (An Act Authorizing Certain Conveyances of Land to Establish the Southeastern Massachusetts Bioreserve).

11. *Id.*

12. *See* Green Futures, *supra* note 1. Financing to acquire the 3,800 acres from Acushnet Saw Mills included $9.65 million from the commonwealth, $2 million from the Trustees of Reservations, and $2.45 million from the Fall River Redevelopment Authority. Bob Durand et al., *Bioreserves: An Option for Land Conservation at the Urban Edge* (Powerpoint presented at Land Trust Rally (2001) (on file with the Environmental Law Institute).

13. Dartmouth Natural Resources Trust, Ridge Hill Reserve Expansion Project (2007), *available at* http://www.dnrt.org/conservation/land-projects.htm. The Dartmouth trust served on the working group for the management plan for the bioreserve.

14. *See* Green Futures, *supra* note 1.

15. Personal Communication with Andy Backman, Resource Management Planner, Massachusetts Dep't of Conservation and Recreation (July 19, 2007).

16. Trustees of Reservations, Copicut Woods Management Plan (2005).

17. 42 U.S.C. §§300f to 300j-11, as enacted by Pub. L. No. 93-523, 88 Stat. 1660 (1974).

18. *Id.* §300j-12.

19. *Id.* §300j-13.

20. U.S. EPA, State Source Water Assessment and Protection Programs (1997) (EPA 816-R-97-009).

21. *Id.*

22. *Id.* at 2-15. EPA "encourages" coverage beyond the borders. *Id.* at 2-16.

23. *Id.* at 3-2 (quoting Senate Environment and Public Works Committee).

24. Trust for Public Land & American Water Works Ass'n, Protecting the Source: Land Conservation and the Future of America's Drinking Water 4 (2004).

25. *Id.* at 25. One newer case study cited by TPL was the protection in 2002 of about 4,000 acres including conservation easements on municipal watershed land and acquisition of some privately held lands in the watershed serving New Bedford, Lakeville, and Taunton,

Massachusetts, an area east of the lands covered by the Southeastern Massachusetts Bioreserve. *Id.* at 38. TPL and AWWA published a companion *Source Protection Handbook*, also
in 2004, as a "manual for implementing" many of the policy recommendations developed in
Protecting the Source.

26. Department of Environmental Protection, Source Water Assessment and Protection Report
    for Fall River Water Department (2003).

27. *See* Durand et al., *supra* note 12.

28. Southeastern Massachusetts Bioreserve, Goals Statement (Apr. 2001).

29. *Id.*

30. Southeastern Massachusetts Bioreserve Management Plan, at 3-1.

31. *Id.* ch. 5.

32. *Id.* ch. 7.

33. *Id.* at 7-17.

34. *Id.* at 9-1.

35. *Id.* at 9-3 to 9-4.

36. *Id.* at 9-5 to 9-9. The Fall River Water Department includes a five-member "Environmental
    Police" staff to protect the watershed areas, both in and outside of the bioreserve. *Id.* at 3-16,
    3-17.

37. Personal Communication with Debbi Edelstein, former Manager, Bioreserve for Trustees of
    Reservations (July 23, 2007) (discussing current Buzzards Bay and Cape Cod superintend-
    ent for Trustees) [hereinafter Edelstein Communication].

38. Southeastern Massachusetts Bioreserve Management Plan, at 1-1.

39. Commonwealth of Massachusetts Executive Office of Environmental Affairs, The State of
    Our Environment 112 (2000).

40. *See* Edelstein Communication, *supra* note 37.

41. Massachusetts Natural Heritage & Endangered Species Program, Living Waters: Guiding the
    Protection of Freshwater Biodiversity in Massachusetts (2003).

42. *E.g.,* Massachusetts Natural Heritage & Endangered Species Program, BioMap and Living
    Waters: Guiding Land Conservation for Biodiversity in Massachusetts—Core Habitats of
    Fall River (2004).

43. Mass.Gov, *GIS-Based Buildout Analyses for All the Cities and Towns in Massachusetts,*
    http://www.mass.gov.mgis/mgpres2.htm (last visited Oct. 26, 2008).

44. *See generally* Metropolitan District Commission, Growth Management Tools: A Summary
    for Planning Boards in Massachusetts (2002) (summarizing build-out analysis and identify-
    ing potential growth management responses authorized under state law). The build-out
    analyses were prepared under Executive Order No. 418 and Massachusetts' Community
    Preservation Act.

45. Trust for Public Land & American Water Works Ass'n, Source Protection Handbook 18 (2004).

46. *Id.* at 25-27.

47. Executive Office of Envtl. Affairs, Water Assets Study: Regional Summary Report—Buz-
    zards Bay Watershed (2006). Although Fall River is not in the Buzzards Bay watershed, its
    Copicut Reservoir is.

48. *Id.* at 3-26.

49. *See* Edelstein Communication, *supra* note 37.

50. *Id.*

51. *Id.*

52. Southeastern Massachusetts Bioreserve Management Plan, at 2-13.

53. While the conservation restriction on the city's watershed lands is enforceable by the commonwealth, the overall management of the bioreserve is governed by the MOU and the ratifying legislation, which does not specify the mutual enforceability of plans over the long term but which contemplates their continued validity.

54. Southeastern Massachusetts Bioreserve Management Plan, at 1-3. The use of source water protection funding to protect these lands is discussed *supra* note 36.

55. *Id*. at 2-5.

56. *Id*. at 8-1 to 8-3.

57. *See* Copicut Woods Management Plan, *supra* note 16, at 8-4.

58. *Id*. at 9-10 to 9-12.

North Carolina's Ecosystem Enhancement Program: Transportation Projects and Compensatory Mitigation

North Carolina developed a program in 2003 to identify lands and waters important for wetland and stream conservation throughout the state. This program targets mitigation funding associated with compensating for the adverse effects of highway construction on wetlands and waters, toward identified waters that produce broader ecological and watershed benefits than might be the case if mitigation were organized project permit by project permit. The state's Ecosystem Enhancement Program (EEP) addresses conservation needs at multiple scales.

Transportation projects often adversely affect wetlands, streams, and other aquatic resources. State departments of transportation, such as the North Carolina Department of Transportation (NCDOT), frequently need to provide compensatory mitigation for impacts that cannot be avoided. Because these departments create demand for mitigation activities while providing funding from state and federal transportation infrastructure accounts, there is an opportunity to direct mitigation funds in ways that confer biodiversity benefits on the wider landscape—both on a statewide basis and by focusing on particular watersheds. In 1998, North Carolina Department of Environment and Natural Resources (NCDENR) and the U.S. Army Corps of Engineers (the Corps), which has jurisdiction over dredging and filling of waters of the United States including wetlands under §404 of the federal Clean Water Act (CWA),[1] entered into a memorandum of understanding (MOU).[2] The MOU addressed circumstances under which the Corps would recognize NCDENR activities as providing compensatory mitigation for the unavoidable loss of wetlands subject to federal §404 permitting. The MOU specifically recognized North Carolina's existing Wetland Restoration Program (WRP), an effort launched in 1997 pursuant to 1996 state legislation. The WRP operated as an in-lieu fee program—where permittees, including NCDOT, would (with the Corps' approval) pay NCDENR to select aquatic sites and conduct restoration activities.

In 1999, the NCDENR and NCDOT signed a separate MOU to help address NCDOT's anticipated future mitigation needs. This MOU provided that NCDOT would contribute mitigation funds to the NCDENR Wetlands Trust Fund to support development of Local Watershed Plans, which would in turn help support the WRP mitigation program. This collaboration, intended to facilitate planning, set the stage for what subsequently became the EEP.

In January 2002, NCDOT, the NCDENR, and the Corps issued a report on proposals to streamline the way in which mitigation would be identified and carried out in North Carolina, and specifically produced a plan to decouple the identification and restoration of mitigation sites from the process used to issue §404 permit process needed for individual transportation projects.[3]

In July 2003, NCDOT, the NCDENR, and the Corps established the EEP with a memorandum of agreement (MOA).[4] The EEP provides a programmatic approach to compensatory mitigation and is housed within the NCDENR. EEP conducts basinwide and local watershed planning to identify high-quality mitigation sites, and provides advance mitigation (mitigation in advance of the impacts) for NCDOT projects. The EEP, administered by the NCDENR, expends approximately $40 million per year on these activities.

While it was established and funded as a wetland and aquatic resource mitigation program, North Carolina articulated a broader mission for the EEP:

> The EEP mission is to restore, enhance, preserve and protect the functions associated with wetlands, streams, and riparian areas, including but not limited to those necessary for the restoration, maintenance and protection of water quality and riparian habitats throughout North Carolina.[5]

The EEP has provided a vehicle for prioritizing the conservation and restoration of streams, wetlands, and other aquatic resources within the major basins of North Carolina, using transportation funding. The program has generated "surplus" mitigation (including some projects supported by NCDOT prior to 2003), meaning that the mitigation generated has exceeded the quantity needed for regulatory approval of transportation projects.[6]

The EEP is a different way of organizing mitigation activities. It takes what is normally a set of separate compensatory mitigation actions tied to federal wetland permits for individual highway and transportation projects, and it attempts to harness the funding to do anticipatory planning which results in watershed and ecological benefits on a statewide (and watershed) basis.

EEP was designated by the Federal Highway Administration (FHwA) as 1 of 15 exemplary ecosystem initiatives in the nation. It received a national innovation award from the National Association of Development Organizations in 2003. It received a National Environmental Excellence Award from the National Association of Environmental Professionals in 2005, and was recognized by the Council of State Governments as a leading state initiative in 2005, and by the national Innovations in Government Awards Committee in 2007.[7]

Operation of the Program

Organization

The EEP operates within and is staffed by the NCDENR.[8] Initially there were two separate divisions dealing with conservation activities—Planning and Implementation, which were later subdivided geographically across the state. The divisions carried out planning, site identification, project acquisition, and design. In 2006, the two were combined as the Watershed Planning and Project Implementation Section in order to bring planning and implementation into closer coordination, thus achieving better understanding of watershed opportunities and follow through of projects; and the combined unit was organized geographically with east, central, and west units.[9]

Two external advisory groups interact with the EEP. The Program Assessment and Consistency Group of federal and state agency personnel serves as a technical monitoring review and oversight body, while the Liaison Council is a group of stakeholders, briefed several times each year, that offers policy recommendations. The North Carolina Wildlife Resources Commission and the U.S. Fish and Wildlife Service have seats on the Program Assessment and Consistency Group, and the commission is also under contract to the EEP for certain restoration work. These elements provide opportunities to integrate wildlife priorities into the program. Nongovernmental members of the Liaison Council include the Southern Environmental Law Center, The Nature Conservancy, Environmental Defense, Martin Marietta Corporation, and various environmental consultants. The council also includes state agencies, North Carolina's Natural Heritage Program, and the state's Clean Water Management Trust Fund.

Funding

NCDOT provides substantial funding to operate the EEP under a biennial budget. Funding procedures are set forth in a 2004 MOA between NCDOT and the NCDENR. The FHwA provided $500,000 in start-up funding. NCDOT funding for EEP mitigation activities has totaled $175 million over the first four years of the program.[10] the EEP invoices NCDOT quarterly and is paid in advance for each quarter.[11] Funding has supported approximately 60 NCDENR positions.

NCDOT funding is directed toward watershed planning and mitigation for transportation projects. Fees collected under the EEP's in-lieu fee, buffers, and nutrient programs provide for planning and mitigation associated with those projects/permittees paying into those programs, respectively. Project accounting associated with each program is maintained separately.

Conservation Identification and Priority Setting for Mitigation Actions

Selection of sites, mitigation project design, and implementation of mitigation are based on landscape or watershed-level planning and programmatic needs, rather than as reactive, project-specific mitigation triggered by specific project impacts. The EEP relies on a watershed planning process that identifies opportunities for high-quality watershed mitigation that meets both water quality goals and open space preservation goals.

EEP watershed planners establish restoration priorities for each of the 17 river basins in North Carolina, and use these to identify potential projects. The MOA requires that mitigation be provided in the same 8-digit hydrologic unit classification (HUC) watershed as the impact. There are 54 cataloging units in 17 river basins.

Mitigation is provided primarily in four ways:

- The EEP prepares its own mitigation sites through separate contracts for mitigation design and bids for mitigation construction on sites it selects using the watershed planning process and the EEP's Project Atlas, which identifies priority sites by watershed unit.
- The EEP issues a request for proposals in order to contract for a "full delivery" of mitigation, paying for both design and construction on watershed sites proposed by the contractor within the watershed cataloging unit.
- The EEP acquires credits from a privately operated wetland mitigation bank to meet NCDOT mitigation needs.
- The EEP has also acquired high-quality preservation (HQP) wetlands by purchase, in instances where preservation is allowed as mitigation.[12] Initially under the MOA the EEP allowed NCDOT to rely on preservation of HQP sites, provided that mitigation was provided at a high ratio of acres preserved to acres of permitted loss. Mitigation based chiefly on restoration

(rather than preservation) would follow during a seven year ramp-up period for the program. At the end of the transition period, a portion of the HQP share would be replaced by restoration. This approach front-loaded preservation opportunities, while assuring that restoration also was accomplished in connection with every permitted wetland loss. HQP sites were identified by local land trusts or state conservation agencies within each of eight ecoregions. "To qualify as HQP sites, each parcel was approved for acquisition by an interagency committee comprised of conservation and regulatory agency staff."[13]

The Watershed Planning process is fundamental to EEP-provided mitigation. EEP has identified 26.4% of the state's land area as "targeted local watersheds" within the state's 17 major basins.[14] EEP planners are preparing 34 Local Watershed Plans within the targeted local watersheds (but not covering all of the targeted local watersheds), comprising 3,100 square miles. Twenty-two were completed through July 2006. The Local Watershed Plans culminate in a final plan, plan summary, supporting documents, and a project atlas.[15] (See Fig. 11.1.)

The planning process engages local stakeholders including land trusts, local governments, and landowners, as well as technical staff. The EEP's annual report notes that Local Watershed Plans include three "key components": (1) an inventory of the specific causes of watershed degradation identified through a detailed assessment; (2) a plan that links watershed problems with specific restoration strategies that are supported by the local community; and (3) a strategy for implementing restoration projects and other watershed initiatives identified in the plan.[16]

The Local Watershed Plans influence but do not yet entirely direct mitigation and conservation activities produced by the EEP. Nearly 44% of wetland and 31.7% of stream "full delivery" projects are located in these watersheds, with a lower percentage for design-bid-build projects.[17] Of course, the plans do not cover all the watershed units where mitigation may be needed. In order to be credited to a given transportation project, mitigation must be conducted within the same eight-digit watershed unit as the impact, whether or not it is a targeted local watershed. And only two-thirds of the plans had been completed by the end of July 2006. In watersheds where local plans have not been developed, the EEP relies on the priorities developed under its basinwide planning process to guide mitigation siting.

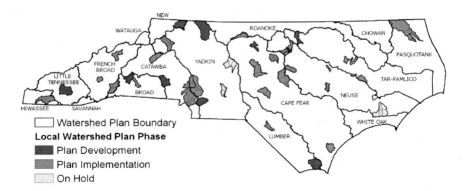

Figure 11.1 Ecosystem Enhancement Program Local Watershed Plans With permission from the North Carolina Department of Environment and Natural Resources, North Carolina Ecosystem Enhancement Program.

Wildlife Focus

Some of the Local Watershed Plans expressly identify wildlife habitat conservation as major goals for the planning unit. For example, the New Hanover Final Local Watershed Plan states:

GOAL D: PRESERVE WILDLIFE HABITAT: The [New Hanover Local Watershed Planning] Group established two objectives for preservation of wildlife habitat:
(1) Maintain continuity and connectivity of habitat
(2) Identify areas of important habitat and strive to protect these areas

Overall Recommended Actions: The Group recommended that the NCWRP [North Carolina Wetlands Restoration Program—a predecessor of the EEP] work with other organizations to develop conservation strategies for two important tracts of land adjacent to and within the watershed. Particular areas of concern were identified in the northwest portion of the watershed (see Appendix E). The Nature Conservancy has acquired one of the recommended sites, a tract of land that consists of Angola Bay and Bear Gardens in Pender County that links to other N.C. Wildlife Resources gamelands creating a large contiguous tract of habitat for wildlife. The other identified site of concern in the watershed is a 4,068-acre tract of forestland . . . .[18]

Many Local Watershed Plans do not have wildlife objectives expressed in such terms. Nevertheless, the selection of watersheds by the EEP for targeting within the 17 basins suggests that these areas should have a significant impact on the ecological integrity and water quality of the affected basins.

In addition, the substantial lands that have been identified and preserved through the high-quality preservation sites component of the EEP, and the significant involvement of North Carolina's land trusts in EEP activities (see below), suggest that wildlife habitat conservation has been a beneficiary of the program if not its primary articulated goal. In its 2005-2006 annual report, the EEP reported that it had funded more than 3,000 acres of high-quality preservation sites during that most recent period, and specifically referenced the program's involvement in assembly of the new Mayo River State Park, expansion of state game lands, the protection of "rare mussel populations" by the acquisition of 26 conservation easements on the Upper Tar River basin, and protection of "endangered and rare plant habitats" in the Pacolet River and New Hope Creek watersheds.[19]

In the same annual report, the EEP specifically devoted a section to a case study relating to "species of concern" in a particular Local Watershed Plan area. This case study noted that earlier plans in the Fishing Creek Local Watershed Plan had addressed species of concern merely as a screening criterion, but that "the current direction of LWPs is toward addressing issues relating to [species of concern] wherever improvement goals overlap with mitigation goals." The case study notes that "the projects that EEP will recommend . . . will be prioritized to encourage instream habitat improvements in heavily sedimented reaches and highly erodible areas; the object is to reestablish good instream habitat and connect it to population sources for rare native bivalve species."[20]

The EEP has developed a focus on ecosystem function that should benefit habitat—particularly aquatic habitats in the larger watershed matrix, although neither its watershed planning nor its acceptance of proposed mitigation in response to requests for proposal require it to make habitat a primary consideration. North Carolina's recent State Wildlife Action Plan does characterize the state's aquatic biota using the 17 river basins,[21] but there is as yet no formal link between the wildlife plan and the EEP.[22]

Monitoring

The mitigation is monitored for five years after construction is complete, as required under §§404/401. Typically the first year monitoring is performed by a firm that does construction management services (often the design firm), while the two to five years are monitored under a separate contract. For "full-delivery" mitigation, the contractor provides the monitoring for five years.[23] Monitoring of preservation sites is determined by the agreements under which such sites are acquired.

Site Protection

EEP site selection criteria and guidelines provide:

> Long-Term Protection: All EEP projects must be protected by a permanent conservation easement. Conservation easements serve to protect projects by restricting uses that would damage restoration work but allow for the landholder to retain ownership of the project area. Conservation easements do not allow for public access to the protected areas and provide for the continued use of the property, such as hunting, fishing, camping and other types of recreation.[24]

Preservation sites, such as those involving land trusts, as discussed below, require site protection as well, although these often include and anticipate public access. The NCDENR has established a Stewardship Program responsible for ensuring that easements are maintained.

Collaboration with Land Trusts and Meeting Conservation Objectives

In the first two years of the EEP, regulatory authorities permitted a higher amount of preservation than normally allowed to meet mitigation requirements as the program was being ramped up. (Preservation is usually the least-favored form of mitigation under the federal CWA compensatory mitigation programs because it does not ultimately support the goal of no-net-loss of wetland acres. As a result, when preservation is allowed, usually it requires a fairly high ratio of acres preserved to acres lost, and requires additional restoration.)[25] The EEP worked with conservation organizations and state agencies to identify high-quality preservation sites to meet mitigation needs. During this time, North Carolina completed more than 60 land preservation transactions involving land trusts.[26] The EEP has served as a critically important funding source helping these land trusts meet their conservation objectives. Partners include the Conservation Trust of North Carolina, The Nature Conservancy, and at least 23 others. One of the early large acquisitions was the January 15, 2004, action by the Land Trust for the Little Tennessee and The Nature Conservancy preserving the 4,500-acre Needmore Tract along the Little Tennessee River, described as "one of the most biologically important and threatened areas in North Carolina."[27]

Through all of its mitigation activities, the EEP has protected 232 miles of stream, 7,076 acres of riverine wetlands, 1,388 acres of non-riverine wetland,

and gross acreage of 35,000 acres of conservation lands.[28] The program notes that it is working through the Conservation Trust of North Carolina and local land trusts to complete acquisition of all of the HQP sites identified in the state EEP preservation plan.[29]

Analysis

The EEP is a program that marshals funding and technical assets to compensate for authorized ecological/water resources losses. Thus, like all compensatory mitigation, its outcomes must be considered in light of impacts. The program, while facilitating permitting for transportation infrastructure, offers a worthy approach to generating meaningful habitat conservation benefits that are relevant in each ecological region, basin, and watershed unit.

Because the EEP is targeted toward mitigation and must meet associated regulatory requirements, it has developed a very detailed tracking system that breaks down its assets by type and location. The EEP has not undertaken efforts to quantify its results in terms of species habitat or recovery, but does rely on Natural Heritage assessment of conditions and verification of significant habitats. The program does keep track of its protection of federally/state threatened or endangered species habitats protected by EEP high-quality preservation acquisitions—and has been particularly focused on protection of linear miles/feet of stream protection where endangered mussels species were the impetus for protection. As for the restoration activities, the program is working to identify functional improvements to watersheds, but has nothing comprehensive at this point.[30] North Carolina is one of the few states that bases much of its assessment of water quality on biocriteria.

The EEP has led to the development of new assessment methods, research projects, and other scientific tools—including reference stream data and other tools useful for landscape-scale and local conservation.[31] The development of the suite of potential HQP sites used a combination of science and best professional judgment involving panels of experts. The Local Watershed Plans rely on science but also reflect local concerns and interests of the participating stakeholders in setting goals and identifying potential projects.

The EEP experience offers substantial lessons for future conservation activities addressing multiple scales—from the site level to the ecoregional level. State transportation agencies, as well as many other developers, are frequently required to provide compensatory mitigation for unavoidable wetland losses.[32] There has also been increasing awareness of the relationship between transportation and wildlife impacts and conservation opportunities associated with transportation planning and mitigation of project impacts.[33] Mitigation expenses are eligible project expenses under federal law providing aid to states for transportation projects, and as the North Carolina experience shows, these can amount to tens of millions of dollars each year for each state. The Environmental Law Institute (ELI) evaluated all wetland compensatory mitigation expenses annually and found that in fiscal year 2003 this amount lay somewhere between $2.5 billion and $4.4 billion, with a likely midpoint of approximately $3.4 billion.[34] Transportation-related expenditures are likely a significant fraction of this amount.

In 1998, Congress established a preference for the use of wetland mitigation banking to compensate for unavoidable losses to wetlands or other natural habitat caused by transportation projects receiving federal assistance.[35] This means that aggregating wetland mitigation on large sites is preferred, thus providing a further opportunity to integrate landscape-level planning that takes into account other resources such as wildlife. Perhaps even more significant is the fact that in 2008, the Corps and EPA issued a new rule on *all* compensatory wetland mitigation.[36] The new rule establishes a "watershed approach" for mitigation projects, and it creates a mitigation preference first for mitigation banks, followed by mitigation of conservation sites supported by an "in-lieu" fee paid to a nonprofit organization, followed by permittee-conducted site mitigation. The probable result of this approach is a greater opportunity to integrate compensatory wetland mitigation with other conservation efforts throughout a watershed.

Notes

1. 33 U.S.C. §1344.
2. MOU between NCDENR the Corps, Wilmington District (1998), *available at* http://www.nceep.net/news/reports/WRP_MOU.pdf.
3. NCDOT et al., A Final Report on Improving the Mitigation Process for Transportation-Related Mitigation Projects in North Carolina (2002), *available at* http://www.nceep.net/images/2002%20Mitigation%20Process%20Improvement%20Report.doc.
4. MOA among the NCDENR and NCDOT and the Corps, Wilmington District (July 22, 2003) (on file with the Environmental Law Institute (ELI)). In addition to the $40 million per year NCDOT program under the MOA, the EEP also operates additional non-NCDOT programs—specifically, in-lieu fee programs for wetlands, for stream buffers for the Neuse and Tar-Pamlico basins, and nutrient offsets for the Neuse and Tar-Pamlico basins. These programs, not part of this case study—expend about $30 million, $4 million, and $3 million/year respectively. The EEP also operates a very small "wetlands trust fund" for non-mitigation wetland projects. EEP, 2005-2006 Annual Report 3-4 (2006).
5. MOA, *supra* note 4, ¶ III.B.
6. Dye Management Group et al., Study of the Merger of Ecosystem Enhancement Program & Clean Water Management Trust Fund, North Carolina General Assembly 53-57 (2007). This "surplus" has since created concern that state and federal transportation dollars had been over-expended on environmental mitigation not needed to meet regulatory obligations, and has led to a number of proposals to redress this perceived imbalance.
7. N.C. Ecosystem Enhancement Program, *Awards and Recognition,* http://www.nceep.net/abouteep/awards2.html.
8. http://www.nceep.net/abouteep/ochart.html (last visited Oct. 29, 2008).
9. *See* 2005-2006 Annual Report, *supra* note 4, at 25.
10. *See* Dye Management Group et al., *supra* note 6, at 22.
11. MOA between the NCDENR and NCDOT ¶ 3.7.4 (2004).
12. *See* Dye Management Group et al., *supra* note 6, at 25-28.
13. *See* 2005-2006 Annual Report, *supra* note 4, at 12. *See also* Dye Management Group et al., *supra* note 6, at 22-23.
14. *See* Dye Management Group et al., *supra* note 6, at 18. The EEP website further explains:
    > To determine the best locations for stream and wetlands projects that restore, enhance or protect water quality, the EEP Planning Group conducts two basic types of planning: *River Basin Restoration Priorities* are set periodically in each of the 17 river basins in North Carolina. EEP's basic purpose is to identify local watersheds (generally under 100 square miles in area) where ecological restoration or protection is most needed—for instance, streams with impaired water quality and degraded habitat, or areas with endangered aquatic species. *Local Watershed Planning* is undertaken once River Basin Restoration Priorities have been identified. Criteria include support from local communities and projected impacts from future development on watersheds.

    Local watershed planning is described as an 18-24 month process. *See* EEP, *Watershed Planning,* http://www.nceep.net/pages/Watershed_Planning.pdf (last visited Oct. 28, 2008).
15. *See* 2005-2006 Annual Report, *supra* note 4, at 23. Local Watershed Plans can be obtained at http://www.nceep.net/services/lwps/localplans.htm.

16. *See* 2005-2006 Annual Report, *supra* note 4, at 2.

17. *Id.* at 18 (excluding high-quality preservation projects).

18. New Hanover County Local Watershed Planning Group, Local Watershed Plan (2002), *available at* http://www.nceep.net/services/lwps/new%20hanover/New%20Hanover%20Plan.pdf.

19. *See* 2005-2006 Annual Report, *supra* note 4, at 12.

20. *Id.* at 20.

21. North Carolina State Wildlife Action Plan, *Species Habitat Assessments and Conservation Strategies: Aquatic Systems*, http://www.ncwildlife.org/pg07_wildlifespeciescon/WAP_Chapter5B.pdf (last visited Oct. 28, 2008).

22. The Wildlife Action Plan does reference the EEP as an ongoing conservation effort whose acquisition activities may be relevant to the wildlife plan's goals:

   The Ecosystem Enhancement Program, developed through a 2003 Memorandum of Agreement between the NC Department of Environment and Natural Resources, the NC Department of Transportation, and the US Army Corps of Engineers, also has huge potential to dictate future land acquisitions in North Carolina through a watershed approach to compensatory mitigation from unavoidable impacts to stream and wetlands associated with highway development projects.

   North Carolina State Wildlife Action Plan, *Statewide Conservation Strategies: Urban Wildlife Management Strategies*, http://www.ncwildlife.org/pg07_wildlifespeciescon/WAP_Chapter4.pdf (last visited Oct. 28, 2008).

23. *See* Dye Management Group et al., *supra* note 6, at 27-28. EEP monitoring reports are available for review at http://www.nceep.net/business/monitoring/Monitoring_report_web/Projects_By_Basin.htm.

24. EEP, *Consideration for Potential Sites*, http://www.nceep.net/pages/protect.htm (last visited Oct. 28, 2008).

25. The MOA required the EEP to include *restoration* at a ratio of 1:1 for all permits issued using preservation after the first two years. During the first two-year "transition period" permits could be issued using preservation alone at a 10:1 ratio, but when the restoration was subsequently provided, one-half of the preservation credits (5:1) from these preservation-only transactions were returned to the EEP for future use.

26. Conservation Trust for North Carolina, Protecting North Carolina's Threatened Land and Waterways: Land Trusts and the Ecosystem Enhancement Program—A Historic Partnership (2005), *available at* http://ctnc.org/downloads/eepbook.pdf.

27. *Id.*

28. *See* 2005-2006 Annual Report, *supra* note 4, at 13.

29. *Id.*

30. Personal Communication from Suzanne Klimek, Planning Supervisor, EEP (July 9, 2007).

31. *E.g.*, Mark M. Brinson et al., Developing Reference Data to Identify and Calibrate Indicators of Riparian Ecosystem Condition in Rural Coastal Plain Landscapes in North Carolina (2006); Richard D. Rheinhardt et al., Applying Ecological Assessments to Planning Stream Restorations in Coastal Plain North Carolina (2005).

32. 33 U.S.C. §1344, 40 C.F.R. 230.10. For transportation demands on compensatory mitigation see generally ELI, 2005 Status Report on Compensatory Mitigation in the United States (2006).

33. *See, e.g.*, Richard T. Forman et al., Road Ecology: Science and Solutions (2003); Defenders of Wildlife, Getting Up to Speed: A Conservationist's Guide to Wildlife and Highways (2007); FHwA Public Roads (2003).

34. ELI, Mitigation of Impacts to Fish and Wildlife Habitat: Estimating Costs and Identifying Opportunities 32 (2007).
35. *See* U.S. Department of Transportation, FHwA, Federal Guidance on the Use of the TEA-21 Preference for Mitigation Banking to Fulfill Mitigation Requirements Under §404 of the CWA (2003), *available at* http://www.fhwa.dot.gov/environment/wetland/tea21bnk.htm.
36. 73 Fed. Reg. 19594 (Apr. 10, 2008).

CHAPTER TWELVE

Solving the Scale Problem

The jurisdictional limits of local government land use plans, development and construction plans, and governmental programs aimed at environmental mitigation or remediation do not often correspond to land areas defined chiefly by ecological processes. For at least some processes and biological resources, decisions may suffer from a mismatch of the scale of the decision to the scale of the ecological process or unit of relevant habitat. But waiting for a grand ecoregional plan and a series of coordinated subordinate plans is almost never an option for decisionmakers. Decisions must be made now, by landowners or governmental units with limited geographical jurisdiction. And existing accountability mechanisms often privilege other values—location of transportation facilities, water supply, public recreation, utilities, township and county governance, to name a few—over ecological results.

Environmental advocates and professionals have generally hoped to make decisionmakers more familiar with conservation biology concepts, with the expectation that some of these concepts would creep into project design, development approvals, or plan-making. Graduate schools and their faculties have sought to train conservation biologists and ecologists with the hope that their expertise would be valued by entities other than fish and wildlife conservation agencies and organizations. But even where these lessons are heard and expertise is available, it takes an additional step to deal with the problem of scale rather than to confine conservation to the four corners of a parcel of land or planning area.

It turns out that *institutional and procedural* practices—what we have called "nature-friendly land use practices"—make it possible to deal with the problem of differing scales in ecological processes and land use decisions. Land use decisions taken at any level can have positive conservation influences on ecology at the parcel, site, watershed or subregional, and ecoregional levels. Although each of the case studies in this book offers unique lessons for habitat conservation, six practices make it far more likely that scale issues can be addressed effectively.

Engage or Create a Sustainable Independent
Entity Whose Primary Concern Is Habitat

In plans or development activities where wildlife habitat is not the primary driver, but an important secondary objective, it is important to identify (to create if necessary), and sustain an external independent entity whose *primary* concern *is* the wildlife habitat. This turns out to be one of the most significant steps for ensuring that conservation benefits are not limited to the four corners of the development site or the planning area. It is also essential to ensure that the focus on habitat will not be lost over time.

In the Santa Lucia Preserve and Coffee Creek Center private developments, the creation of independent conservancies make it possible to ensure the continued active management of the habitat conservation elements of each project. These habitat-focused entities also provide credibility in dealing with outside institutions such as state regulators, academic institutions, and wildlife habitat groups, and they provide a way for scientific and regionally important habitat information to inform on-site decisions and activities. In the case of Coffee Creek, the Coffee Creek Watershed Conservancy made it possible for the habitat portion of the project to succeed and continue, even as the development aspects of the project encountered delays and market readjustments.

The North Carolina Ecosystem Enhancement Program (EEP) performs a similar function in ensuring the ecological validity of the mitigation actions needed to offset state transportation project impacts. Indeed, the EEP was even able to support statewide research that benefitted project design and ecological success across numerous mitigation projects. In Fall River, the creation of a multi-stakeholder management team for the Southeastern Massachusetts Bioreserve provides a way for landscape-level conservation to be kept in view even as the separate participants addressed differences in the specific land management and development objectives for their individual parcels of land. In the case of General Motors Lansing Delta Township (LDT) Plant, which does not have a habitat-focused separate entity, it remains to be seen whether the corporation's commitment alone will be sufficient to sustain its habitat conservation gains over the longer term.

The creation of a habitat-focused entity also makes it possible to pursue and stimulate regional conservation projects *outside* the initial project area—both by example and by the conservation entity's seeking additional funding sources and participation by others for projects extending the initial vision of the project (as in Fall River and Coffee Creek).

If habitat is presumed to be everyone's concern or is articulated as a general goal, it may turn out to be no one's particular concern, especially at the margins of decisionmaking and the borders of property or planning units. Identifying an institutional advocate makes it possible to address effectively the management issues at multiple necessary scales.

Maintain Continuing Active Access to Conservation Science

No conservation project or program can simply rest on an initial set of assumptions and static ecological data. As Bruce Stein notes in Chapter Three, habitat management must be dynamic and recognize and address ecological and physical change. Many of the case studies bear out the importance of identifying authoritative sources for up-to-date conservation science information and building this information gathering into the process—rather than simply resting upon initial consultant studies, however complete and useful.

Summit County relies on the expertise of the Colorado Department of Wildlife, and explicitly takes advantage of the department's updated scientific information about habitat requirements, population dynamics, migration corridors, and other information. The East Contra Costa County Habitat Conservation Plan/Natural Community Conservation Plan (HCP/NCCP)[1] used detailed consultant-generated information to design a flexible conservation network, but the implementation will be guided over time by additional information as well as by the advice of science advisory bodies built into the system. The North Carolina EEP has a pair of scientific advisory review bodies, and has built a system based on detailed watershed plans. The Southeastern Massachusetts Bioreserve relies on a great deal of state-generated data about watersheds, biological resources, and growth patterns, as well as a management design that provides for additional information and adjustment of management measures.

In Baltimore County, the environmental science is closely integrated within the land planning and permitting process and the county has also served as a key proving ground for state-based research and pilot projects. Baltimore County's integration of environmental science into its operations has demonstrated how scientific understanding about green infrastructure, water quality, habitat, forests, and the like can be quickly incorporated into regulations and projects. The use of conservation science informs both site design and approval requirements and the designation of conservation areas and buffer requirements.

Santa Lucia and Coffee Creek both support science research and education. The Santa Lucia Conservancy provides for research and monitoring, often in collaboration with academic and agency scientists; this component of the project both advances understanding of the regional ecological systems and habitats and provides data useful for management. Dan Perlman notes, in Chapter Two, that practical collaboration between scientists and planners on local landscapes is a key approach. Input from local biologists was critically important in each of the case study projects. It informed decisions throughout the process of designing the project or program, and helped to resolve conflicts and address competing priorities throughout.

Sources of dynamic, ongoing science are increasingly available. Many institutional sources of data are available to local governments and private developers, including state natural heritage programs, The Nature Conservancy's many ecoregional plans, watershed plans, and specific initiatives like the Western Governors Association's Wildlife Corridor Initiative. The same level of spatial specificity and habitat data layers will not be available everywhere, but no part of the U.S. land area is without a significant amount of at least regionally meaningful biological information. Going forward, the State Wildlife Action Plans provide scientific data in an organized way that can inform more detailed project planning on any landscape when used by conservation biologists and planners together, and when provision is made for future reviews and adjustments over time.

Commitment to Habitat Elements of a Project or Place Must Be Articulated as Part of the "Brand Identity"

Habitat conservation can enter project or program planning in different ways, but its identification as an essential part of the purpose makes it possible to sustain the commitment over time.

Habitat that is merely incidental or identified as a design constraint cannot meaningfully hope to achieve conservation that is effective at multiple scales—and particularly not at a regional level.

For example, tree conservation at the parcel level will not succeed in sustaining a forested landscape after the original purchaser transfers the land if such conservation is not designed and explained as part of a vision for a regional forest network. Riparian corridors will not be maintained, or the corridors will be degraded, if the corridor's relationship to a living complex of aquatic organisms is not made plain to people living along the corridor. A local government's comprehensive plan will not inform subsequent zoning decisions if the plan does not specify what is ecologically and biologically important as well as what areas are and are not designated for development. Technically sound conservation choices must be backed by awareness of the conservation vision.

Summit County, Colorado, began its efforts in the 1970s by recognizing the importance of wildlife to the mountain living experience, and then built on that experience by continuing to articulate this as a county goal in successive plans and zoning ordinances. This led to creation of a zoning and review system that was able to put wildlife ahead of development in some instances, and enabled the county to include habitat protection as an integral part of land use permitting review.

Baltimore County's success owes a great deal to planning by civic groups in the 1960s, backed by a continuing commitment by elected officials and county departments over the next forty years to make adjustments and changes articulating the integral role of the environment in development of this suburban county. The East Contra Costa County HCP/NCCP was driven initially by Endangered Species Act (ESA) regulatory and planning concerns, but was made feasible because of the commitment of the regional water district and the existence of a substantial constituency interested in preserving a network of open space lands in a rapidly developing area.

The impetus to launch the Southeastern Massachusetts Bioreserve came from a state government-articulated vision, but it was carried forward over time because of the involvement of the Trustees of Reservations in helping to define the place. The land trust facilitated the complex land transactions to assemble the bioreserve and led by example in preparing a management plan for the Copicut Woods parcel of the bioreserve. This was important, because as the state-elected and state-appointed officials changed, the project had articulated a strong enough identity that it was able to persist and carry forward the vision. The North Carolina EEP grew out of the desire by state officials to rationalize compensatory mitigation on a larger ecologically defined landscape, in order to harness the substantial financial resources coming from an expanded program of transportation construction projects.

The Santa Lucia Preserve was made possible because of the developer's vision and sustained by the investments made in environmental review, and the project's "brand" was reinforced by the creation of the Santa Lucia Conservancy to place conservation in the forefront of the project's management. The Coffee Creek developer's vision for the preserve area as the heart of the project actually ensured that the conservation part of the project succeeded and gained civic support and backing even as the development plans suffered setbacks. And General Motors decided as a matter of corporate policy that in one of its newest flagship plants in its home state it would make the management of the grounds outside the plant a matter of company pride and civic identity as much as the plant itself.

In each case a strong articulated vision made it possible to bring about a substantial commitment to wildlife habitat conservation—and, in each case, to allow that commitment to expand and adapt over time. This articulated vision could be thought of as a way of branding projects, programs, or places as wildlife-supporting. Thus, in order to address habitat at multiple scales, it is important to ensure that habitat is not incidental but is part of the identity of the place.

Recognize Opportunities to Connect Conserved Habitat With Other Lands Beyond the Project or Plan Boundaries as Well as Opportunities to Influence the Actions of Entities Other Than the Project Participants

Planners and landowners should specifically seek to *identify* regional habitat conservation efforts, including funding sources and activities on lands and waters outside their planning boundary. The case studies in this book illustrate different ways in which regional conservation opportunities are identified and addressed, and the variety of spillover effects of case study actions on independent entities.

For example, with Coffee Creek, the influence of the Preserve's creation spilled over to the local government, influencing the passage of several habitat friendly ordinances affecting lands outside the development's boundaries. In addition, the Coffee Creek Conservancy subsequently led the preparation of a watershed plan for Coffee Creek, including lands and conservation activities not associated with the development.

The creation of the Southeastern Massachusetts Bioreserve inspired independent purchases of adjacent conservation lands by land trusts and others not part of the initial bioreserve team. This included lands not within the boundaries of the initial bioreserve, but nevertheless supporting the regional assemblage of lands and waters constituting the wildlife habitat base for this region.

The East Contra Costa County HCP/NCCP strategy was launched in order to serve as the basis for "incidental take" permitting under the federal ESA and under the California ESA, as well as to support wetlands permitting under §404 of the federal Clean Water Act (CWA). But essential to the plan was its recognition of and relationship to ongoing regional conservation programs and preserved open space lands that will be complemented and extended by the preserve system assembled under the new plan.

The North Carolina EEP stimulated work with land trusts across the state— allowing for the realization of conservation visions that transcended mere wetland mitigation in numerous instances. The EEP planning process for watersheds also led to the creation of stakeholder visions for the conservation and management futures of watershed basins even where individual EEP projects would only cover a small portion of the land area involved in the plans.

The Baltimore County urban services boundary and protection of the county's river valleys as conservation areas led to the state of Maryland's subsequent adoption in 1997 of "priority growth areas" as a key to "smart growth." It also served as a proof of concept for the state's adoption of a statewide "greenprint" strategy to identify and protect core habitats and habitat linkages. The county had already shown the feasibility and value of these techniques, and provided a place in which these could be demonstrated and applied when adopted.

Effective Projects and Programs Educate the Public and Surrounding Community About Native Habitats and Wildlife

Each of the case study projects, plans, or programs engage the public in a substantial way. The private developments provide access and sponsor educational opportunities for school children and adults. Coffee Creek holds educational events and civic celebrations focused on the preserve portion of the development. The Santa Lucia Conservancy has a well-developed program of education and outreach, including research opportunities to increase connections with academic institutions and conservation agencies. And the General Motors LDT Plant has a substantial civic engagement component including educating schoolchildren, as an integral part of the project.

The local governments (Baltimore County, Summit County, and Contra Costa County) engaged with the public when they created the relevant institutions for conservation. They also engage the public in their administration of the provisions (through planning and advisory boards), and in commenting on individual activities protecting wildlife and habitat.

And the two state-related government programs with ancillary benefits for wildlife (Fall River and North Carolina EEP) engaged a broader constituency, moving beyond the technical implementation of source water protection and wetland mitigation projects, into involving citizens in planning and in visiting and using sites conserved by these processes. Indeed the Southeastern Massachusetts Bioreserve expressly built public access and visitation into the plan for the reserve in order to build public support and identity. And in North Carolina, many if not most of the EEP conservation sites are open for public use, and the watershed planning is multi-stakeholder by design.

The creation of awareness and education programs provides a constituency for ongoing landscape level conservation, creates an opportunity for the emulation of site and parcel-level practices by other landowners and decisionmakers, and improves awareness of the relationships between site-level practices and regional conservation success. The educational component, while initially looking like another version of branding or marketing, turns out to be highly important in making "place-based" conservation extend to a wider vision of the "place."

Recognition by a Certification Program Provides Accountability and Improves Continuity

A number of these case study areas have been the subject of external recognition. This not only helps to validate their brand as nature-friendly, but even more importantly provides accountability and reinforcement of their intentions. Institutions change over time, people leave, and visionary leaders are not always able to keep the habitat vision in the forefront of local landowner awareness. It is helpful to have external recognition of the goals and practices set in place so that these can be maintained and reinforced over time. Such recognition can help internal managers overcome pressures based on changing priorities, lack of funding, or flagging commitments.

For example, the Wildlife Habitat Council's certification of the General Motors habitat conservation reduces the likelihood that such conservation will be quietly abandoned if corporate priorities change. Baltimore County has used its recognition as a "Nature-Friendly Community"[2] and other awards and recognition to protect and expand the environmentally oriented focus of its county governance and administrative procedures. In Massachusetts, the designation of the Fall River City watershed lands, nearby purchased lands, and state forest lands as the commonwealth's first "bioreserve" created an identity for lands not otherwise seen as important by local governments, owners, towns, and water authorities. This designation has proven to be significant as there have been several changes in political leadership at the state level and several snags in the implementation of parts of the agreement that the identification has made it possible to overcome.

Coffee Creek has maintained viability (and visibility) in a weak real estate market via its receipt of the Illinois Chapter of the American Society of Landscape Architects (ILASLA) Merit Award of Design in 2001, the Conservation and Native Landscaping Award from the U.S. Environmental Protection Agency (EPA) and Chicago Wilderness in 2003, and recognition as one of the Urban

Land Institute's 26 Great Planned Communities.[3] The North Carolina EEP has been subject to questions in the North Carolina Legislature about costs and the need for such extensive conservation activities, but its recognition by the Federal Highway Administration as 1 of 15 exemplary ecosystem initiatives in the nation, its national innovation award from the National Association of Development Organizations in 2003, its National Environmental Excellence Award from the National Association of Environmental Professionals in 2005, recognition by the Council of State Governments as a leading state initiative in 2005, and recognition by the national Innovations in Government Awards Committee in 2007, have helped sustain the program.

Other forms of external recognition or validation will soon be available to provide this opportunity for nature-friendly projects and plans to improve their durability. The American Society of Landscape Architects, the Lady Bird Johnson Wildflower Center, the United States Botanic Garden and other stakeholder organizations, launched the Sustainable Sites Initiative.[4] Including open space areas and development sites, the program will generate Standards and Guidelines by 2009 and later (by 2012) a Rating System with specific site performance goals, Pilot Projects, and a Reference Guide describing how pilot projects achieved sustainability goals.[5] In 2007, the U.S. Green Building Council finalized evaluation criteria for the new Pilot Program for Leadership in Energy and Environmental Design—Neighborhood Development (LEED–ND).[6] Several of the criteria relate to habitat conservation. Although not all sites, particularly those in rural or exurban areas, would meet most of the neighborhood criteria of the new program, a few of the habitat conservation criteria provide some basis for recognition of at least site-level and some subregional conservation.[7]

The tendency to become focused at only one level of conservation (overlay zone but not site level, or parcel level but not regional) is a natural outgrowth of complexity. It is difficult for even a well-organized and managed operation to keep everything in view, and when (*unlike* Baltimore County's exemplary Department of Environmental Protection and Resource Management) responsibilities are diffused, it is very likely indeed that elements of conservation at multiple scales will drop out. But external recognition creates a type of accountability mechanism. Recognition defines a touchstone for new work or a reason to remedy conditions that have decayed from those which garnered the recognition in the first place. Even without continuing audit or reporting requirements, the external plays upon the internal to push it toward the eternal (or at least toward the durable). They don't teach this in biology departments, but they do in management schools.

Scale: Addressable Through Institutional and Process Solutions

As the essays and case studies show, landowners and local governments seeking to conserve and protect wildlife habitat have a great many tools to draw upon. The local government case studies showed use of comprehensive land use plans, zoning, overlay zoning, wildlife habitat assessment requirements, subdivision requirements, tree conservation and mitigation requirements, water and wetland buffers, land and easement acquisition, transfer of development rights, urban-rural service boundaries, agricultural zoning, invasive plant controls, and impact fees. These diverse experiences demonstrate the vast array of tools that can be employed for complementary purposes and further show that wildlife conservation objectives can be served by a mix of politically feasible mechanisms adopted by governments operating at a county-scale landscape. The reference publications *Nature-Friendly Ordinances*,[8] *Habitat Protection Planning*,[9] and *Protecting Nature in Your Community*,[10] outline the substantial capacity of local governments to protect habitat using their existing legal authority. Developers too can use design tools, scientific expertise, and innovative site planning to produce results that work not just at the parcel and site levels but beyond. State regulatory and planning programs also can be structured to address multiple landscape objectives

While understanding principles of biodiversity conservation[11] is important, even more important to solving the scale issue on the ground is the creation of a process and set of institutions that can be as dynamic as the ecological processes themselves over a period of time longer than a one-time decision.

In sum, process and institutions—the right kind of institutions, and processes that build in repeated access for science—provide an answer to the problem of scale. Fortunately, the answer does not depend on creation of wholly new institutional frameworks. In this respect, implementing nature-friendly practices at multiple scales is initially a bit simpler than the task of developing and implementing a full-blown management system dependent upon ecological indicators.[12]

Where to Begin?

We close with a couple of observations for those interested in how to begin the process of integrating ecological conservation at multiple scales into a particular decision as a developer, land use planner, or government program manager.

Follow the Water

The first observation is to "follow the water." Both human development pref-
erences and plant and animal habitat end up competing for water. Water is not
a complete substitute for all other forms of ecoregional organization—which
depend on issues of soil, topography, climate, vegetation and other characteristics. But attention to water is necessary, if not sufficient, in taking a view that
extends the scale in both directions from a decision point affecting a single site,
or a parcel, or a region. Water also has the advantage of being better understood and documented than possible occurrences of a threatened species or the
existence of an ecological boundary (ecotone) within a planning area.

Watersheds have been defined across the U.S. in a nested hierarchy of units
known as HUCs (Hydrologic Unit Code system). These are defined by a string
of numbers. Smaller watersheds are defined by longer number strings, adding
digits to the shorter number strings that define the larger watersheds of which
they are a component part. Thus a proposed development on a 14-digit HUC
stream is in a watershed that is tributary to and part of, say, an 11-digit HUC
stream; and in turn this is tributary to a large 8-digit HUC river. These units,
defined by the U.S. Geological Survey, provide a way both to expand or narrow one's focus when considering activities affecting watershed lands. In
thinking about the nested hierarchy of watersheds, it becomes possible to think
about the significance of headwaters, springs, isolated waters, and other watershed features. What is the "watershed address" of your parcel or planning area?
It has not only one such address but a collection of addresses of different numer-
ical lengths.

Water shortages, "water wars," and the need to reconcile competing industrial, agricultural, domestic, and instream uses are occurring everywhere as the
U.S. population (already at 300 million) continues to expand.[13] Global climate
change also will place new stresses on the stability and reliability of water supplies in the coming decades. The protection of watershed lands is the most
cost-effective and resilient means of maintaining reliable, high-quality water
supplies in the face of these challenges. The federal Safe Drinking Water Act's
source water protection and source water assessment programs have helped
provide new information and opportunities to protect watersheds, and to integrate such protection with other public objectives. The Trust for Public Land
and the American Water Works Association recognize the potential linkages,
publishing together in 2004 *Protecting the Source: Land Conservation and the
Future of America's Drinking Water* and the *Source Protection Handbook*.[14]
Protection of watershed lands and protection of habitats are not only compat-

ible, but mutually reinforcing, as the Fall River experience demonstrates. The assembly of watershed lands and their connection to other public and private conservation lands provides a significant opportunity for ecologically significant conservation at multiple scales. The key need is for information and an understanding of the landscape as a whole—a role that the commonwealth of Massachusetts provided to facilitate this effort.

Programs to control nonpoint sources of water pollution also present a major opportunity to conserve habitat at multiple scales.[15] EPA's CWA §319 grant program addresses impaired waterways by funding states to develop management programs and supporting targeted, locally implemented watershed-based projects. States may integrate §319 funding with other state-based programs to meet multiple objectives. The Coffee Creek Watershed Conservancy obtained a §319 grant to fund the development of a watershed plan to address water quality concerns related to Coffee Creek and its tributaries, and community members participated in the meetings leading to this planning effort. Wetland mitigation also presents a significant opportunity to marshal funding and planning to support wildlife habitat conservation.[16] The North Carolina EEP shows that watershed planning and conservation land trusts can be integrated into the process.

Focus on the Boundaries

Second, focus special attention on the boundaries of the site or jurisdiction. We do bad conservation when we pretend that everything outside the planning boundary is really "white space." The greatest value can be obtained by identifying nodes of high-quality habitat, or species of conservation concern, or wildlife corridors that are at the boundaries of sites or jurisdictions, because this will inform activities within the planning area as well as relationships outside it. Although it may seem counterintuitive to focus on the boundaries—because it is easier to work within one single unit controlling the fate of a habitat patch or parcel—effective conservation demands creating understanding at the intersections of the ecologically important areas with the artificial boundaries of the property line or governmental unit boundary.

Looking directly at the problem—and seeing the ecology reasonably whole is a feature of looking at boundaries—makes it possible to define solutions. It also makes it possible to define solutions that are someone else's opportunity or responsibility. A neighboring development site, a land trust, a state conservation funding agency, a potential mitigation bank, a neighboring governmental unit will have *opportunities* to act in instances where the initial actor has paid attention to the boundary issues and intersections. This occurs again and again in the case studies—in the lands surrounding the Southeastern Massachusetts Bioreserve, in the watershed lands of Coffee Creek outside the development boundary, in the lands adjoining non-participating cities in the Contra Costa plan. Building nifty self-contained habitats within planning units or development sites simply repeats the errors that were made in the past in such areas as stormwater management and transportation networks. The boundaries and intersections matter.

Conclusion

The projects and plans profiled in this book pursue habitat conservation as an important, albeit frequently secondary, objective. Yet they did so in a way that reaches both down to the site level and well beyond the site level. The scale issue is real. But so are the solutions that have emerged from practice. Six process and institutional practices make it feasible to integrate habitat conservation at multiple scales into nature-friendly plans, programs, and projects.

Notes

1. The East Contra Costa County plan is a Habitat Conservation Plan (HCP) under the federal Endangered Species Act, 16 U.S.C. §1539, and also a Natural Community Conservation Plan under California state law, Cal. Fish & Game Code §2800-2835.

2. Chris Duerksen & Cara Snyder, Nature-Friendly Communities (Island Press 2005).

3. Urban Land Institute, *Great Planned Communities—Coffee Creek Center*, http://www.coffeecreekcenter.com/media/mediaattn/PRINT-COVERAGE/GPC.pdf (last visited Oct. 30, 2008).

4. Sustainable Sites Initiative, *Homepage*, http://www.sustainablesites.org/index.html (last visited Oct. 30, 2008).

5. For the Sustainable Sites Initiative's Preliminary Report on Standards and Guidelines (Nov. 2007) addressing hydrology, soils, vegetation, materials, and human well being, see http://www.sustainablesites.org/SustainableSitesInitiative_PreliminaryReport_110107.pdf (last visited Oct. 30, 2008).

6. U.S. Green Building Council, *LEED for Neighborhood Development Pilot Rating System*, https://www.usgbc.org/ShowFile.aspx?DocumentID=2845 (last visited Oct. 30, 2008).

7. *Id.* Criteria relevant to habitat and ecological processes include: *Imperiled Species and Ecological Communities Prerequisite:* The development must determine if endangered or imperiled species are located on site. If species are found, the development must comply with a local Habitat Conservation Plan or coordinate with the wildlife agencies to perform adequate surveys of imperiled species and ecological communities and take measures to protect the species and habitat. *Site Design for Habitat or Wetland Conservation:* Developments can earn certification credit for identifying significant habitat on-site and preserving and protecting identified habitats and buffers, or for a previously developed site, use 90% native plants and no invasive plants, or for sites with wetlands and water bodies conserve all waters and conduct a functional assessment of the waters. *Restoration of Habitat or Wetlands:* Developments can earn certification credit for using 100% native plants to restore native habitat on project site in an area equal or greater than 10% of the development footprint and removing invasive species on the site. *Conservation Management of Habitat or Wetlands:* Developments can earn certification credit for creating a long-term management plan for on-site native habitats or wetlands, water bodies, and buffers, and for creating a guaranteed source of funding to protect habitat on-site.

8. James M. McElfish Jr., Nature-Friendly Ordinances (Environmental Law Institute 2004).

9. Christopher Duerksen et al., Habitat Protection Planning: Where the Wild Things Are (American Planning Ass'n, PAS Rep. No. 470/471, 1997).

10. Northeastern Illinois Planning Commission, Protecting Nature in Your Community: A Guidebook for Preserving and Enhancing Biodiversity (2000)

11. *E.g.*, Environmental Law Institute, Conservation Thresholds for Land Use Planners (2003).

12. *See generally* James M. McElfish Jr. & Lyle M. Varnell, *Designing Environmental Indicator Systems for Public Decisions*, 31 Colum. J. Envtl. L. 45 (2006).

13. Craig Anthony Arnold, Wet Growth: Should Water Law Control Land Use? (Environmental Law Institute 2005) and Craig Anthony Arnold & Leigh Jewell, Beyond Litigation: Case Studies in Water Rights Disputes (Environmental Law Institute 2002).

14. Trust for Public Land & American Water Works Ass'n, Protecting the Source: Land Conservation and the Future of America's Drinking Water (2004) and Trust for Public Land & American Water Works Ass'n, Source Protection Handbook (2004).
15. U.S. EPA, *Nonpoint Source Pollution*, http://www.epa.gov/OWOW/NPS/qa.html.
16. Michael J. Bean et al., Design of U.S. Habitat Banking Systems to Support the Conservation of Wildlife Habitat and At-Risk Species (Environmental Law Institute 2008).